Cesar's Way

With Scarlett

Cesar's Way

The Natural, Everyday Guide to Understanding and Correcting Common Dog Problems

CESAR MILLAN

with Melissa Jo Peltier

HODDER & STOUGHTON

Copyright © 2006 by Cesar Millan and Melissa Jo Peltier

Offset by arrangement with Harmony Books, an imprint of the
Crown Publishing Group, a division of Random House, Inc., New York.

First published in Great Britain in 2006 by Hodder & Stoughton
A division of Hodder Headline

The right of Cesar Millan and Melissa Jo Peltier to be identified as the Authors
of the Work has been asserted by them in accordance with the
Copyright, Designs and Patents Act 1988.

A Hodder and Stoughton Book

4

A CIP catalogue record for this title is
available from the British Library

ISBN 978 0 340 933176

Printed and bound by Mackays of Chatham Ltd, Chatham, Kent

Hodder Headline's policy is to use papers that are natural, renewable
and recyclable products and made from wood grown in sustainable forests.
The logging and manufacturing processes are expected to conform to
the environmental regulations of the country of origin.

Hodder & Stoughton Ltd
A division of Hodder Headline
338 Euston Road
London NW1 3BH

Dedicated to the memory of my grandfather
Teodoro Millan Angulo
and
to my father, Felipe Millan Guillen;
I thank them both for teaching me how to truly appreciate,
respect, and love Mother Nature

Special thanks to my mother, Maria Teresa Favela d'Millan,
who taught me the power of a dream

ACKNOWLEDGMENTS

This first book means so much to me, and it's important that I give credit to all of the people who have in some way influenced my life—who helped get me to the point where I'm actually fulfilling my dream of writing a book! Some of these people I've never met, but all have helped to shape the way I think and the way I approach my work.

First among those is Jada Pinkett Smith, who has been more than just a client; she has also been a mentor, a guide, and a role model. Thank you, Jada, for your beautiful spirit, and for showing me the meaning of unconditional friendship.

I want to credit Jay Real for taking me under his wing and teaching me the rules, boundaries, and limitations in the business world. Jay, you are a man of honor. You instinctively knew when to take me by the hand and to lead, but you also knew when it was time for me to leave the nest and fly away. I will always be grateful for that.

There are also two women I need to thank, the women who ran a grooming parlor in San Diego and who hired me when I first came to the United States. Forgive me for not recalling your names—I knew no English then, and American names were very difficult for me. But if you are reading this, please know that I'll never forget what you did for me. I think of you as my first (but not my last!) American guardian angels.

"Self-help" authors and experts are often trivialized in the media, but I credit several of them with the success I have today. Oprah Winfrey influenced me long before I had the honor of meeting her in person and working with her dogs. Her show "How to Say No" changed my life early in my career, because at that time I was saying no to my family, but yes to everyone else. Thank you, Oprah, for your wisdom and insight. To me you will always be the embodiment of "calm-assertive" energy in the way you approach your life and your work. You are truly a stellar "pack leader" for the human race!

There are others I want to mention and recommend who have influenced both my life and the way I work with dogs. Anthony Robbins showed me how to set a goal, stick to the tasks required to realize that goal, and reach it. Dr. Wayne Dyer taught me the power of intention. Deepak Chopra helped me clarify my beliefs regarding the balance between body and soul, and our connections with the natural and spiritual worlds. Dr. Phil McGraw taught me how to give people information they may not want to hear in a loving way, and he also helped me gracefully accept the fact that my advice isn't for everyone. The book *Men Are from Mars, Women Are from Venus,* by psychologist John Gray, helped save my marriage.

There was a point in my life when I was desperate to know if I was crazy, when I wondered if I was the only person in the world who believed that dog *psychology*—not dog *training*—was the key to helping dogs with problems. The late Dr. Leon F. Whitney's *Dog Psychology: The Basics of Dog Training* and Dr. Bruce Fogle's *The Dog's Mind* were the two books that saved my sanity and helped me to see that I was on the right track.

When the *Los Angeles Times* published a feature article on me back in 2002, a flock of Hollywood producers descended on my Dog Psychology Center all at once, each one promising me the moon in exchange for signing away my life and my "rights."

Sheila Emery and Kay Sumner were the only two who didn't want to take something from me, and who didn't make wild promises. I thank them for introducing me to the MPH Entertainment group—Jim Milio, Melissa Jo Peltier, and Mark Hufnail. The MPH/Emery-Sumner team sold my show, *Dog Whisperer with Cesar Millan*, to the National Geographic Channel. Unlike other producers who had approached me, the MPH partners didn't want to change me. They never once asked me to pretend to be something I was not. They wanted to present me exactly as I was—no frills, no showmanship, just my essence. Kay, Sheila, and the three MPH partners—I call them my "television pack"—have helped keep me grounded and balanced in a business that can easily cause newcomers to lose their equilibrium.

I especially want to acknowledge my two special kids, Andre and Calvin. They have a father who is extremely dedicated to his mission, a mission that has often taken up time that could have been spent with them. I want them to know as they grow that every second that I'm not with them, they are foremost in my thoughts. My amazing boys, you are my reason to keep going; any imprint on the world I make I make for you. I want you to grow up in a family of honor that stands for something important. Andre and Calvin, I hope you will always remember and cherish your roots.

Most important of all, there is my strength, my backbone—my wife, Ilusion Wilson Millan. I believe that no man is luckier than one who has a woman behind him 100 percent, and I am blessed to have that. Ilusion was there with me before I was "somebody" or had anything. She showed me the importance of unconditional love, and at the same time, she really "rehabilitated" me. I was born grounded, but before I married my wife, I was starting to get lost. I became selfish and had my priorities mixed up. Ilusion brought me back. She gave me rules, boundaries, and limitations. She always fought for what she believed was best for the relationship, and what was best for our family, and she never backed down from that. She loves human beings the way I love dogs. Earlier in my career, it was easier for me to dismiss the human part of the human-dog relationship, but Ilusion saw right away that it was the humans who had to "get it" in order for the dogs to be happy. She's also the most unselfish and forgiving person I have ever met. She knows what true forgiveness is—not just the words, but the action of forgiving; for her this has meant forgiving those responsible for some very traumatic things that happened in her life. That in itself is an inspiration for me. Ilusion, every day I wake up proud and honored to have you as my wife.

Finally, there are the dogs. If I were a tree, all the wonderful people in my life would be the ones who influenced my growth, but dogs would still be my roots. They keep me grounded. In every dog I see, there lives the spirit of my grandfather, the man who most influenced my life's purpose, who first introduced me to the miracle of animals and the wonders of Mother Nature. Dogs don't read books, so this acknowledgment means nothing to them. But I hope, when I'm near them, that they always sense the energy of my undying gratitude for all they have given me.

Melissa Jo Peltier wishes to thank:

Laureen Ong, John Ford, Colette Beaudry, Mike Beller, and Michael Cascio at the National Geographic Channel, as well as Russel Howard and Chris Albert, their crack publicity department; our crew and staff on *Dog Whisperer with Cesar Millan*, for their consistent excellence; Scott Miller at Trident Media Group, for his faith and patience, and the incomparable Ronald Kessler, for introducing me to Trident; Kim Meisner and Julia Pastore of

Harmony Books, for their expertise; Heather Mitchell, for her research and fact-checking; Kay Sumner and Sheila Emery, for bringing Cesar into our lives; Ilusion Millan, for her trust and friendship; Jim Milio and Mark Hufnail, for ten amazing years and counting; Euclid J. Peltier (Dad), for inspiration; the lovely Caitlin Gray, for being patient with me during a summer of writing; and John Gray, the love of my life—you've changed everything.

And of course, Cesar. Thank you, Cesar, for the honor of allowing me to be part of your purpose.

CONTENTS

FOREWORD BY JADA PINKETT SMITH

Let me prepare you for the idea that you will learn just as much about yourself through Cesar Millan's dog psychology as you will about your dog(s). You see, we humans are the ones who have lost the concept of the natural order in which our dogs function. Our lack of knowledge about the nature of our pets and their needs strips our animals of the natural instincts they use to survive. This creates an imbalanced, unhappy pet that is more of a headache than a joy. Cesar helps us understand the natural ways our dogs live, so they become more balanced and happier. Our dogs, in this state, enable us to develop a healthier companionship with them.

Through his patience and wisdom, Cesar has been a blessing to my family, my dogs, and me. So, new students, be open to learning new things, and be blessed.

President, International Association of Canine Professionals

Today, even though we have more books, more help, more training gadgets, and definitely more treats, there are more badly behaved dogs than ever before. We have the means to help us
achieve well-behaved dogs, yet we lack sufficient understanding
of our dogs' natures. While most of us are well-intentioned and
loving dog owners, this lack of understanding can create many
common dog problems. Put simply, dogs are not small humans.
They do not think like humans, act like humans, or see the world
in the same way as humans. Dogs are dogs, and we need to respect them as dogs. We do them a huge disservice by treating
them like humans and thus create many of the bad behaviors we
see today.

From the first moment I saw Cesar Millan work with dogs on
his show *Dog Whisperer*, I knew he understood this concept. He
is a unique man who is not afraid to be politically incorrect,
who talks about leadership with dogs and is not afraid to give
and show a correction when a dog requires it. I am continually
impressed with the way Cesar interacts with both dogs and their
owners. Cesar explains what is creating the problem in a way
that every dog owner can understand. His personality, warmth,
and humor are irresistible; in the presence of his charm, even the
most stubborn owners listen and want to change. Not only can
he explain the situation, he can also fix the problem. With a
minimal amount of verbal communication, the dog complies,

changing its attitude and its behavior. Dogs respond to Cesar's calm, confident approach. This is truly a man who knows how to "speak dog."

In this book, Cesar reminds us that the most important part of training a dog is building a healthy relationship between human and dog, one in which the boundaries between the two are clearly drawn. I know this to be critical from personal experience. My first dog, Kim, never showed aggression and never behaved improperly in public or when company visited my home. Today, people would say, "What a well-trained dog." But it wasn't training; it was because we shared a relationship based on the three key elements Cesar details in this book: exercise, discipline, and affection.

Cesar shows us how to build this kind of relationship and helps us understand our dogs in a better way. He also explains how dogs can change their behaviors and attitudes with the right approach. This is essential information for everyone who wants to live more peacefully with our valued companions.

Cesar's Way

INTRODUCTION

Does your dog drive you crazy? Is he or she aggressive, nervous, fearful, or just plain high-strung? Perhaps your four-legged friend is obsessive about something—whether it's jumping on anyone who walks through the door or bugging you to play "fetch" with the same filthy green tennis ball, over and over and over.

Or maybe, just maybe, you believe you have the perfect pet but would like a more fulfilling relationship with him or her. You'd really like to learn what makes your dog tick. You want to get inside your dog's mind, to foster a closer bond.

If you answered yes to any of the above, then you've come to the right place.

If you don't know me from my television series, *Dog Whisperer,* airing on the National Geographic Channel, let me introduce myself. My name is Cesar Millan, and I'm eager to share with you wisdom from my lifetime experience living and working with dogs—including the thousands of "lost causes" I have rehabilitated over the years.

A little bit about me: I came to the United States from Mexico in 1990, with no money in my pocket and the dream and ambition to become the best dog trainer in the world. I started as a groomer, but in less than ten years, I was working with packs of overly aggressive Rottweilers, including some dogs that happened to belong to a wonderful couple you may have heard about, Will Smith and Jada Pinkett Smith. Will and Jada, both responsible dog owners, were impressed by my natural talent with dogs, and they very generously recommended me to their friends and colleagues, many of them celebrities. I did no advertising; my business was strictly word of mouth.

Soon I had a thriving business and was able to open my Dog Psychology Center in South Los Angeles. There I keep a pack of thirty to forty dogs nobody else will take. Most of these animals I rescue from shelters or rescue organizations because they are considered "unadoptable" or have been abandoned by their owners for behavioral reasons. Sadly, since there aren't enough no-kill shelters to go around, most abandoned animals face certain euthanasia. But *my* rescued dogs, once rehabilitated, become happy, productive pack members. Many of them eventually find loving, responsible adoptive families. And during their time in my pack, these dogs that were once destined for death row regularly play host to and serve as role models for my clients' problem dogs.

There's a unique neediness in American dogs—I've seen it in their eyes and felt it in their energies from the first day I crossed over the border into the United States. America's pet dogs long to have what most dogs in the wild have naturally: the ability simply to *be dogs*, to live in a stable, balanced *pack*. American dogs struggle with an issue unknown to most of the world's dogs—the need to "unlearn" their owners' lovingly motivated but ultimately destructive efforts to transform them into four-legged people with fur.

As a kid in Mexico, I watched *Lassie* and *Rin Tin Tin* and dreamed of becoming the world's greatest dog "trainer." I don't call what I do "training" anymore. There are plenty of great trainers out there—people who can teach your dog to respond to such commands as "sit," "stay," "come," and "heel." That's not what I do. I do heavy-duty rehab. I deal with dog psychology; trying to connect with the dog's mind and natural instincts to help correct unwanted behavior. I don't use words or commands. I use energy and touch. When I come to a client's house, the owner usually thinks the problem lies with the dog. I always have in the back of my mind that the issue is most likely with the owner. I often tell my clients, "I rehabilitate dogs, but I train people."

The key to my method is what I call "the power of the pack." Having grown up on a farm, around dogs that were work dogs but not house pets, I had years of experience interacting with and observing dogs in their natural "pack" societies. The concept of a "pack" is ingrained in your dog's DNA. In a pack, there are only two roles: the role of leader and the role of follower. If you don't become your dog's pack leader, he will assume that role and try to dominate you. In America, most pet owners spoil their dogs and give them constant affection, thinking that this is enough for the dog. Simply stated, it's not enough. In a dog's world, getting only affection upsets his natural balance. By teaching my clients how to "speak" their dog's language—the language of the pack—I open up a whole new world for *them*. My goal in working with clients is to ensure that both the human and the dog end up healthier and happier.

There are more than sixty-five million pet dogs in America.[1] Over the past ten years, the pet industry has doubled in size, with an income of about $34 billion—yes, billion! American dog owners pamper their pets with such things as $5,700 green crocodile leather travel bags for miniature Yorkshire terriers and $30,000 insurance policies.[2] On the average, dog owners can spend as much as $11,000 or more on their pet in that pet's lifetime—and that's one of the more conservative figures![3] This country definitely has the most spoiled dogs in the world. But are they the happiest?

My answer, sadly, is no.

What I hope you'll come away with after reading this book are some practical techniques for helping your dog with his problems. More important, however, I want you to gain a deeper understanding of how your dog sees the world—and what he really wants and needs in order to live a peaceful, happy, balanced life. I believe almost all dogs are born in perfect balance, in tune with themselves and with nature. It is only when they live with humans that they develop the behavior problems that I call "issues." And speaking of issues, who among us doesn't have a few? After applying my techniques, you may even begin to understand yourself better. You'll look at your own behavior in a different light, and may find yourself changing the ways you interact with your children, your spouse, or your boss. After all, humans are pack animals, too! I've heard from more viewers than you might imagine that my techniques have helped as many humans as they have dogs. Take an excerpt from this delightful fan letter, for example:

Dear Cesar,

Thank you so much for your show, "Dog Whisperer."

The funny thing is you've changed me and my family's life and we don't even own a dog.

I am a 41-year-old mother of 2 (a 5-year-old son and 6-year-old daughter). I was having a terrible time disciplining them (I learned they had no boundaries and limitations). My kids were pushing me around, literally, in public places and at home. And then I saw your show.

Since then I have trained myself to become a more assertive parent, using a more authority energy, demanding my space as an authority figure. I have also trained myself not to ask and beg them to do things, but to tell them to do things (such as clean up their room, clean their eating area, and put away their laundered clothes). My life has changed and so have they. To my amazement, my children have become more disciplined (and there's less fighting) and I found they actually like responsibilities and chores. They are proud when they accomplish a given task and I am just thrilled.

You have not only taught humans about their dogs, you have taught humans about themselves.

Thank you so much!

The Capino Family

I owe a lot to dogs. Obviously, I owe my livelihood to them, but my gratitude goes much deeper. I owe my balance to dogs. I owe my experience of unconditional love to dogs and, as a boy, my ability to overcome loneliness. I owe my understanding of family to dogs, and they have helped me learn to be a better, more balanced "pack leader" with my wife for our kids. Dogs give us so much, but what do we really give them in return? A place to sleep, food, affection ... but is that enough for them? They are so pure and unselfish in sharing their lives with us. Can't we take a deeper look inside their minds and hearts to discover what they really want?

Some dog owners, I've come to believe, don't really want to do what it takes to fulfill their dogs' lives because they fear it will upset the balance in the way their dog fulfills *them*. But in an ideal relationship, shouldn't both parties be getting their needs met?

What I hope to do in this book is try to help all my readers give back to their dogs just a fraction of the many gifts their dogs give them.

A NOTE ABOUT GENDER

I grew up in Mexico, in a culture that you might call "macho." Others in America might call it "sexist." Whatever name you give it, it is a culture that does not value women the way they are valued in the United States. Women are respected as mothers, but their personal worth is not given anywhere near the significance it should be given. Women are not encouraged to have high self-esteem or to feel their importance in society.

Since I came to America and married an American woman, I have been "rehabilitated" to the point where I believe no culture can be truly healthy unless it places on women the value they deserve. When it comes to the written word in my first book, the issue of how gender is handled is very important to me. Therefore, my co-writer and I have dealt with the issue of gender in the following way:

In every other chapter, we will alternate between the masculine and feminine pronouns and adjectives when describing humans. In every other chapter, we will do the same when describing dogs. Therefore, in one chapter "he" will describe a dog and "she" will describe a human. Then we'll switch off, and so on.

I credit my brilliant and beautiful wife, Ilusion Wilson Millan, for opening my eyes to the vital role that women play in our human existence. They truly are the glue who hold our human "packs" together.

In the mountains with the pack

A Dog's Life

It's 6:45 in the morning and the sun is just beginning to peek over the crest of the Santa Monica Mountains. We're heading due east, and the trail is quiet and empty. I haven't seen any sign of a human being yet, which is a good thing. When I'm running in the hills— followed by about thirty-five off-leash dogs—I always keep to the least-traveled paths. The dogs aren't a danger, but they can look pretty formidable to someone who's never seen a man running with a pack of dogs behind him.

We've been running for about a half hour now, and Geovani, my assistant, follows the last dog, keeping up the rear of the pack and watching for stragglers. There rarely are any. Once we get into a rhythm, the pack and I churn up the dirt on this trail as if we were a unit, as if we were one animal. I lead, and they follow. I can hear their heavy breaths and the light scratches their feet make on the *trail. They are calm and happy, and they trot lightly with their heads down and tails wagging.*

The dogs follow me in the order of their status, but since this pack is much larger than a wolf pack would be in the wild, the dogs divide themselves up into groups based on high, medium, and low energy. (The smaller dogs have to run harder to keep up the pace.)

All the dogs are in migrating mode, and their instincts are in charge. So, I sometimes think, are mine. I breathe in deep—the air is clean and clear, and I can't smell even a trace of Los Angeles smog. It's a total rush, an exhilarating feeling. I feel at one with the outdoors, the dawn, and the dogs. I think of how blessed I am that this is how I get to spend my days, that I have been allowed to enjoy this day as a part of my life's work, my life's mission.

On an average workday, I leave my home in Inglewood, California, and arrive at the Dog Psychology Center in South Los Angeles by 6:00 A.M. Geovani and I will let the dogs out into the dirt-floored "backyard" of the Center so they can relieve themselves after their night's rest. After that, we load them into a van and arrive in the mountains by no later than 6:30 A.M. We stay there for about four hours, alternating vigorous exercise with moderate exercise and rest.

The exercise is as I've described—I lead the pack like an alpha wolf, and the dogs follow me. They are a motley crew—a ragtag mix of injured, rejected, thrown-away rescued dogs, and my clients' dogs who've come to the center to "return to their roots"— in the dog sense, that is. We've got more than our fair share of pit bulls, Rottweilers, German shepherds, and other powerful breeds, along with the springer spaniels, Italian greyhounds, bulldogs and Chihuahuas. While I'm running, most of the dogs will be off-leash. If a dog needs to be leashed, an assistant will handle that. If there is any doubt about the dog's ability to be an obedient pack member, he stays home, and I exercise him in other ways. As diverse as they are, the dogs work together as a pack. Their deepest, most primal instinct guides them to follow me, their "pack leader," to obey me, and to cooperate with one another. And each time we go through this exercise, I am more closely bonded with them. This is how nature intended a dog pack to work.

What's remarkable is, whenever we're walking or running, the dogs of all breeds are indistinguishable. They are simply a pack. When we rest, they break up into breeds. The Rottweilers will all go together. They will dig a burrow in the ground to rest in. The pit bulls will lie down together, always in the middle of the pack, out in the sun. And the German shepherds will go and lie under a shady tree. They all have their own style. Then, when it's time to run again, they'll all fall in as if there were no differences between them at all. The dog and animal in them is far stronger than the breed—at least when it comes to the serious business of migrating. Every day that I live with the dogs, they teach me something new about them. For everything that I do to help them, they give me a thousand gifts in return.

10:45 A.M.: We're back in South Los Angeles. After four hours of intensive exercise in the mountains, the dogs are ready for more water—and for home. They come back to the Center and rest under the shade of a two-story portico, a leafy tree, or in "Thailand"—what I call the row of five small, private doghouses for the tinier ones among them. Some of the more active ones like to cool off in one of our pools before they crash. During the

The Rottweilers resting together during a hike

hour that they rest, from about 11:00 A.M. to noon, that's when I'll have consultations and an intake of new dogs at the Center. The best time to introduce a new, unbalanced dog to a stable pack is when the pack is all pooped out.

Now that they're exercised and rested, the dogs have earned their food . . . just like they'd have to do in nature. I like to prepare the food myself, scooping and mixing it with my bare hands, so their food will always have their pack leader's scent in it. The feeding ritual at the Dog Psychology Center takes one and a half to two hours, and it's designed to be a psychological challenge to the dogs—in human terms, an exercise in "willpower." The dogs line up in front of me, and wait. Only the mellowest, calmest, and most relaxed dog will get to eat first. This makes all the other dogs realize that the calmer and mellower they are, the more likely they will be to get what they want. The dogs have to eat next to one another, without fighting or becoming dominant over the food. This is an enormous mental challenge for a dog, but one that helps ensure that the pack runs smoothly.

Once the dogs have eaten and relieved themselves, they're ready for some more physical exercise. As you can see, I'm a great believer in both structure and intensive physical activity to help dogs achieve the kind of balance they would have if they lived naturally, in a world without human influence.

Our next activity is the most rigorous of the day—rollerblading. Believe it or not, most dogs love running with me while I rollerblade—they love the challenge of keeping up with a pack leader on wheels! I can rollerblade with a maximum of only ten dogs at a time, so that's three or four sessions in a row. By mid-afternoon, everybody's had a shot at it. The dogs are exhausted, and so am I. While they rest for a couple of hours, I do phone consultations and office work. At about 5:00, we go out back and throw the ball for twenty minutes. At the Dog Psychology Center, between thirty and forty dogs can play fetch with the same ball without a fight breaking out. That's what I call the "power of the pack" to influence good behavior.

As the sun begins to dip, the pack goes into a resting mode for the remainder of the day. This is the best time for any one-on-one work I need to do with some of the various dogs. For instance, take Beauty, a lanky female German shepherd who has a severe case of fear aggression. If anyone approaches her, she will shrink back and either run away or attack. In order to attach a leash to her collar, I have to chase after her, tire her out, and then wait until she submits. I may have to repeat this process a thousand times until she realizes that when I put my hand out, the best solution is for her to come to me. Because Beauty has been exercising and participating in the pack all day, she is in the best state of mind for me to work with her on her issues.

Today, more than ten years after the Dog Psychology Center opened its doors, I maintain a small staff comprising, in addition to myself, my wife, Ilusion, and four other loyal employees. We care for an average of thirty to forty dogs at a time. Many of the dogs in the pack at the Center have been with us since the beginning. Some we consider our family pets, and they come home with us every night. We've become attached to so many of them that we have to alternate between whom we bring home. Other dogs are return visitors, belonging to longtime clients who like the balancing effect the pack has on their dogs. These clients bring their dogs to us whenever they travel. For their dogs, who are already psychologically healthy, coming to hang with the pack is like going to camp and reuniting with old friends.

The rest of the dogs at the Center are temporary visitors, dogs I bring here to help with their rehabilitation. The ratio for pack "regulars" to pack "temporaries" is about fifty-fifty. Some of those pack "temporaries" are dogs rescued from shelters—dogs that might be euthanized if they can't be turned into social animals, *fast.* The others are dogs who belong to private clients. I like to tell people that the dogs from clients are the ones that keep the business going, and those from rescue organizations are the ones that keep my karma going. Most of my private clients don't need to send their dogs to the Center to get them well, just as not all human beings need to go to group therapy to deal with their psychological issues. Most of the cases I handle involve dogs who simply need stronger leadership from their owners plus rules, boundaries, limitations, and consistency in their own homes to become better. But there are other cases where the best solution is to bring the dogs to have the support and influence of their own kind so they can relearn how to be dogs.

Because so many of our dogs are from rescue organizations, many of them have heartbreaking stories, some involving the incredible cruelty some humans inflict on animals. Rosemary had one of those stories. A pit bull mix, she had been bred to fight other dogs in illegal pit fights. After she lost an important fight, her owners poured gasoline over her and lit her on fire. A rescue organization saved her life and she recovered from her burns, but it was clear that her horrific experience had turned her into a dangerously human-aggressive dog. She started biting people. I heard about Rosemary after she attacked two elderly men, and immediately offered to take her and try to rehabilitate her.

Rosemary was presented to me as a deadly, dangerous dog. When I brought her to the Center, however, turning her around proved to be a piece of cake. All she needed was a safe place and solid leadership in order to regain her trust in people. Before, she had felt intimidated by people, so she'd make the first move. That's when she'd attack, because in her experience, if she didn't attack a person, that person would hurt her. It took no more than two days for me to earn her trust. After that, she was the sweetest, most obedient dog you could imagine. She wasn't born to be a killer, humans had made her that way. Once she was living in the Center, surrounded by the energy of stable, balanced dogs, she proved to be a very smooth case.

Rosemary now lives with an adoptive family who loves her—and can't believe she was ever human-aggressive. She turned out to be one of the best ambassadors for the Dog Psychology Center that I could ever imagine.

Like Rosemary, Popeye was found wandering the streets by a rescue organization and ended up here because the rescue workers couldn't handle him. Popeye is a purebred pit bull who lost his eye in an illegal fight. Now that he was "damaged goods," his owners had no more use for him and abandoned him. While he was adjusting to having only one eye, Popeye became very suspicious of other dogs because his vision of the world had narrowed and he felt vulnerable. He responded by approaching other dogs very aggressively in order to intimidate them—which would almost always start a fight. Then he started attacking people. When he came to me, he was very pushy, dominant, and highstrung. He was a much more difficult case, because his energy was so strong, so I always had to be extra alert and aware around him. Today, he's a mellow, trusted member of the pack. And no one here gives him a hard time because he has only one eye.

We have a lot of pit bulls in the pack, not because they are more dangerous than other dogs but because they are among the most powerful breeds, and are often the hardest for rescue organizations to handle when the dogs develop issues, particularly aggression. Unfortunately for pit bulls, many people raise them for illegal fighting or for protection, so they are conditioned to bring out the aggressive side of their nature.

Preston is also a pit bull, and he's enormous. He lived with an eighty-year-old man, spending his whole life closed up with the man inside an apartment. Because Preston's got a naturally calm disposition, he never became destructive—while his owner was alive. Preston was there when his owner passed away, and he was found by the man's landlord, who called the Amanda Foundation. When they came and got him, he was very shy. Shy dogs are often candidates for fearful aggression. When they put Preston into a kennel and then tried to take him out again, he started lashing out at everybody. Because he's such a big guy, his rescuers grew to be afraid of him. When I brought him here, however, I could see right away that he was actually a scared, insecure guy. He was one of the rare dogs that I threw right into the pack full time, from day one. Being a naturally calm fellow, Preston picked up on the relaxed, stable energy of the other pack members and almost instantly reverted to being just like them. He calmed down immediately and although he still looks scary to most visitors, I know his secret—he's really a gentle giant.

Even though I keep no favorites at the Center, Scarlett, a petite, black-and-white French bulldog is one dog to whom I have become very attached. She comes home with me often, and my sons consider her a family pet. Scarlett was the newest dog in a houseful of dogs and other pets. Her owners had a rabbit that got out of its hutch, and Scarlett attacked it and took its eye out. I came to the owners' house and worked with Scarlett; she wasn't even a case I felt needed to go to the Center. The problem wasn't Scarlett; it was her owners. There was no discipline in the house—no rules, boundaries, or limitations—and the owners were rarely home to supervise all the various animals they had running loose on the property. I gave the owners a lot of home-work, but they didn't change anything. A few weeks later, Scar-lett took the leg off of a Chihuahua that was living with them. Because Scarlett was the most aggressive dog and the newest one in their pack, the owners once again blamed her. I didn't think there was any hope for her in that household, so I offered to adopt her myself. Now she's so sweet and calm she can go any-where with me. I think of her as my good-luck charm. Whenever I need an extra stroke of luck, I rub her tummy like a Buddha. She's never failed me yet.

Oliver and Dakota are two brown-and-white springer span-iels. Both have physical issues resulting from too much inbreed-ing, such as recurring infections in the eyes and ears. Dakota is the worse off. I believe that each dog comes into your life to teach you something. Dakota was the dog who taught me about neurological damage—a problem I can't fix. Dakota's energy is "off." Everything about him—from his bark to the way he chases shadows—is very unbalanced. Because there is no aggression allowed in the pack—ever—the other dogs don't hurt him and he can live peacefully. In nature, he would be targeted and attacked for his weakness, and would probably not survive.

I wish I could introduce you to all of the dogs in the pack, because they all have equally fascinating stories and histories. However, they all share one thing. For them, being part of their own kind has a profound meaning. Being part of a family of people wouldn't have that same kind of meaning. They would be comfortable, and maybe even spoiled. But their lives would lack this primal meaning. So when these dogs get to be part of their own kind—regardless of the breed—they feel complete.

I wish that all of the dogs in America—in the world—could be as balanced and fulfilled as the dogs in my pack. My goal in life is to help rehabilitate as many of the "problem" dogs as I possibly can.

As the evening wears on, it's time for me to go home to my human pack—my wife, Ilusion, and our two sons, Andre and Calvin. Geovani will remain for the night, tending to the dog's needs and putting them in their kennels when it's time to sleep. After about seven to eight hours of exercise, they are ready to crash. Tomorrow the cycle will repeat again, with either me or one of my colleagues at the center. This is my life—a dog's life— and I couldn't be more blessed to be living it.

Through this book I invite you to experience it with me.

My family at the farm in Ixpalino.
Left to right: my mother, grandmother, sister,
cousin, grandfather, and me.

1

Growing Up with Dogs

A View from the Other Side of the Border

We woke up before the sun, those summer mornings on the farm. There wasn't any electricity, so once the sky turned dim in the evenings, there was little for us kids to do in the candlelight. While the adults talked softly into the night, my older sister and I would try to drift off to sleep in the stifling heat. We needed no alarm clocks; our wake-up call was that first sliver of backlit golden dust streaming through the unscreened open window. The first sounds to reach my ears would be the chickens—their insistent clucking in competition for the grain my grandfather was already spreading around the yard. If I lazed in bed long enough, I'd smell the coffee brewing on the stove and hear the swishing of the water in the ceramic buckets my grandmother carried up from the well. Before she came into the house, she would softly sprinkle some of the water onto the dirt road in front of the doorstep, so the cows wouldn't suffocate us with the

dust they churned up as they passed by on their morning parade
to the river.

Most days, however, the last thing I wanted to do was stay in
bed. I couldn't wait to get up and go outside. The only place I
really wanted to be was among the animals. From as early as I
can remember, I loved to spend hours walking with them or just
silently watching them, trying to figure out how their wild minds
worked. Whether it was a cat, a chicken, a bull, or a goat, I
wanted to know what the world looked like through the eyes of
each animal—and I wanted to understand that animal from the
inside out. I never thought of them as the same as us, but I can't
remember ever thinking animals were "less" than us, either. I was
always endlessly fascinated—and delighted—by our differences.
My mother still tells me that from the time I could reach out and
touch any animal, I could never learn enough about it.

And always, the animals that attracted me most were dogs. In
our family, having dogs around was like having water to drink.
Canines were a constant presence in my childhood, and I can't
overstate their importance to my development in becoming the
man I am today. I wouldn't want to imagine a world that didn't
have dogs in it. I respect dogs' dignity as proud and miraculous
animals. I marvel at their loyalty, consistency, resiliency, and
strength. I continue to grow spiritually from studying their seam-
less link with Mother Nature, despite thousands of years of living
side by side with man. To say that I "love" dogs doesn't even come
close to describing my deep feelings and affinity for them.

I was very blessed to have had a wonderful childhood, spent
living in proximity to dogs and many other animals. Since I also
grew up in Mexico, in a very different culture from the one you
have here in the United States, I had the advantage of seeing your
country and customs from a newcomer's perspective. Though
I'm not a veterinarian, a Ph.D., or a biologist, I have successfully

rehabilitated thousands of problem dogs over the years, and it's both my observation and my opinion that many dogs in America are not as happy or as stable as they could be. I'd like to offer you a more balanced, healthier way to love your dog. A way that promises you the kind of deep connection you always dreamed of having with a nonhuman animal. I hope after sharing with you my experiences and my personal story of a life shaped by dogs, you may begin to have a different perspective on the relationship we humans share with our canine friends.

The Farm

I was born and spent most of my earliest years in Culiacan, one of the oldest cities in Mexico, located about 643 miles from Mexico City. My most vivid childhood memories, however, are of spending every vacation and weekend at my grandfather's farm in Ixpalino, about an hour away. In the Sinaloa region of Mexico, farms like the one my grandfather lived on operated on a kind of feudal system. The farm, or ranch, was owned by the *patrones*, the richer families in Mexico. My grandfather was one of many workers and ranch families, known as *campesinos*, who rented *ejidos*, parcels of land, and earned their meager incomes working them. Those farm families made up a community—the land they worked was what they had in common. You could compare this to the sharecropper situation in the American South. The primary job my grandfather had was to care for the cows— dozens of them—and see them safely from the pasture to the stream and back again, every day.

We also raised chickens and other animals, mostly for our own food. The house was cramped—built long and narrow and mostly of brick and clay. It had only four rooms, which got kind of crowded once my other sisters and brother were born, and whenever our many cousins came to visit. I was already fourteen or fifteen years old when we first got running water. Yet I never recall feeling "poor." In that part of Mexico, the working class was the majority. And in my young eyes, that farm was paradise. I would rather have been there than at Magic Mountain, any day. The farm was always the place where I felt I could really be me, the person I was born to be. It was the place that made me feel truly connected to nature.

And always there, in the background, were the dogs, usually living in loosely formed packs of five to seven animals. They weren't wild, but they weren't "indoor dogs," either. They lived outside in the yard and came and went as they pleased. Most were a concoction of mixed breeds, many of them resembling something between a small German shepherd, a Labrador, and a Basenji. The dogs always felt like part of our family, but they weren't anything like "pets" in the modern American sense of the word. These farm dogs all worked for a living. They helped keep the other animals in line—running alongside or behind my grandfather as he herded the cows, working to keep the cows from straying from the path. The dogs also performed other functions, such as protecting our land and property. If any of the workmen left a hat behind in the field, you could be sure one of the dogs would stay behind to watch it until the owner returned. They also took care of the women in the family. If my grandmother walked to the fields at lunchtime carrying meals for the workers, a dog or two would always go with her, lest an aggressive pig appeared to try to take the food away from her. The dogs always protected us; we took this for granted. And we never "taught" them to do any of these things, not in the sense of "dog training" as most people know it. We didn't shout commands to them as trainers do, or reward them with cookies. We never physically abused them to get them to obey us. They simply did the jobs that needed doing. Something about how they helped us seemed to be in their nature already, or perhaps they had passed the behaviors down from generation to generation. In exchange for their assistance, we'd throw them a burrito or two now and then. Otherwise, they scavenged for their food, or hunted smaller animals. They happily interacted with us, but they also had their own distinctive lifestyle—their own "culture," if you will.

These "working dogs" on our farm were my true teachers in the art and science of canine psychology.

I always loved to watch dogs. I suppose your average American kid will run and play fetch with his canine companion— throw a Frisbee to her, play tug-of-war or wrestle with her in the grass. From the time I was very little, I found joy in dogs simply by observing them. When the dogs weren't hanging around us or interacting with the other animals on the farm, I'd watch them play with one another. Very early, I learned to read their body language—such as the "play bow" position, when one dog would invite another for a frolic. I remember them grabbing one another's ears and rolling on the ground. Sometimes they'd run and explore together; sometimes they'd team up and excavate a gopher hole. When their "workday" was done, some of them would rush to jump in the creek to cool off. The less bold among them would lie quietly on the bank and watch the others. Their daily patterns and rhythms formed a culture unto itself. The mothers disciplined their pups so the pups learned the rules of the pack at a very young age. Their packs and family units definitely operated like an organized society, with clear rules and boundaries.

The more hours I spent watching them, the more questions came into my mind. How did they coordinate their activities? How did they communicate with one another? I noticed early on that a simple glance from one dog to another could change the dynamic of the whole pack in a split second. What was going on between them? What were they "saying" to one another, and how were they saying it? I soon learned that I could have an effect on them, too. If I wanted something from them—for example, if I wanted one of them to follow me into the field—it seemed I only had to put that thought in my mind, think of what direction I wanted to go in, and the dog could read my mind and obey. How did she know how to do that?

I was also fascinated by the endless number of things dogs were able learn about the complex world around them, simply by trial and error. Was part of what they knew about nature already inborn, I wondered? The vast knowledge they displayed about their environment and how to survive in it seemed to spring from an equal combination of nature and nurture. For example, I have a vivid memory of watching a couple of adolescent pups approaching a scorpion, probably for the first time in their young lives. They obviously were fascinated by this outlandish creature, and they inched toward it tentatively, leading with their noses. As soon as they got close, the scorpion started to move toward them, and the puppies jumped back. Then the puppies began sniffing around the scorpion all over again, then backed off, then started again—but never got so close as to be stung by it. How did they know how far they could go? Was the scorpion sending them "signals" as to what its boundaries were? How did those two pups sense the scorpion's poison? I witnessed the same thing with one of our other dogs and a rattlesnake. Did she smell danger from the rattlesnake? I knew the way I had been taught that an animal was poisonous. My father told me, "You go near that scorpion, and I'm going to spank you," or "If you touch that snake, you'll get poisoned." But you never saw a dog father or dog mother telling a pup, "This is how it is." These pups learned from experience and watching other dogs, but they also seemed to have a kind of sixth sense about nature—a sense that, even as a boy, I observed to be missing from most of the humans I knew. These dogs seemed completely in tune with Mother Nature, and that's what amazed me and drew me back to observe them, day after day.

Pack Leaders and Pack Followers

There was something else I noticed quite young—a set of behaviors that seemed to separate the dogs on my grandfather's farm from the dogs on some of the other families' farms. Some of the other ranchers seemed to have dogs with fairly tight pack structures, where one dog was pack leader and the others were followers. Those families liked to watch when their dogs got into battles over dominance—when one dog beat another down. This was entertainment for them. I could see that such dominance displays were natural behavior for dogs; I had also witnessed it in the feral dog packs that ran wild in the fields near our house. But that kind of behavior wasn't acceptable for my grandfather. The dogs on our farm didn't seem to have a discernible pack leader among them. I realize now that this was because my grandfather never let any dog take the leadership role away from him—or from the rest of us humans, for that matter. He instinctively understood that for the dogs to live in harmony with us—to work willingly with us on the farm and never show aggression or dominance toward us—they all had to understand that we humans were their pack leaders. You could see it in their postures around us. Their body language communicated clear, classic "calm submission" or "active submission"—qualities of energy that I'll describe in greater detail later. The dogs' heads were always low, and they always kept a certain position in relation to us when traveling—trotting either behind or next to us, and never running out in front.

Now, my grandfather never had any training manuals or self-help books or scientific techniques to rely on, yet he could always elicit that perfectly calm, submissive, and cooperative response from his dogs. I never witnessed my grandfather use any violent punishment, and he didn't bribe the dogs with treats. What he did was project the kind of consistent, calm-assertive energy that just cries out "leader" in any language, for any species. My grandfather was one of the most confident, even-tempered people I've ever met—and definitely the person most in tune with nature. I think he recognized that of all his grand-kids, I was the one born with that same special gift. The wisest thing he ever said to me was "Never work against Mother Nature. You only succeed when you work *with* her." To this very day, I repeat that to myself—and to my clients—whenever I work with dogs. And sometimes, when I'm feeling stressed, I apply it to other areas of my life. Though my grandfather passed away at the age of 105, I quietly thank him every day for that timeless piece of wisdom.

Living among dogs that had that gentle, compliant state of mind, none of us kids ever developed a fear that one of the dogs would harm us. We were always confident around them, and therefore, we, too, naturally became their leaders. I never once saw a dog bare her teeth to, growl at, or act aggressively toward my grandfather, and not one of the children in the family was ever hurt or bitten by a dog. My experience learning from my wise grandfather on the farm has convinced me that, when dogs and humans live together, a calm-submissive state of mind is the best state of mind for the dog to have. My family and I grew up among dogs with that state of mind, and our relationship with those dogs was one of pure, relaxed harmony. And the dogs, too, always seemed happy, relaxed, serene, and content. They didn't exhibit stress or anxious behavior. They were healthy, balanced dogs, as nature intended them to be.

I don't want to give all the credit for my amazing and unique childhood to my grandparents. My father was the most honest, honorable man I've ever met. He taught me about integrity. My mother, however, taught me about patience and sacrifice. She always talked about the importance of having a dream and to dream as big as you like. But like some people who grow up to work with animals, I always felt a little different from the other kids. I seemed to connect better with animals than with people. That feeling of isolation increased when we started spending less time on the farm and more time in the busy seaside city of Mazatlan.

The move was motivated by my dad's concern about our education. He was a traditional Mexican son—very devoted to his parents—yet he realized that there were no real schools at the ranch. Sometimes teachers would come and hold classes for a few of the farm kids, but often they wouldn't come back again for a long time. My dad wanted us kids to take our education more seriously, so we moved to Mazatlan, Mexico's second largest coastal city and a vacation mecca. I was probably about six or seven years old.

Life in the City: Dog Eat Dog

I remember our first apartment in Mazatlan. Trust me; it never would have made the cover of *Metropolitan Home*. It was on the second floor of an apartment building on Calle Morelos, in the crowded, working-class part of town. It was very long and narrow, like a "railroad flat" in Manhattan—a living room, kitchen, hallway and two bedrooms, one for our parents, the other for all us kids. There was a bathroom where you'd also wash your clothes. That was it. My father got a job delivering newspapers, and we kids dressed in one another's hand-me-downs and went to school every day.

For me, the worst thing about living in the city was that we couldn't have dogs around anymore. When we first brought dogs to the apartment, we let them live in the hallway. But they smelled bad, and we weren't very disciplined about cleaning up after them. (We also tried raising chickens in the hallway, but they smelled even worse!) We couldn't let the dogs out to roam, because they might be hit by the cars that drove even faster than they had in Culiacan. We were used to having the dogs run free on the farm and basically taking care of themselves; we didn't know anything about walking with them or caring for them properly in an urban environment. To be honest, we were a little lazy about it. And the city kids in our neighborhood didn't play with dogs. Most of the dogs that we came across were running loose, scavenging for garbage. I noticed that those city dogs weren't as skinny as the dogs at the ranch; there was much more food available to them, plenty of garbage for them to eat. But they were definitely more afraid, nervous, and unsure of themselves. And for the first time, I saw people actually abusing dogs. In the country, people would only yell at dogs or chase them away if they were attacking their chickens or stealing the family's food. Mostly, those were the feral dogs, or coyotes. The dogs who lived with us would never do anything like that. But in the city, I witnessed people throwing rocks at dogs and swearing at them, even if the dogs were only passing by their car or running past their store or fruit stand. It tore me up inside to see that. It just didn't feel "natural" to me. That was the only time in my life when I actually detached myself from dogs. I think in some ways that's when I became detached from myself.

Since I was still very young, the city was already curbing my natural "wildness," in the same way it impeded dogs' true natures. On the farm, I could go outside for hours and hours, walking the land, following "the guys"—my father or my grandfather or the other ranch hands—and always with the dogs trailing behind us. There wasn't anywhere I couldn't go on foot. Now, my mom was nervous about only letting us walk to the corner and back. Of course, she feared kidnappers, child molesters—the usual urban boogie men. The only time I felt "free" again was on the weekends when we we'd go back to the farm. But those weekends never seemed to last long enough.

I remember one good thing about the city: it was there where I saw my first purebred dog. There was one doctor who lived in our neighborhood. His name was Dr. Fisher. He was out walking his Irish setter—the first purebred dog I had ever seen in my life—and when I saw her sleek red coat, I was mesmerized. She was so well groomed and so very different from the mangy, mixed-breed dogs I was used to seeing. I couldn't stop staring at her, thinking, "I've got to have that beautiful dog!" I followed Dr. Fisher to see where he lived. Then I returned, day after day, following him and watching him walk his dog. One day she had a new litter of puppies. That was it. I got up the courage to introduce myself to Dr. Fisher and ask him, "Do you think you can give me one of those puppies?" He looked at me as if I were crazy. There I was, some stranger, a kid, and I wanted him to give me a valuable purebred puppy, which rich people might pay hundreds of dollars for. Still, I think he could read in my eyes how serious I was about it. I really wanted one of those dogs! After staring at me for a while, he answered, "Maybe." Maybe, indeed! Two years later, he finally gave me a puppy from one of his litters. I named her Saluki, and she grew up to be a big, beautiful, and totally loyal girl. She was my constant companion for almost ten years, and she taught me a lesson that's been very important to my current work with dogs and their owners. Purebred or mutt, farm dog or house dog, Siberian husky, German shepherd, or Irish setter, a purebred is first and foremost just an ordinary dog wearing a designer suit. Later in the book, I'll talk about why I think too many people blame "breed" for their dogs' problem behavior. Sweet Saluki taught me that beautiful purebred dogs and funny-looking mutts are both the same thing under their skin—they are both simply *dogs first*.

Despite the presence of Saluki, I didn't fit in very well with the kids at school. They were all city kids to begin with, born and raised in that type of life. From day one, it was clear to me that how they felt about their lives had nothing to do with how I felt about mine. I didn't make any judgment about better or worse; I just sensed that there was really not that much we had in common. However, like a good pack animal, I realized that if I was going to make it in the city, somebody needed to change his behavior, and it obviously wasn't going to be the other kids. They were the "pack," so I tried to adapt and fit in. I have to admit, I pulled it off fairly well. I hung out with them and went with them to the beach, played baseball and soccer, but deep inside I knew I was faking it. It was never like on the farm, chasing a frog here and there, catching fireflies in jars and then setting them free, or simply sitting under the stars, listening to the crickets' song. Nature had always offered me something new to learn, something to think about. Sports were just working off energy and trying to fit in.

The truth was, those years on the farm were embedded in my soul. The only place I was truly happy was outside, in nature, without concrete walls or streets or buildings to pen me in. I was swallowing my soul in order to be accepted, and all that excess energy and frustration had to go somewhere. It wasn't long before it turned into aggression—but most of my anger seemed to erupt at home. I started fighting with my sisters and arguing with my mother. My parents were smart—they got me into judo. It was the perfect way to drain my anger and channel it into something constructive and healthy, something that taught me lessons that I still credit for my success today.

At six years old, I walked into a judo studio for the first time. By the age of fourteen I had won six championships in a row. My aggression had to be redirected somehow, and I found the perfect mentor in my judo master, Joaquim. He told me he believed I had a special quality; a "fire within," he called it. He took me under his

At a judo tournament, age 8

wing, telling me stories about Japan, and how the people there were also in tune with Mother Nature. He taught me about Japanese meditation techniques—about breathing and focus and using the power of the mind to reach any goal. The experience reminded me of my grandfather and his natural wisdom. Many of the techniques I learned in judo—single-mindedness, self-control, quieting the mind, deep concentration—are skills I still use every day, and find especially crucial in my work with dangerous, red-zone aggressive dogs. I also recommend many of these techniques to clients who need to learn to control *themselves* better before they can get their dogs to behave. My parents couldn't have found a more perfect outlet for me during that phase of my life. It was judo that kept me sane during those years, until the weekends when I could romp on the farm or go to the mountains or walk among the animals again. Only when I was with Mother Nature or doing judo was I truly in my element.

El Perrero

When I was about fourteen, my father started working as a photographer for the government. He saved enough money to buy a very nice house in a much higher-class section of town. We had a yard and were only one block away from the beach. It wasn't until then that I finally started to feel comfortable in my own skin again, and began to see my mission in life taking shape. All my friends were talking about what they wanted to be when they grew up. I didn't feel the desire to be a fireman or a doctor or a lawyer or anything like that. I didn't know exactly what it was I'd be doing, but I knew that if there was a profession that involved dogs, I wanted to be a part of it. Then I thought back to when we got our first television set. As a very little boy, I had been mesmer-

Rin Tin Tin

ized by the reruns of *Lassie* and *Rin Tin Tin,* always in black and white and dubbed in Spanish. Because I had grown up with dogs in a very natural environment, *I* knew that of course Lassie didn't really understand the words that Timmy was saying. I also figured out that normal dogs didn't automatically do the heroic things Lassie and Rin Tin Tin did every week. Once I learned that trainers stood offscreen, controlling the dogs' behavior, I began to romanticize them. What a feat, to turn those ordinary dogs into such stellar actors! With my natural understanding of the canines on the farm, I instinctively knew that I could easily train dogs to do the same impressive tricks that Lassie and Rin Tin Tin's handlers had taught them to do. Those two television shows inspired my first great dream—to move to Hollywood and become the best dog trainer in the world. What I ended up becoming was something else all together—but that comes later in the story.

As I repeated this goal to myself, it felt so totally right. Saying to myself "I'm going to work with dogs and be the best trainer in the world" felt to me like being given a glass of water after nearly dying of thirst. It felt *natural,* easy, and it felt really *good.* Suddenly, I wasn't fighting myself anymore. I knew the path I would take on the way to my future.

The first step toward my goal was to get a job at a local veterinarian's office. It wasn't anything like the fancy, sterile vets' offices here in the States; it was kind of a combination vet's/kennel/grooming establishment. I was only fifteen, but the employees there immediately saw that I had no fear of dogs; I could grab dogs that even the vet wouldn't go near. I started as a helper, sweeping floors and cleaning up after the animals. Next I became a groomer, and very quickly progressed to veterinary technician. As a tech, I would hold a dog and keep it calm while the vet gave it a shot. I would clip the dog before surgery, bathe it, bandage it, and basically serve as the vet's backup for whatever needed to be done.

It was around this time—during my high school years—when the other kids started calling me *el perrero,* "the dog boy." Remember, in the city of Mazatlan, this wasn't exactly a compliment. In North America and much of Western Europe, of course, people who have special relationships with animals are put up on pedestals. Think of such memorable figures as Dr. Dolittle, the Horse Whisperer, Siegfried and Roy . . . even the Crocodile Hunter! All of them—fictional characters and real people alike—are cultural heroes here because of their amazing natural gifts in communicating with animals. In Mexico, however, dogs in the city were considered lowly, dirty beasts—and because I hung around with dogs, I was, too, by association. Did

I care? No. I was on a mission. But it's important for me to explain the extreme differences in perception between Mexico and the United States when it comes to dogs. I believe that by coming from a place that values dogs less, I have a clearer perspective on how to *respect* dogs more.

The reality is, in most of the world, dogs are not cherished in the same way they are in North America and Western Europe. In South America and Africa, they are treated like they are in Mexico—as useful workers in the countryside, but filthy nuisances in the city. In Russia they are valued, but in very poor areas they run wild in packs and are dangerous, even to humans. In China and Korea, they are even cooked for food. That may sound barbaric to us, but remember, in India, we seem barbaric because we eat beef, the meat of their sacred cows! Having grown up in one culture and then started my own family in another, I believe it is best not to make too many value judgments about other ways of life—at least without having first experienced them and made an effort to understand how their attitudes and practices came to be. This said, when I came to the United States, I was in for some pretty big surprises about how dogs were regarded here!

Crossing the Border

I was about twenty-one years old when the desire to live my dream finally overcame me. I remember it very clearly; it was December 23. I went to my mom and said, "I'm going to the United States. Today." She said, "You've got to be crazy! It's almost Christmas! And we only have a hundred dollars to give to you!" I didn't speak any English. I would be going by myself. My family didn't know anybody in California. Some of my uncles had moved to Yuma, Arizona, but that was not my destination. My target was Hollywood. And I knew that the only way to get there was through Tijuana. My mother argued with me, pleaded with me. But I can't explain it—the urge to go to the United States *that moment* was totally overwhelming to me. I knew I had to act on it.

It's been published elsewhere, and I am not ashamed to say it: I came to the United States illegally. I now have my residence card, have paid a large fine for crossing illegally, and am applying for full citizenship status. There's no country I'd rather live in than the United States. I truly believe it is the greatest country in the world. I feel blessed to be living and raising my kids here. However, for the poor and working class of Mexico, there is no other way to come to America except illegally. It's impossible. The Mexican government is about who you know and how much money you have. You have to pay enormous amounts to officials in order to get a legal visa. My family had no way to get their hands on that kind of money. So, with just one hundred dollars in my pocket, I set out for Tijuana to figure out how to get across the border.

I had never been to Tijuana before. It's a rough place. There are bars and cantinas filled with drunks and drug dealers and criminals—people who will hurt you, and who are always waiting to take advantage of someone who is trying to get across the border. I saw some terrible things there. Luckily, I had a friend who worked at Señor Frog's, a very famous Tijuana bar. He let me crash in the back room for two weeks, while I figured out how I was going to cross over.

I remember it rained nearly every day, but every day, I went out and studied the situation at the border. I wanted to save my hundred dollars, so I tried to cross by myself—tried three times and failed.

After about two weeks, I was getting ready to try once more. It was about eleven o'clock at night: rainy, cold, and windy. Outside a coffee stand, where everybody was crowding around, just trying to warm up a little, a skinny guy—what we call a "coyote"—came up to me and said, "Hey, somebody told me you want to cross." I told him I did. He said, "Okay. I'll charge you one hundred dollars." A chill ran through me. How amazing was it that he wanted the exact amount of money that I had with me? The only thing he said was, "Just follow me. I'll take you to San Ysidro." So I followed him east.

We ran part of the way, ran until we were exhausted. My coyote pointed out the red lights in the distance, which gave away the positions of the *Migras* (the border patrol guards). He said, "We're gonna stay right here until they move." We were in a water hole. I waited all night, with the water up to my chest. I was freezing, trembling, but I didn't care. Finally, my coyote said, "Okay. Time to go." So we ran north—over mud, through a junk yard, across a freeway, and down a tunnel. At the other end of the tunnel was a gas station. My guide said, "I'm gonna get you a taxi, and then he's gonna take you to downtown San Diego." I hadn't even heard of San Diego. The only places I knew were San Ysidro and Los Angeles. The coyote gave the taxi driver twenty bucks out of the hundred I'd given him, wished me good luck, and was gone. Fortunately, the taxi driver spoke Spanish, because I knew not one word of English. He drove me to San Diego and dropped me off there—dripping wet, filthy, thirsty, hungry, my boots covered with mud.

I was the happiest man in the world. I was in the U.S.

San Diego

First, there were the leashes—leashes everywhere! I had seen chain leashes in the city when I lived in Mexico, but nothing like the leather leashes and nylon leashes and flexi leashes that Americans used. I looked around the city and wondered, "Where are all the dogs wandering in the streets?" It actually took me a long time to get my brain around the concept of a "leash law." On my grandfather's farm, the closest thing we had ever had to leashes were thick lengths of rope that we might tie around a particularly difficult animal's neck, "dog-show style," until we'd established our position as leader. Then it was back to nature—no need for a leash. Leashes were for mules, since most well-behaved dogs on the ranch would always do what we asked them to do. But leashes and fancy collars were only the beginning of my culture shock. As a new immigrant to this great country, I was in for a few more bombshells.

············

I had only a few dollars in my pocket when I came to the United States, and I knew no English. Of course, my dream was the same in any language—I had come here to become the best dog trainer in the world. The first words I learned to say in English were "Do you have a job application?"

After more than a month of living on the streets of San Diego, pounding the pavement in the same boots I was wearing when I first crossed the border, I got my first job—unbelievably, in my chosen field! It all happened so fast, it had to be a miracle. I didn't know where to look for "dog training" positions—I couldn't even read the Yellow Pages. But one day, while wandering through a neighborhood—still buzzing with the excitement of actually being in this country—I saw a sign for a dog grooming parlor. I knocked on the door and managed to put the words together to ask the two ladies who owned it if they had an application for a job. To my astonishment, they hired me on the spot.

Remember, I didn't speak a word of English; my clothes were worn and filthy; and I was living on the streets. Why in the world would they trust me? But they gave me not only a job but also 50 percent of the profits from whatever work I brought in. Fifty percent! After a few days, they learned that I was homeless, and they actually let me live there, right in the grooming parlor!

To this day, I call these women my American guardian angels. They trusted me and acted as if they'd known me all their lives. They were put in my path for a great reason, and I'm forever grateful to them, even though I don't remember their names.

If anyone ever says to you that people in the United States don't have kindness in their hearts anymore, don't believe them. I wouldn't be where I am today if it weren't for the unselfish help and trust of so many people who reached out to me. In this country, those two beautiful ladies in San Diego were the very first, but they wouldn't be the last. Believe me, not a day goes by that I don't remember how truly blessed I've been with the people who've been put in my path.

At the Groomer's

So, there I was, twenty-one years old, speaking almost no English and working at a dog grooming parlor. A *dog grooming* parlor! The very concept would have made my grandfather double over with laughter! The dogs on the farm cleaned one another and swam in the creek only if they got too hot. Their idea of a bath was rolling in the mud! The only time my grandfather ever hosed down a dog was if she had ticks or fleas or other parasites, or if her hair got too tangled or matted. Believe it or not, some dog owners in Mexico would actually put their dogs down if they had too many ticks. They'd show no mercy—just get rid of the dog and get another one that wasn't "flawed." Even the grooming I did at the vet in Mazatlan was simply a part of the medical treatment. The fact that American pet owners spent good money—to my mind, an enormous amount of money!—to wash, trim, and gussy up their dogs on a regular basis was eye-opening to me. It was my first glimpse into the American attitude toward pets. When I was in Mexico, I had heard that Americans treated their pets like human beings, but now I was actually seeing it in action, and at first, it really blew my mind. Apparently, nothing was too good for the dogs in America.

As foreign as the concept of a "grooming parlor" was to me, when I first started working there, I loved it. The women couldn't have been kinder to me, and I quickly developed a reputation for being the only one who could soothe the more difficult dogs— the stronger breeds or the ones that would cause everyone else to throw their hands up. Regular customers began to ask for me when they saw how I interacted with their pets, but I still didn't understand why their dogs behaved so much better with me than they did with the other groomers, or even their own owners. I think I was *beginning* to understand the difference, but I was not able to articulate it yet.

The San Diego grooming parlor had many more resources than I was used to having in Mexico. There were clippers, aromatic shampoos, and special, gentle blow-dryers designed especially for use with dogs. Awesome! Because I'd been trained at the vet's in Mazatlan, I'd never used a clipper, but was extremely proficient with scissors. The San Diego grooming parlor's owners were thrilled when they saw how fast and accurately I could work with a pair of scissors. So they gave me all the cocker spaniels, all the poodles, all the terriers, all the hard-to-groom dogs— which happened to be the dogs for whose grooming people paid the most. The shop charged $120 for an average-size poodle—

which meant $60 for me! This was manna from heaven. I was spending only a few dollars a day—subsisting on as little as a couple of 99-cent hot dogs from the ampm convenience store for breakfast and dinner. Everything else I squirreled away. By the end of the year, I planned to have enough money to move to Hollywood—one step closer to my dream.

Behavioral Issues

Encountering dogs with fancy leashes and collars and expensive hairdos astonished me when I first came to America, but in a way, the "Hollywood hype" I'd been raised with through movies and TV had prepared me for some of that. It was like going to the circus for the first time after being told about it all your life. There was one thing about my new situation, however, that shocked me to the core. It was the bizarre behavioral problems that many of these dogs exhibited. Even after growing up around canines all my life, dogs with what I now call "issues" were something completely foreign to me. During my time at the groomer's, I saw the most beautiful dogs I had ever imagined—stunning examples of their breeds, with clear eyes, gleaming coats, and healthy, well-fed bodies. Yet I could tell just by looking at them that their minds weren't healthy. Growing up with animals, you can automatically sense when their energy levels are normal. That healthy, balanced state of mind is recognizable in any creature—it's the same for a horse, a chicken, a camel, even for a child. Yet I could see right away that these American dogs were exhibiting what seemed to me to be a very strange, very *unnatural* energy. Even at the vet's in Mazatlan, I had never encountered dogs that were so neurotic, so excitable, so fearful and tense. And the owners' complaints! I didn't need to know very much English to understand that these dogs were aggressive, obsessive, and driving their owners crazy. The way some of these owners acted, it seemed as if their dogs were actually running their lives. What was going on here?

Back on my grandfather's farm in Mexico, there was no question of a dog's misbehaving and getting away with it, or trying to show its dominance over a person. And it wasn't because of abuse or physical punishment. It was because the humans knew they were humans, and the dogs knew they were dogs. Who was in charge and who wasn't was crystal clear. That simple equation has carried the dog-human relationship forward during the thousands—possibly tens of thousands—of years since the first dog ancestor wandered into our human ancestors' camp and realized it could get a quicker meal there than by hunting all day. Boundaries between humans and dogs were simple—and obvious. The dogs I knew in Mexico were naturally balanced. They didn't have troublesome personality quirks such as overt aggression or fixations. They were often scrawny and mangy, and sometimes not very pretty to look at, but they seemed to live their lives in the harmony that God and Mother Nature had intended for them. They interacted naturally with both their own kind and with humans. So what was going wrong with these gorgeous poster dogs in America?

The fact that so many American dogs had "issues" hit me even harder once I moved to Los Angeles and started working as a kennel boy at a dog-training establishment there. I wanted to learn how to be a dog trainer, and I'd heard that this was the best place around. I knew that rich people paid a great deal of money to leave their dogs at this highly respected facility. They would drop off their dogs for two weeks so the animals could learn to follow commands such as "sit," "stay," "come," and "heel."

When I began work at this facility, I was stunned at the condition that some of these dogs arrived in. Physically, of course, they were all gorgeous. They were well fed, beautifully groomed, and their coats gleamed with their good health. But emotionally, many of them were complete wrecks. Some were fearful and cowering; some were edgy or out-of-control aggressive. Ironically, the owners usually brought the dogs in to be trained in the hopes of getting rid of those neurotic behaviors. They believed that once the dog was taught to respond to commands, its fear, anxiety, or other problem behavior would miraculously go away. This is a common, but dangerous, misconception. It's absolutely true that if a dog has a mild, happy-go-lucky nature to begin with, traditional dog training can help settle her down and make life easier for everybody. But for a dog that is nervous, tense, excited, fearful, aggressive, dominant, panicky, or otherwise unbalanced, traditional training can sometimes do more harm than good. That fact became clear to me from my first day at the training facility.

My job at this facility was to lock the dogs in separate kennels until their daily "lessons" were to begin, then take them to their trainers. The isolation these troubled dogs experienced in the kennels between sessions often heightened the anxiety they had brought with them. Unfortunately, since the establishment wouldn't get paid unless the dog followed commands by the time the owner arrived to pick it up, instilling fear between commander and commandee was often the method of last resort. Some dogs would leave in worse psychological shape than they were in when they arrived. I witnessed dogs respond obediently to a trainer's commands while crouched down, ears back, cowering, tail between the legs—body language that broadcasts loud and clear, "I'm only obeying you because I'm terrified!" I believe that the trainers at this facility were caring professionals, and there was nothing cruel or inhumane going on there. But there was, in my personal observation, a deep-seated misunderstanding of a dog's basic needs, of what the canine mind truly *needs* to become balanced. That's because traditional dog training is based on human psychology. It doesn't begin to address a dog's nature.

I stayed at this establishment because I felt I needed to learn the business of dog training. It was, after all, what I'd come all this way to do. But this wasn't the dream I had imagined. From the moment I arrived there, I sensed that this kind of "training" may have been helpful for the humans, but it was sometimes detrimental for the dogs. Thinking back, it was then that my original "dream" started to take on a new shape. Once again, much of that change happened by accident. Although, I like to believe that it wasn't accidental at all—it was destiny.

"Cesar's Way" Is Born

While at this training facility, I once again gained a reputation for being the guy who could handle the most aggressive and most powerful breeds of dogs, such as pit bulls, German shepherds, and Rottweilers. I happen to be crazy about those breeds; their brute strength inspires me. Another kennel boy there was also great with the powerful breeds, but he didn't want to work with the nervous or anxious ones. I would end up with them— usually the really troubled cases. Instead of yelling at an aggressive or insecure dog like some of the other kennel boys did, I'd approach her silently. No talk, no touch, no eye contact. In fact, when I saw such a dog, I'd open the gate, then turn my back as if I were about to walk off in the other direction. Eventually, since dogs are naturally curious, the dog would come to me. Only after she had approached me would I put the leash on her. At that point it was easy, because I had already established my calm-assertive dominance with her, the way another dog would do with her in nature. Unconsciously, I was beginning to apply the dog psychology I had learned from my years observing dogs on my grandfather's farm. I was interacting with the dogs the way they interacted with one another. This was the birth of the rehabilitation methods I still use today, although I couldn't have explained in words what I was doing at the time—neither in English nor in Spanish. Everything I did just came instinctually to me.

Another crucial "accident" that occurred at this training facility was that I began to see the "power of the pack" to rehabilitate an unbalanced dog. One day, I went out into the yard holding two Rottweilers, a shepherd, and a pit bull all at once. I was the only one there who had ever attempted anything like this. Most of the other employees thought I was crazy. In fact, at one point, I was expressly ordered *not* to work with the dogs in packs; it made management nervous. But from the moment I discovered this method, I saw what an effective tool a pack of dogs could be in helping a dog that had problems. What I discovered was when a new and unstable dog was introduced to a group that had already formed a healthy bond, the pack actually influenced the newcomer to achieve that balanced state of mind. My job was to make sure the interaction between newcomer and existing pack members didn't get too intense. As long as I monitored and stopped any aggressive, exclusive, or defensive behavior on either side of the encounter, the new dog would eventually adjust its behavior to "fit in" with the others. With humans as with dogs—in fact, with all pack-oriented species—it's in our genetic best interest to try to fit in, to get along with others of our kind.[1] I was simply exploiting this very natural, genetic drive. By working with dogs in packs, I observed that they could accelerate one another's healing processes much faster than a human trainer could.

I soon earned a reputation at the facility as a reliable hard worker. But the more I developed my own ideas about dog psychology, the unhappier I became there. I guess I didn't hide my discontent very well. One client, a successful business owner who was especially thrilled with how I handled his golden retriever, had been watching me for a while and was impressed with both my skills and my work ethic. One day he approached me and said, "You don't look too happy here. Do you want to come work for me?" I asked him what I would be doing for him, thinking of course that it would have something to do with dogs. I was a little let down when he said, "You'd be washing limousines. I own a fleet of them."

Wow. Nice offer, but I had come to America to be a dog trainer. Still, he was a very impressive man—the kind of strong, confident businessman I wanted to become someday.

Then he sweetened the pot for me by telling me that as his employee, I would have my own car. I couldn't afford a car on my own then, and in Los Angeles, that's practically like not being able to afford legs. It took me a couple of weeks to decide, but finally I agreed. Once again, a guardian angel who didn't even know me had helped set the stage for the next phase of my journey.

Word of Mouth

My new boss was a tough but evenhanded taskmaster. He showed me the ropes of his business and how to wash his limos—and he was extremely particular about keeping them spotless. It could be arduous, physical work, but I didn't mind at all because I was—and still am—a perfectionist myself. If I was going to be a car washer, I was going to be the best car washer there ever was. I credit this man for teaching me so much about the way a solid, profitable business should be run.

The day I picked up the new car he lent me is a day I'll never forget. Yes, it was only a car—make that a white '88 Chevy Astrovan, and, no, I didn't have the pink slip—but for me, it symbolized the first time I truly felt I had "made it" in America. That was also the day I started my own "training business" for dogs, the Pacific Point Canine Academy. All I had was a logo, a jacket, and some hastily run off business cards, but most important, I had a clear vision of what I wanted to become. My dream was no longer to be the world's best trainer for movie dogs. Now I wanted to help more dogs like the hundreds of troubled animals I'd met since coming to America. I felt that my unique upbringing and innate knowledge of dog psychology could provide both the dogs and their owners a chance for better relationships and new hope for the future. It distressed me greatly that so many of these "bad" dogs who had "failed" at regular training facilities were doomed to be euthanized if their owners decided they "couldn't handle them" anymore. I knew in my heart that these dogs deserved to live as much as I deserved to live. My optimism about the future came from a deep-seated belief that there were many dogs in America who truly needed my help. Thanks again to the generosity of my new employer, my vision began to take shape more quickly than I could ever have imagined.

Word of mouth is an amazing thing. Even in a city as large and diverse as Los Angeles, the newest hot gossip item or tip can spread like wildfire. Fortunately for me, my new boss knew a lot of people, and he was never shy about praising my abilities. He'd call up his friends and say, "I've got this great Mexican guy who's amazing with dogs. Just bring 'em over." His friends started to bring their problem dogs. They'd be happy with the results. Then

My first truck and the jacket for my first business,
Pacific Point K-9 Academy

they'd tell their friends. Eventually, my Pacific Point Canine Academy had seven Dobermans and two Rottweilers with whom I would run up and down the streets of Inglewood, a small city in Los Angeles County. (That must have been quite a sight.)

After that, my fledgling business began to explode.

What was I doing that impressed people so much? How, after only a few years in America, did I already have a thriving business, without having placed a single advertisement? After all, there are hundreds of dog trainers and licensed behaviorists in Southern California, and I'm sure many of them are exceptional at what they do. You may ultimately decide that one of them may be a more appropriate expert than I am for what you want out of your relationship with your dog. I can only speak for my clients, and to them, I was just known as "that Mexican guy who has a magical way with dogs." The hallmarks of my technique consisted of energy, body language, and when needed, a quick, physical touch with a cupped hand, which is never painful to the dog but approximates the sensation of a dominant dog's or a mother dog's disciplinary "soft bite." I never yelled, never hit, and never "punished" animals out of anger. I simply corrected, the same way a natural pack leader will correct and educate a follower. Correct and then move on. There is nothing new in the techniques I was developing—they came directly from my observations of nature. I'm not saying there were no other trainers in America experimenting with these same methods. But the methods seemed to fulfill a desperate need among my clients in Los Angeles, and so they kept on coming.

One day, in 1994, I was at a client's house working with his troubled Rottweiler, Kanji. Kanji had been making great progress, and her owner, who was well connected in the entertainment business, had been talking me up all over town. I looked outside as

With the pack, back when it all began

a brown Nissan 300C pulled up the drive and a stunningly gorgeous woman got out of it and sauntered confidently toward me. I looked at her, trying to remember where I had seen her before, but for the life of me, I couldn't put my finger on it. Walking next to her—not so confidently—was a hesitant, shy Rottweiler. (Saki, it turned out was one of Kanji's pups.)

The woman asked me if I could train her dog, and three weeks later, I went to her house. And who should answer the door there but actor Will Smith. I was nearly speechless. Now I remembered where I'd seen that woman before—in the movie *A Low Down Dirty Shame*. My client was Jada Pinkett Smith!

Okay, let's get this straight: I'm in America for only three or four years, I now have my own successful business, and today I'm working with Jada Pinkett and Will Smith's dog?

Jada and Will explained that Jay Leno had just given them two new Rottweilers, and those dogs needed some work, as did Saki. This was an understatement—the dogs were a mess. Fortunately, Jada was one of those rare, special people who "got" my techniques and philosophies right away. She is an ideal dog owner—all she wants is what is best for her animals, and she will go to any length to ensure that they are happy and fulfilled.

That day was the beginning of an eleven-year friendship that continues today. Jada and Will recommended me to their friends in the "Hollywood elite," including Ridley Scott, Michael Bay, Barry Josephson, and Vin Diesel. But those aren't, by far, the most valuable gifts Jada has given me. She took me under her wing. She hired a teacher for me, for an entire year, to work intensively with me on my English. Most of all, she believed in me. Becoming known for what I do has always been my dream, but every great gift comes with a price. My life has become much more complicated now, with new quandaries such as whom to trust and whom to watch out for; which contracts are good and which should go in the shredder—things you don't learn on the farm in Ixpalino, Mexico. When I have questions that stump me, I know I can count on Jada. She's not only one of the most generous people I've ever met, she's also one of the smartest. I'll ask her, "Jada, what's going on? What do I do now?" And she'll just kick in and start soothing me: "Okay, Cesar, it's like this . . ." I always feel I have someone who knows a lot more than I do about playing in the big leagues, and who's always been willing to take a moment out of her incredibly busy life to lend me a hand. Jada has been more than my client. She's been my mentor, my sister, and another one of my precious guardian angels.

Also thanks to Jada, I made leaps and bounds in my English. I became more excited about my new, crystal-clear mission—as I put it, "to rehabilitate dogs and to train people." I began a program of self-education, reading everything I could get my hands on about dog psychology and animal behavior. Two books that most influenced me and reassured me about what I knew instinctively were Dr. Bruce Fogle's *The Dog's Mind,* and *Dog Psychology,* by Leon F. Whitney, DVM. I took in a great deal of wisdom from these and other books (some of which are listed in the "Recommendations for Further Reading," at the end of this book), and I also made sure to integrate that information into what I had learned from experience. In my opinion and observation, Mother Nature is the world's greatest teacher. But I was learning to think critically in a way I hadn't before, and more important, I was finding ways to articulate the things I intuitively understood. And finally, I was actually able to express those new ideas clearly, and in English.

By this time, I had met my future wife, Ilusion, who was only sixteen when we started dating. When a friend of mine told me that in the United States there was a law against an older guy dating a girl that young, I flipped out. I was terrified of being deported, and I dumped her flat. She was heartbroken. Convinced that I was "the one," she came knocking on my door the day she turned eighteen. We had a rocky relationship during the first years of marriage, and after our son Andre was born. I was still stuck in my old-world, macho Mexican ways. I believed that the only thing that mattered was me—my dream, my career—and she'd better put up or shut up. She did neither. She left me. Once she was gone and I realized she meant it, I had to look myself in the mirror for the first time in my life. I didn't want to lose her. I didn't want to see her remarry—and watch another man raise our son. Ilusion would come back to me on only two conditions—that we go to couples therapy and that I sincerely commit to being a full partner in the relationship. Reluctantly, I agreed. I didn't think I had that much to learn. I was wrong. Ilusion rehabilitated me in the same way I rehabilitate unbalanced dogs. She made me see what a gift a strong partner and family is, and that every member of a family needs to pull his or her own weight. Today, I consider Ilusion, Andre, and Calvin to be my greatest blessings on earth.

While I struggled to become a better partner in my marriage, I had more business than I could handle, thanks to people like my limo-rental boss and clients like Jada. Rescue organizations had started calling me to help them save their "last chance" cases from being put down, and suddenly I found myself with a pack of newly rehabilitated but orphaned dogs. I needed more space, so I rented a rundown piece of property in the warehouse district of South Los Angeles. Ilusion and I renovated it and made it into the Dog Psychology Center, sort of a permanent halfway house or "group therapy" drop-in station for dogs. Through it all, I kept working to find ways to explain my methods and philosophies to the average dog owner.

The Dog Psychology Center in its early days

Americans and Dogs:
Humans Who Love Too Much

When I was a boy in Mexico watching the *Lassie* and *Rin Tin Tin* shows, I was always entertained by those superstar dogs' adventures, but I thought that of course *everyone else watching* also realized that these shows were just Hollywood fantasies! When Lassie barked four times, and Timmy said, "What's that, Lassie? Fire? The house . . . no, the barn is on fire? Thanks, girl, let's go!" I knew—and assumed everyone else knew—that real dogs don't act like that. When I came to America, I was shocked to discover that many dog owners unconsciously believed that Lassie really *did* understand what Timmy was saying! I learned that here, the general perception of dogs was that they were all like Lassie—basically, humans in dog suits. It took me a while to process this, but once I'd been here a while, I saw that most pet owners did, on some level, believe that their animals—be they dogs, cats, birds, or goldfish—were indeed human in everything but the outfit. And they treated them accordingly.

After I'd been in the United States for about five years, it finally hit me—*that* was the problem! America's dogs were so troubled because their owners thought they were human. *They weren't allowed to be animals!* In the land of the free—where everyone is supposed to be able to reach his or her limitless potential—these dogs were doing anything but! Certainly, they were being pampered—they had the best food, the best homes, the best grooming, and large helpings of love. But that wasn't all they wanted. *They simply wanted to be dogs!*

I thought back to what I had learned in Mexico, where I spent countless hours watching the best dog trainers on earth—the dogs themselves. Thinking back to my natural relationship with them, I began to see how I could help dogs in the United States become happier, healthier creatures—and help their owners, too. My method is not brain surgery. I didn't create it: Mother Nature did. My fulfillment formula is simple: for a balanced, healthy dog, a human must share exercise, discipline, and affection, in that order! The order is vital, and I'll explain more about that later on.

Unfortunately, most American dog owners I meet don't get the fulfillment order right. They put affection as number one. In fact, many owners give their dogs nothing but affection, affection, affection! Of course, I know they mean well. But their good intentions can actually cause damage to dogs. I call these owners "humans who love too much."

You may be reading this and thinking, "I give my dog tons of affection because she's my baby! And she's fine! I have no behavioral problems with her." Indeed, you may well have a dog that has a naturally passive, happy-go-lucky disposition, and you may never have a single problem with her. You may shower her with an excess of love, and get nothing but that wondrous, unconditional dog love in return. You may consider yourself the luckiest dog owner in the world, with the world's most perfect dog. Thanks to your dog, you're happy, and your life is fulfilled. And I'm happy for you. But, please, open your mind to the possibility that your dog may be missing some of the things *she* needs in *her* life to be happy and fulfilled *as a dog*. At the very least, I hope this book helps make you more aware of your dog's very species-specific needs, and inspires you to find creative ways to help provide for them.

What I'm about to share is the truth of my life experiences. These are the things I have personally learned and experienced and observed, working with thousands of dogs for well over twenty years. I do believe from the deepest place in my heart that it is my mission to help dogs, and to spend my life learning everything they have to teach me. I see my career among dogs as an eternal education. I am the student, and they are my teachers. Let them help teach you what they've taught me. They've helped me to understand that what dogs really need isn't always what *we* want to give them.

2

If We Could Talk to the Animals

The Language of Energy

What is the communication style you use with your dog? Do you implore him to come to you, while he refuses, continuing to run down the street after a neighborhood squirrel? When your dog steals your favorite slipper, do you talk baby talk to him to try to get it back? Do you scream at the top of your lungs for your dog to get off the furniture, while he just sits there, staring at you as if you're crazy? If any of these sounds like you, I know you're aware that the techniques you're using aren't working. You understand that you can't "reason" with a dog, but you simply don't know any other way to communicate with him. I'm here to tell you that there's a much better way.

Remember the story of Dr. Dolittle, the man who was able to speak and understand the language of any animal he happened to meet? From the Hugh Lofting books to the 1928 silent film, to the thirties radio series, to the 1967 movie musical and seventies cartoons, to the blockbuster Eddie Murphy comedies, this wonderful tale and its main character have appealed to children and adults generation after generation. Just think of the countless worlds that would be unlocked if we saw things as animals see them. Imagine looking down at the earth through the eyes of a soaring bird, moving through life in three dimensions like a whale, or "seeing" the world through sound waves, the way bats do. Who hasn't dreamed of such thrilling possibilities? The attraction of the Dr. Dolittle story is that it brings animals to life, in big-screen living color.

What would you say if I told you that Doctor Dolittle's secret was more than just creative fiction?

Perhaps you're imagining this secret from a human perspective. You're wondering if I'm telling you that there's a *verbal* way to talk to your dog, perhaps with the use of a phrase book that translates your language into his. What would his language look like, sound like, you wonder? Would it include the words *sit, stay, come,* and *heel*? Would you have to shout the translations, or could you whisper them? Would you have to learn how to whimper and bark? Sniff your pet's behind? And how would your dog answer you back? How would you translate what he was saying? As you can see, creating a dog-to-human phrase book—the way, say, an English-to-Spanish phrase book is created—would be a very complicated effort indeed.

Wouldn't it be simpler if there was a *universal language* that *every* species could understand? "Impossible," you say. "Even human beings don't all speak the same language!" True, but that hasn't kept people from *trying* to find a common language for centuries. In the ancient world, all the higher-class, educated people learned Greek. That way, they could all read and understand the most important documents. In the Christian era, anybody who was anybody knew how to read and write Latin.

Today, English is at the top of the language food chain. I learned this the hard way when I first arrived in America fourteen years ago. Believe me, if you're not born speaking it, English is a monster of a language to learn from scratch—yet everyone from the Chinese to the Russians now accept it as the international language of business. Humans have sought other ways to breach the language barrier. No matter what language you speak, if you're blind, you can use Braille. If you're deaf, you can understand any other deaf person using International Sign Language. Mathematics and computer languages cross many linguistic borders and allow humans of different tongues to converse easily with one another, thanks to the power of technology.

If humans can succeed in designing these collective languages, can't we create a way to converse with the other species on the planet? Isn't there a language we can learn that means the same thing to every creature?

Good news! I'm happy to report that the universal language of Doctor Dolittle already exists. And humans didn't invent it. It's a language all animals speak without even knowing it, including the human animal. What's more, all animals are actually *born* knowing this language instinctually. Even human beings are born fluent in this universal tongue, but we tend to forget it because we are trained from childhood to believe that *words* are the only way to communicate. The irony is, even though we don't think we know the language anymore, we are actually speaking it all the time. Unknowingly, we are broadcasting in this tongue 24-7! Other species of animals can still understand *us*, even though we may not have a clue how to understand them. They read us loud and clear, even when we're unaware that we're communicating!

This truly universal, interspecies language is called *energy*.

Energy in the Wild

How can *energy* be a language? Let me give you some examples. In the wild, different animal species intermingle effortlessly. Take the African savannah or a jungle, for instance. At a watering hole in a jungle, you might see monkeys and birds in the trees, or on a savannah, different plant eaters, such as zebras or gazelles, wandering around, happily drinking out of the same crystal-clear pond. All is peaceful, despite the many different species sharing the same space. How do they all get along so smoothly?

How about a less exotic example? In your own backyard you may have squirrels, birds, rabbits, even foxes, all happily co-existing. There's no trouble until you rev up your lawnmower. Why? Because all these animals are communicating with the same relaxed, balanced, non-confrontational energy. Every animal knows that all the other animals are just hanging out, doing their own thing—drinking water, foraging for food, relaxing, grooming one another. Everybody's feeling mellow and no one's attacking anyone else. Unlike us, they don't have to *ask* one another how they're feeling. The energy they are projecting tells them everything they need to know. In that sense, *they are speaking to one another, all the time.*

Now that you've got this peaceful vision in your mind, imagine this: Suddenly, a new animal enters your backyard, or approaches our imaginary jungle waterhole, projecting a completely different energy. This new energy could be something as minor as one squirrel trying to plunder another's stash, or a gazelle jockeying another gazelle for a better drinking position at the oasis. It could also be as serious as a hungry predator seeking to subdue its next prey. Ever notice how a whole group of peaceful animals can turn scared or defensive in an instant, sometimes even before a predator has shown itself on the scene? They probably got a whiff of its scent—but it's also probable that they sensed the energy the predator was projecting.

What's always amazing to me about the animal kingdom is that even if a predator is near, all the other animals can usually tell if it's safe to stay around it or not. Imagine being introduced to a man you knew to be a serial killer. Would you be able to relax in his presence? Of course not! But if you were another kind of animal on this planet, you would probably be able to sense whether the serial killer was on the prowl or simply kicking back. Animals immediately recognize when a predator is projecting a hunting energy, sometimes even before they spot the predator itself. As humans, we are so often blind to these nuances in animal energy—we think a tiger is dangerous at all times, when, really, if he's just eaten a three hundred-pound deer, he's probably more tired than treacherous. The moment his tummy gets empty, however, he's a different animal—all instinct, all survival energy. Even your backyard squirrel will pick up on this subtle difference. Yet we humans tend to be blind to what, in the animal kingdom, is pretty much a flashing red light.

Here's an example of animal energy that folks who live in the American South can probably relate to. On a sunny day in Florida, Louisiana, or the Carolinas, you'll see giant alligators sunning their leathery bodies on the banks of swamps—all over expensive, exclusive golf courses! Meanwhile, golfers are teeing off a few feet away. Herons and cranes and turtles are happily sunning themselves right next to these terrifying reptiles. Eighty-pound old ladies are walking their teacup-size dogs on footpaths just inches from the alligators' swamp. What's going on here? It's simple. The other animals—from the turtles to the teacup Chihuahuas—are aware, on an instinctual level, that these fearsome predators aren't in a hunting mode at the moment. One thing you can be sure of—when the same big creature's tummy starts to rumble and his energy shifts into hunting mode, the rest of the animals will be gone in the blink of an eye. Except maybe the golfers. But they are one of the strangest species in nature, and even modern science hasn't figured them out yet.

Energy in Humans

When it comes to energy, we humans have much more in common with animals than we usually like to admit. Imagine one of the most ruthless jungles in the human world—the high school cafeteria. Picture it as a watering hole where different species— in this case, the cliques of jocks, nerds, and stoners—peacefully intermingle. Then a bully "accidentally" bumps into a smaller guy's food tray. The energy released by that interaction will ripple right through the entire room. Ask your teenager if this isn't true. And exactly as in the animal kingdom, this energy shift doesn't even have to be as blatant as a shove. Let's say the little guy in the cafeteria is having a bad day. He's failed two tests in a row and is in a weak state of mind. He happens to look up and accidentally catch the eye of the bully. Maybe the bully was just minding his own business, but as soon as he picks up on the weaker guy's diminished energy, the whole dynamic between them changes in a split second. In the animal kingdom, that's called survival of the fittest.

Let's take this concept beyond the school lunchroom and think about our society as whole. Right or wrong, we in America expect our leaders to project a dominant, powerful energy, like that of a Bill Clinton or a Ronald Reagan. Some powerful leaders project a charismatic energy that infects and energizes everyone around them—consider Tony Robbins. Martin Luther King, Jr., projected an energy that was what I call "calm-assertive"—the ideal energy for a leader. Though Gandhi was also a leader, his energy was of a more compassionate nature.

It's interesting to note that Homo sapiens is the only species on the planet that will follow a wise, kind, compassionate, or lovable leader. Humans will even follow an unstable leader, but that's another book in itself! As difficult as it may be for us to understand, in the animal kingdom, a Fidel Castro would win out as leader over a Mother Teresa any day. In the animal world, there is no morality, no right and wrong. Conversely, animals never cheat or lie their way to power—they can't. Other animals would figure them out in a heartbeat. Nature's leaders must project the most obvious and uncontestable strength. In the animal kingdom, there are only rules, routines, and rituals—based on survival of the strongest, not of the smartest or fairest.

Ever hear of "the smell of fear"? That's not just an expression. Animals sense vibrations of energy, but smell is their next strongest sense—and in a dog, energy and scent seem to be deeply connected. In fact, dogs empty their anal glands when they are afraid, emitting a smell that's distinctive not only to other dogs but to most animals (including us). A dog's sense of smell is connected to the limbic system, the part of the brain responsible for emotion. In his book *The Dog's Mind*, Dr. Bruce Fogle cites studies from the 1970s that showed that dogs can detect butyric acid—one of the components of human perspiration—at up to a million times' lower concentration than we can.[1] Think of lie detector sensors that can pick up minute changes in the perspiration on a person's hands when she is being deceptive. In essence, your dog is a living, breathing "lie detector"!

Do dogs actually physically "smell" fear in us? They certainly can sense it instantly. Countless joggers and mail carriers relate this harrowing experience—running or walking past a house and causing the dog there to bark, growl, or even charge the fence or gate. Now, this could be a dog that has adopted the role of protector of the house and takes that role very seriously—and too many mail carriers and joggers have the scars to show how powerful, aggressive dogs—what I call red-zone dogs—get out of control. (Red-zone dogs are serious business, and I'll address them in depth in a later chapter.)

For the purposes of understanding how dogs sense emotional states, imagine this as you walk by a house with a red-zone dog in it: *Perhaps the barking dog has a secret.* He may be more afraid of you than you are of him! Once you freeze up in terror, however, the balance of power instantly changes. Does the dog pick up on your energy shift through his "sixth sense"? Or does he smell some change in your body or brain chemistry? Science hasn't spelled it all out in layman's terms as of yet, but in my opinion, it's a combination of both. I can be sure of this from decades of close observation: you cannot "bluff" a dog the way you might be able to bluff a drunken poker buddy. Once you shift into the emotion of fear, that dog instantly knows he has an advantage over you. You are projecting a weak energy. And if the dog gets out, you are much more likely to be rushed or bitten than if you had tuned out the barking and simply gone on with your day. In the natural world, the weak get weeded out quickly. There's no right or wrong about it—it's just the way life on earth has worked for millions of years.

Energy and Emotion

The most important thing to understand about energy is that it's a *language of emotion*. Of course you never have to tell an animal that you're sad, or tired, or excited, or relaxed, because that animal already knows *exactly* how you're feeling. Think back on some of the beautiful stories you've read in publications like *Reader's Digest* and *People* magazine—stories of pets who have comforted, even saved, their sick, depressed, or grieving owners. These stories often include comments like "it was almost as if he knew what his owner was going through." I'm here to assure you that, yes, these animals *do* know exactly what their owners are feeling. A French study concluded that dogs may actually also use their sense of smell to help distinguish between human emotional states.[2] I'm not a scientist, but after a lifetime of being around dogs, my opinion is that, without question, dogs can sense even the most subtle changes in the energy and emotions of the humans around them. Of course animals can't always comprehend the *context* of our issues; they can't distinguish whether we're heartbroken over a divorce or losing a job or misplacing a wallet, because those very human situations mean nothing to them. However, such situations create emotions—and those emotions are universal. Sick and sad are sick and sad, no matter what your species.

Animals aren't in tune only with other animals—they seem to be able to read the energy of the earth as well. History is full of anecdotal tales of dogs who have appeared to "predict" earthquakes or cats who have hidden in the cellar for hours before a tornado. In 2004, a half day before Hurricane Charley hit the coast of Florida, fourteen electronically tagged blacktip sharks who had never before left their home territory off Sarasota suddenly headed off for deeper waters. And think of the terrible Southeast Asian tsunami of that same year.[3] According to eyewitnesses, an hour before the wave hit the coast, captive elephants for tourist "elephant rides" in Indonesia started wailing and even broke their chains in order to flee to higher ground. All over the region, zoo animals fled into their shelters and refused to come out, dogs would not go outdoors, and hundreds of wild animals at the Yala National Park, in Sri Lanka—leopards, tigers, elephants, wild boar, deer, water buffalo, and monkeys—also escaped to safe ground.[4] These are some of the miracles of Mother Nature that continue to astound me: they are a brilliant illustration of the powerful language of energy at work.

One of the most important things to remember is that all the animals around you—especially the pets with whom you share your life—are reading your energy every moment of the day. Sure, you can say anything that pops into your mind, but your energy *cannot* and *does not* lie. You can scream at your dog to stay off the sofa until your face is blue, but if you aren't projecting the energy of a leader—if, down deep inside, you know you're going to let him on the sofa if he begs you long enough—he's going to know what your real bottom line is. That dog is going to sit on the sofa as long as he damn well pleases. He already knows you are not going to follow through on your screaming. Because dogs often perceive loud vocalizing by humans in an excited, emotional state as a sign of instability, he'll be either unaffected by your tantrum or confused and frightened by it. He certainly won't relate it to your rules about the couch!

The Calm-Assertive Personality

Now that you understand the powerful "language" of energy, my next job is to help you understand how to harness it to foster better communication between you and your dog. It takes a dog only a few seconds to determine what kind of energy you are projecting, so it is important that you be consistent. With your dog, you want to project what I call "calm-assertive" energy at all times. A calm-assertive leader is relaxed but always confident that he or she is in control.

Now, the word *assertive* has gotten an unfair bad rap lately. Maybe it's because it is so similar to the word *aggressive,* but their meanings are worlds apart. Think of people in popular culture. No matter what side of his politics you adhere to, you've got to admit that Bill O'Reilly is angry-aggressive. He yells "Shut up!," interrupts, and tries to get his way through bullying. In most everyday situations, being angry-aggressive can work against you—it's simply not an energy-efficient way to get things done, and it's really not good for your blood pressure. An angry-aggressive dog would not make a good pack leader because the other dogs would perceive him as unstable.

I haven't come across many people who are "calm-aggressive" in my job, though I suppose you could describe the villains in James Bond movies that way—they're always plotting to blow up the world without breaking a sweat or spilling their martinis. In any case, "calm-aggressive" is not an energy state that's natural to the nonhuman creatures in the animal kingdom.

But calm-assertive personalities? They are the leaders of the animal world. In our human landscape, they are few and far between, but they are almost always the most powerful, impressive, and successful people on the block. Oprah Winfrey—the number one role model for my own professional behavior—is the epitome of calm-assertive energy. She is relaxed, even-tempered, but undeniably powerful, and always in charge. People everywhere respond to her magnetic energy, which has made her one of the most influential—and one of the wealthiest—women in the world.

Oprah's relationship with one of her dogs, Sophie, is another story. Like many of the powerful people who hire me to help them with their dogs, Oprah had some issues in sharing her vaunted calm-assertiveness with Sophie. In the years that I've been helping people and their dogs, I've observed that many type A powerbrokers—directors, studio heads, movie stars, doctors, lawyers, architects—have no trouble being dominant and in control in their jobs, but the moment they arrive home, they let their dogs walk all over them. These people often see their life with their pet as the *only* area where they can let their softer side show. This is all incredibly therapeutic for the human, but it can be psychologically damaging for the animal. Your dog needs a pack leader more than he needs a buddy. But if you're looking for a role model in calm-assertive energy, turn your channel to *The Oprah Winfrey Show* and watch her interact with her guests and her audience. That's the kind of energy you should be aiming for when you interact with your dog, cat, boss, or your kids!

Fake It Till You Make It

What if you're not naturally a calm-assertive person? How do you react when a problem pops up? Are you panicky and excitable, or defensive and aggressive? Do you tend to handle problems as if they were a personal assault upon you? It's true that energy doesn't lie, but *energy and power* can be *focused* and *controlled*. Biofeedback, meditation, yoga, and other relaxation techniques are excellent for learning about how to better control the energy you project. Spending eight years in intensive judo training as a boy made controlling my mental energy second nature for me. If you're high-strung, anxious, or overly emotional— dead giveaways when animals are reading your energy—such techniques can make a big difference in how you relate to your pets. Learning to harness the power of the calm-assertive energy within you will also have a positive impact on your own mental health—and on your relationships with the *humans* in your lives. I guarantee it.

I often counsel my clients to use their imaginations and employ visualization techniques when they feel "stuck" in trying to project the right energy to their dogs. There are a lot of wonderful self-help, psychology, and philosophy books available to help you learn to harness the power of your mind to change your behavior. Some of the authors who have most influenced me are Dr. Wayne Dyer, Tony Robbins, Deepak Chopra, and Dr. Phil McGraw. Acting techniques such as those pioneered by Konstantin Stanislavski and Lee Strasberg are also excellent tools for transforming the way you relate in the world.

In the first season of my National Geographic Channel show, *Dog Whisperer with Cesar Millan,* I came across a case that offered an excellent example of how we can use our powers of visualization to instantly transform our energy and our relationships with our dogs.

Sharon and her husband, Brendan, had rescued Julius, a sweet, lovable pit bull/Dalmatian mix, who, unfortunately, came to them afraid of his own shadow. Whenever they took him out for walks, he would tremble all over and walk with his tail between his legs, and would bolt for the safety of their house the moment he got a chance. When guests came over, he would freeze up and cower under the furniture. When I worked with the couple, I noticed that Sharon became extremely anxious and frightened whenever Julius acted afraid or pulled on his leash during walks. She was so worried about Julius that she would try to comfort him with words, and when he wasn't comforted, she would just throw her hands up in helplessness. It was clear to me that Julius was picking up on Sharon's fearful energy, which was greatly intensifying his own fear.

When Sharon told me she was an actress, however, I realized

that she had a powerful tool at her disposal that she wasn't taking advantage of. The best actors learn to dig deep inside themselves, to use the power of thought, feeling, and imagination to transform themselves into different characters and to switch instantly from one emotional state to another. I asked Sharon to reach into the same "tool kit" she drew upon when she performed onstage or in a film and concentrate on a very simple acting exercise: to think of a character she identified as being calm and assertive. Because of her training, Sharon immediately understood what I was asking her to do. Without hesitation she answered, "Cleopatra." I then suggested that she "become" Cleopatra every time she walked Julius.

It was thrilling for me to watch her the first time she gave that acting exercise a try! While walking Julius, Sharon began to imagine that she actually was Cleopatra. Right before my eyes, her posture became straighter and her chest higher. She raised her head and gazed imperiously around her, as if she were the queen of all she surveyed. Thanks to the same acting abilities she'd spent a lifetime honing, suddenly she was aware of her power and her beauty, and she naturally expected everyone— especially her dog—to obey her every wish! Of course, Julius had never gone to acting class, but because he picked up on her energy shift, he had no choice but to become Sharon's "scene partner" in her Cleopatra fantasy. The change in that cowering pit bull/Dalmatian was immediate. Once he realized he was walking with a "queen," he instantly became more relaxed and less fearful. After all, what dog would be afraid with the all-powerful Cleopatra holding his leash?

Julius and his owners have worked hard and come a long way. It took many months of dedicated daily practice, but a year later, Julius is totally secure on their walks, and now even welcomes strangers into their home—all thanks to the power of calm-assertive leadership, and with a little help from Cleopatra.

Calm-Submissive Energy

The proper energy for a follower in a dog pack is called calm-submissive energy. This is the healthiest energy for your dog to project in his relationship with you. When people come to the Dog Psychology Center and watch my pack in action, they are often astounded at how mellow a group of forty to fifty dogs can be 90 percent of the time. That's because my pack is made up of calm-submissive, mentally balanced dogs.

The word *submissive* carries with it negative connotations, just as the word *assertive* does. *Submissive* doesn't mean pushover. It doesn't mean you have to make your dog into a zombie or a slave. It simply means *relaxed* and *receptive*. It's the energy of a group of well-behaved students in a classroom, or of a church congregation. When I give my dog-behavior seminars, I always thank my audience for being in a calm-submissive state—that is, open-minded and able to converse easily with one another. When I learned how to be calm-submissive to my wife, it improved my marriage 100 percent!

For dogs and humans to truly communicate, the dog must project a calm-submissive energy before a human can get him to obey her. (As dog owners, we don't ever want to be perceived as the submissive ones.) Even when a dog is doing search and rescue, he's not assertive—he's active-submissive. Though that search-and-rescue dog is meant to be out in front of the handler, scratching excitedly at piles of rubble, the handler will first sit the dog down and wait until he is in a submissive state of mind, and only then will give him the signal to begin the search. Dogs who work with handicapped people also must be the submissive ones in the relationship, even if their owners are blind or confined to wheelchairs. The animals are there to help people, not the other way around.

Body Language

Your dog is constantly observing you, reading your energy. He is also reading your body language. Dogs use body language as another means of communicating with one another, but it's important to remember that their body language is also a function of the energy they're projecting. Remember the example of Sharon and Julius, where simply thinking about being Cleopatra inspired Sharon to stand up taller and prouder? The energy fed the body language, and in turn, the body language reinforced the energy. The two are always interconnected.

You can learn to interpret your dog's body language by the visual clues he or she gives you, but it's important to remember that different energy can determine the context of a posture. It's like those pesky words called homonyms in English—words that sound exactly the same but mean different things. Like *read* and *red*, or *flee* and *flea*. For the non-native English speaker, it takes a little while to learn how to distinguish between such words. But of course, it all comes down to context. How a word is used is what determines its meaning. It's the same with dogs and body language. A dog with his ears back may be signaling calm submission, which is the appropriate energy for a follower in a pack. Or, he may be signaling that he is afraid. One dog mounting another may signal dominance, or it may simply be play behavior. The energy always creates the context.

Alert dominant

Alert relaxed

Calm submission

Fear (tail between legs)

May I Sniff You?

As I mention earlier, scent can also function as a language for dogs. Your dog's nose—millions of times more sensitive than yours—provides him with a huge amount of important information about his environment and the other animals in it. In nature, a dog's anal scent is his "name." When two dogs meet, they'll sniff each other's behinds as a way of introduction. Since they don't have phone books, dogs can tell other dogs where they live and where they've roamed by urinating on a "signpost"—a bush, a tree, a rock, or a pole. When a female is in heat, she'll deposit her scent through urine all throughout her territory, placing a kind of personal ad for the male dogs in the neighborhood[5]—who may show up on her owner's doorstep the following morning, without her poor human owner knowing how in the world they got "invited." Through scent, dogs can also find out if another dog is sick or what kind of food it has been eating. As in the studies of dogs and their ability to "sniff" out emotional changes in humans, scientists have for many years been trying to understand the miraculous power of a dog's nose to discern all sorts of subtle information. In September 2004, the *British Medical Journal* published the results of a Cambridge University study that proved that dogs could "sniff out" bladder cancer in urine samples at least 41 percent of the time.[6] For years, there had been anecdotal evidence of such miraculous feats, but now science is actively working to research how dogs can help detect diseases at much earlier stages than even some high-tech equipment can detect it.

You know those whole-body CT scan machines, where you lie down for a few moments and supposedly get a complete diagnosis of all your bodily systems? That's pretty much what dogs do when they first meet you. They use their noses to give you a whole-body scan, check you out, find out where you've been and what you've been doing lately. In dog etiquette, you're supposed to let them do it. At my Dog Psychology Center, when a new dog enters the pack's territory, it is only polite for him to remain still while everybody in the pack comes up and smells him. If the dog stands quietly, allowing the others to finish sniffing, he will be accepted more easily into the pack. If he moves away, the other dogs will chase him around until they're done sniffing. A sign that a dog is antisocial toward other dogs is that he is uncomfortable or aggressive about being sniffed. That's a dog that hasn't learned any manners—like a human who won't shake hands upon intro-duction. When a person enters the gate of my center and walks through the dog pack, the dogs will do the same thing to her. Many people find it intimidating—or just plain terrifying—to have a pack of forty very scary-looking dogs descend on them and start sniffing away. A person shouldn't look at or touch the dogs during this process, but the dogs should be allowed to surround that person and smell her. That's the only way they can become comfortable with a new animal of any species— by learning to distinguish her by her scent. I'm not "Cesar" to my dogs. I'm their pack leader, which is Cesar's scent and energy.

While smelling you is a way for your dog to recognize you, projecting the correct energy is the key to becoming your dog's pack leader. We'll go deeper into the pack leader concept—it is the cornerstone of your healthy relationship with your dog. But first, it's important to remember that your dog doesn't see the world the same way you do. Once you learn to experience your dog as an animal first, and not as a four-legged human, you will be better able to understand his "language" of energy—and truly "hear" what he is saying to you.

"So you're saying your mother was a bitch."

3

Dog Psychology

No Couch Required

In the last chapter, I define and discuss energy as a concept of communication between humans and animals. Whether you know it or not, you and your dog are communicating all the time through energy, with body language and scent thrown in for good measure. But how do you interpret the messages your dog is sending you? And how do you know you are projecting the right kind of energy back to her? It begins by understanding dog psychology—by going back to your dog's inborn nature and trying to see the world through her eyes, not your own.

Humans Are from Saturn, Dogs Are from Pluto

For any relationship to truly achieve harmony, it can't be one-sided. The needs of both parties must be fulfilled. Think about male-female relationships. When I was first married, it took me a long time to realize that the way I saw the world as a man was very different from the way my wife saw the world as a woman. The things that made me happy and content in the relationship were not always the same things that made her happy and content—and as long as I fulfilled only my own needs, we would have real problems. It was my way or the highway, partly because I was selfish, but mostly because I didn't know there was another way.

If I don't understand the psychology of the most important woman in my life, then how can we truly communicate? We can never become connected to each other, and a relationship without connection is vulnerable to divorce. I had to read a lot of relationship psychology books to learn to see the world through Ilusion's eyes, and believe me, my doing so made a huge difference in our marriage.

My goal here is to help you make the same kind of positive changes in your "marriage" with your dog, based on a new understanding of your dog's true nature. It's only with this knowledge that you can achieve the kind of connection between species—that true man-beast connection—that you desire in your heart.

The first mistake so many of my clients make in relating to their dogs is similar to the one many men make in relating to women—they assume that both their minds work in exactly the same way. Most animal lovers insist on trying to relate to their dogs using human psychology. No matter the breed—German shepherd, Dalmatian, cocker spaniel, golden retriever—they truly see all dogs as furry, four-legged people. I suppose it's natural to humanize an animal, because human psychology is our first frame of reference. We've been raised to believe the world belongs to us, and that it should run the way we want it to. However, as clever as we humans are, we aren't clever enough to completely undo Mother Nature. Humanizing a dog, the source of many of the problem behaviors I am called in to correct, creates imbalance, and a dog who's out of balance is an unfulfilled and, more often than not, troubled dog. Time and time again, I am called in to work with a dog that is essentially running her owner's life, exhibiting dominant, aggressive, or obsessive behaviors, and creating a household in turmoil. Sometimes these issues have gone on for years and years. Often, a baffled owner will say, "The problem is, she thinks she's a person." No, she doesn't. I promise you, your dog knows full well that she's a dog. The problem is, you don't know it.

Different Pasts, Different Presents

Animals and humans all evolved differently, from different ancestors and with different strengths and weaknesses to help them survive in the world. In his book *Wild Minds: What Animals Really Think*, Professor Marc D. Hauser describes different animals as having different built-in "mental tool kits" for survival.[1] I like this "tool kit" analogy because it's a simple way to begin to understand nature's great diversity. Some tools we all share, such as the universal language of energy, which I describe earlier. Some tools are specific to one species. Many tools are the same across more than one species—scent, for example—but may play a greater role in the survival of one species over another. Each of these evolutionary "tools" becomes the toolbox of an animal's mind, so that every species has a psychology that is in some ways very specific and unique. Giraffes have their own psychology. Elephants have their own psychology. You wouldn't expect a lizard to have the same psychology as a human, would you? Of course not. Because a lizard evolved in a different environment, and lives a completely different life from a human's. Lizards are "built" for completely disparate functions than we are. Going back to the "tool kit" analogy, you wouldn't expect a doctor to bring a computer programmer's tool kit to the operating room. You wouldn't expect a plumber to bring a violinist's tools to fix your sink. They all have separate tools because they all do very different jobs. Although dogs and humans have interacted closely—perhaps even interdependently—for thousands of years, dogs were also "built" for jobs very much unlike the jobs we humans were designed by nature to do. Think about it. Considering your different jobs and different tool kits, why would you expect your dog's mind to operate in the same way that yours does?

When we humanize dogs, we create a disconnect for them. By humanizing them, we're going to be able to love them the way we would love a human, but we're never going to achieve a deep communion with them. We're never really going to learn to love them for who and what they truly are.

It may seem to you, as you read this book or watch my TV show or attend one of my seminars, that I keep hitting these same points over and over: "Dogs don't think like humans." "Dog psychology isn't human psychology." If you've heard enough of it already and are all set to start relating to your dog as a dog, congratulations and more power to you! But you'd be amazed at the number of clients I have, and the hundreds of people I speak to or who write to me, who are reluctant and sometimes downright unwilling to let go of the picture they have in their minds of their dogs as cute little people. Their dogs are their "babies," and by thinking of them otherwise, their owners are afraid they'll somehow lose the connection between them instead of strengthen it. During a question-and-answer period at the end of one of my seminars, a clearly disheartened woman stood up and said, "Do you realize that everything you are telling us goes completely against everything we've ever thought about our dogs?" I had to say to the audience, "I'm sorry, humans." Some of my clients are heartbroken and actually shed tears when I tell them that in order to solve their dogs' problems, they have to start perceiving and treating their canine companions in a way that is completely different from how they've perceived them, sometimes for years. Often when I leave a consultation, I fear that the dog I've just met is never going to get the chance to live a peaceful, balanced life because her owner seems unlikely and unwilling to change. If you are reading this and fear that you may be one of these people, please take heart. Think of getting to know your dog for who she *really* is as an exciting new adventure! Consider the great privilege you will be given, being able to live side by side with and learn to see the world through the eyes of a very special member of a completely different species! Remember that by making a commitment to change, you are making a commitment to your dog. You are giving your dog an opportunity to reach her natural potential. You are offering another living creature the highest form of *respect*, by letting that creature be what she is supposed to be. You are building the foundations of a new connection that will bring you and your dog even closer.

So, what exactly is so different about dog psychology? To begin to understand it, we must again look at how canines live in nature, when humans are out of the picture. Dogs begin their lives in a very different way from humans. Even our most basic senses are different.

Nose, Eyes, Ears: In That Order!

When a mother dog gives birth, her puppies are born with their noses open but their eyes and ears are closed. The earliest, most vital thing in a dog's life—her mother—appears to it first as scent. The mother is, first and foremost, scent and energy. A human infant can also distinguish his mother's smell from the smells of other humans, so scent is important to us as well.[2] But it's not our most important sense. For man, "seeing is believing." When you hear that some guy named Cesar Millan can control a pack of forty dogs without a leash, you're not going to believe it until you see me do it. Well, for a dog, smelling is believing. If she doesn't smell it, she can't figure it out. It's not real to her. And how's this for a comparison: while we humans have only about 5 million scent receptors in our noses, the average grown dog has about 220 million. In fact, as handlers of tracking and cadaver dogs can tell you, dogs have the ability to sniff out smells that we can't even pick up using sophisticated scientific equipment.[3] In short, a puppy grows up to "see" the world using its nose as its primary sensory organ.

Along with scent and energy, a puppy will experience touch as she wriggles close to her mother to nurse, long before she even knows what she looks like. Not until about fifteen days after her birth will she open her eyes and start to take in the world through sight. And not until around twenty days after birth will her ears start to function.[4] But how do we most often try to communicate with our dogs? By talking to them as if they understood us, or by yelling commands at them!

Nose, eyes, ears. My clients get tired of my repeating this, but I'll say it again. Nose, eyes, ears. Commit that to memory. It is the natural order of senses in dogs. My point is that from the very beginning—from the development of their first basic tools of survival—dogs experience the world in a completely different way than we do. They, in essence, experience a different world.

Even the experience of birth for a puppy is far removed from that of a human infant. For a dog, the calm-assertive energy of the mother permeates everything. Think about a typical birth scenario for a human. Imagine the stereotypical male delivery room role: "Breathe, honey, breathe!" Think about your favorite sitcom, with the husband pacing the waiting room or fainting at the sight of blood during the delivery. Remember that famous *I Love Lucy* episode when Ricky and the Mertzes rehearse everything for Lucy's trip to the hospital, but when the time finally comes, they all fall apart?

For first-time human parents, a birth is usually very stressful and frenetic. It's a different story in the animal world. In her natural environment, a mother dog will not be afraid of labor, nor will she need doctors, nurses, midwives, or Lamaze coaches to cheer her on. She builds her nest, goes to it by herself, and in many cases becomes very territorial about the experience. Have you ever seen a mother dog take her newborns into a closet or under a bed, where she cleans them of the placenta and begins to feed them? It's a private thing for her. That, immediately, is another difference between humans and dogs. We bring the whole family into the delivery room: grandma, grandpa, cousins, along with a video camera, cigars, flowers, balloons. We create parties around having babies! Which is a very beautiful ritual for us— but again, a distinction between humans and dogs is the very way that life begins for us. Being a dog is not less or more than being a human. But life for a dog is fundamentally a very different experience, from day one.

Let's look at the early development of dogs as a window into their minds. While puppies are tiny, a mother dog presents herself in the den, and the puppies must find her, must come to her.

She doesn't go to them. As they grow older, sometimes she walks away from them—or even pushes them away—when they approach her to nurse. In nature, this is where both discipline and natural selection begin. The weak puppies will be the ones who have the hardest time finding her, and who can't compete when it's time to feed. If a mother dog senses a weakness in one of her puppies, she won't look out for it. It may even die. You can see right there the enormous difference between humans and dogs. We are the only species in the animal kingdom that takes extra care of a weak infant. There's no neonatal intensive care unit in a dog pack. It isn't that the mother dog doesn't care for her offspring, it's just that, in the natural world of dogs, "caring" means ensuring survival for the pack, and for future generations. A weak puppy who can't keep up endangers not only the whole pack by slowing it down, but in genetic terms, it's also likely to grow up weak, to breed more weak puppies. It seems harsh to us, but in the natural world the weak are always weeded out early.

To a puppy, its mother begins as scent and energy—the same calm-assertive energy that you will read much more about throughout this book. The hormone progesterone, which is still strong in the mother from pregnancy, helps enhance this calm energy, inhibiting her fight-or-flight response so she can concentrate on raising her puppies.[5] Calm-assertive energy is the very first energy that puppies experience, and it will be this energy that they associate with balance and harmony for the rest of their lives. From the very beginning of their lives, they learn to follow a calm-assertive leader. They also learn calm-submission, the natural role of *followers* in the animal kingdom, and especially in the dog world. They are learning patience. Dogs' food doesn't arrive on a Federal Express truck; they have to wait for the mother to return to the den in order to feed. They learn that survival means both competition with their littermates for food and co-operation with their mother—by default, their first pack leader.

The Proper Way to Meet a Dog

This isn't a book about dog biology, but there's a reason why it's important to know how your dog's body and mind interrelate, and how your dog developed from the puppy he or she once was. Its mother is the first "introduction" a puppy will have in the world. She's the first "other being" a puppy will meet. Now, contrast the calm-assertive scent and energy emitted by a mother dog with how we normally introduce ourselves to a dog. What do we usually do when we see a cute little puppy? "Ooooo!" we exclaim loudly, usually in a high-pitched voice we reserve for babies. "Come here, you cute little thing!" By doing this, we are introducing ourselves to the dog using sound first—and not only sound but usually very excited, *emotion-charged* sound. What we're doing is projecting *excited, emotional energy*, which is the furthest from calm-assertive energy that we can get. To a dog, emotional energy is weak and often negative energy. So from the get-go, we're telling the dog that we don't exactly have it all together.

And what happens next? *We* approach *the dog,* not the other way around. We rush up to her, bend down to her level, and give her affection—usually a pat on the head—before she even knows who we are. By this point, the dog has already figured out that we really don't understand anything about her. She's also getting the clear message that we're coming *to her*—and from that point on, we are signing a contract that says that we are the followers and she is the leader. Do you blame her, after we've made such an unstable first impression?

Wrong way to meet a dog

Let's replay that first-meeting scenario using dog psychology instead of human psychology. The proper way to approach a new dog is not to approach her at all. Dogs never approach each other face on, unless they are challenging each other. And pack leaders never approach pack followers; the followers always approach him. There is such a thing as etiquette in the dog world, and a canine Emily Post would demand that when meeting a dog, you not make eye contact, you maintain calm-assertive energy, and you allow the dog to come to you. How will this dog check you out? By sniffing, of course. And don't be alarmed if she sniffs your crotch. Of course among humans it would be considered downright offensive to sniff someone's genitals upon first meeting him, but that's how dogs greet each other all the time. They usually don't mean anything sexual by it; it's simply a way that they get important information about each

Right way to meet a dog

other—gender, age, what the other dog had for lunch. A dog who sniffs you is getting similar information about you. While sniffing you, the dog is reading not only your scent but also the all-important energy you are projecting. Now, that dog may end up not being very interested in you and may wander off in search of other, more fascinating scents. Or she may stick around to explore you further. Once a dog has decided to initiate contact with you, by nuzzling or rubbing up against you, only then should you offer affection to her. And save the eye contact for when you really know each other better—sort of like not going too far on a first date.

Sometimes, after examining a new person, a dog will lose interest and begin to wander away. Naturally, the dog lover will reach out after her and attempt to give her affection in order to bring her back. With some dogs, this can be perceived as an unwanted advance and can precipitate a bite. Even with a friendly dog, I usually suggest that people don't offer affection right away. Let the dog get to know you, feel comfortable with you, and do something to *earn* your affection first.

This advice almost never goes over very well, because we humans get such a great sense of satisfaction from sharing affection with dogs. What most animal lovers don't understand is that by sharing affection first, we are not doing the dog any favors. We might be fulfilling our own needs—after all, dogs are so sweet and appealing and soft and fluffy! And as it turns out, they are important to both our physical and mental health as human beings. As animal behaviorist Patricia B. McConnell points out in her book *The Other End of the Leash: Why We Do What We Do Around Dogs,*[6] petting an animal can actually have significant physical benefits for people. According to McConnell, studies have shown that stroking a dog reduces heart rate and blood pressure in humans—as well as in the dog!—and releases chemicals in our brains that help soothe us and counteract the effects of stress. But when we come to a dog we barely know and offer unconditional affection right away, we may be creating a serious imbalance in our relationship with that dog. Particularly, if we are to be the dog's owner, a simple first meeting like this is often where behavior problems begin. Just like in the human world, to a dog a first impression counts a lot.

Many dog lovers may feel angry at me here, and let me make it clear that I understand that people have the best intentions in mind when giving a dog affection first. To reach out to another being with affection is a natural impulse for most of us, and part of what is most beautiful about being human. But we must try to remember that by doing so, we're fulfilling our own need for affection, not the dog's. Like most mammals, dogs do need and crave physical affection in their lives. But it's not the first and most import thing they need from *you*. If they get affection first, it tips the scales of your relationship—in the wrong direction.

Seeing Things Backward

You now understand how, in relating to dogs, we usually communicate everything to them "backward"—using sound, then sight, and generally ignoring scent. Dogs experience the world through scent, sight, and then sound—in that order. That's vital to remember if we want to communicate correctly with them. Never forget my formula: nose, eyes, ears. Repeat it to yourself the way I repeat it to my clients, until it's second nature.

There is another critical thing we do backward when we associate with dogs, although this concept is a little more difficult to understand. We relate to dogs the same way as we do to humans—as a specific name or personality first. When I relate to people, I expect them to see me first as Cesar Millan, next as Hispanic male, last as human being (Homo sapiens). When we relate to one another, we rarely think about the species we belong to, and almost never remember that we are all members of the animal kingdom. That information just doesn't enter into our minds when we meet our friends for coffee at Starbucks. A friend is a name and personality, period.

Naturally, we think of our dogs and most of our pets in this same way—name and personality first. In fact, we usually think of our dogs as name and personality, then breed, then ... human! Take a famous dog—say, Paris Hilton's Chihuahua, Tinkerbell. We automatically think of the dog as a name first—Tinkerbell. At the same time, we might think of something about Tinkerbell's personality—say, she's spoiled. Or she wears cute outfits. Then we think of her as her breed—Chihuahua. Last, we remember that she is a dog, although the way she is always carried around from place to place in designer handbags and limousines, it would be easy to mistake her for a doll or small child. Because Tinkerbell is so enmeshed in the human world, it rarely crosses our minds to think of her as animal—or to relate to her as such. But animal she is. This is another place where we go very wrong in how we communicate with our canines.

When you interact with your dog—and this is most important when you are trying to deal with her issues or correct her behavior problems—you must relate to her this way, in this order:

First, as

    1. animal
    2. species: dog (Canis familiaris)

Then, as

    3. breed (Chihuahua, Great Dane, collie, etc.)

And last and least important

    4. name (personality)

This doesn't mean Paris can't love Tinkerbell for being Tinkerbell. What it does mean is that Paris needs to recognize the animal and species in Tinkerbell first, in order for Tinkerbell to live a well-adjusted life. All the designer handbags and limousines in the world won't make her a happy, balanced dog.

Recognizing the Animal in Your Dog

What do you think of when you think of the world *animal*? I think of nature, fields, forests, the jungle. I think of wolves, whose territories extend for miles and miles in their wild state. I think of two words in particular: *natural* and *freedom*. Every animal, including the human animal, is born with a deep-seated need to be free. But when we bring animals into our lives, by definition they are not "free" anymore—at least not in the way that nature intended them to be. We contain them when we bring them into our environment. Most of the time, we do it for good and well-intentioned reasons. But regardless of whether it's a kitten, a chimpanzee, a horse, or a dog, whether we provide a one-room apartment or a mansion as big as Paris Hilton's, all animals still have the same needs that Mother Nature originally gave them. And if we're going to make the choice of having them live with us, we have a responsibility to fulfill those natural *animal* needs in them if we want them to be happy and balanced.

Animals are beautifully simple. To them, life is also very simple. It's we who make it complicated for them by not allowing them to be who they are, by not understanding or even trying to speak their language, and by neglecting to give them what nature intended for them to have.

The most important thing to know about animals is that they all live in the present. All the time. It's not that they don't have memories—they do. It's just that they don't obsess over the past, or the future. When someone brings me a dog who attacked someone the day before, I look at her as a dog who is probably unbalanced and needs help today, but I don't think, "Oh, she's the dog who attacked a man yesterday." That dog isn't thinking about what she did yesterday, and she's not planning the strategy for her next bite. She didn't premeditate the first bite either—she only reacted. She's in the moment, and she needs help in that moment. That's perhaps the most wonderful revelation I have had from a life working with dogs. Every day when I go to work, dogs remind me to live in the present. Maybe I had a fender bender yesterday, or I'm worried about a bill I have to pay tomorrow, but being around animals, I am always reminded that the only real moment in life is *now*.

Although humans are animals, too, we are the only species that dwells on the past and worries about the future. We are probably not the only species that is aware of its own death, but we certainly are the only animals who actively fear it.

Living in the moment—what animals do naturally—has become the Holy Grail for many human beings. Some people spend years learning to meditate or chant, and spend thousands of dollars going on retreats to monasteries on high mountaintops, trying to learn to live in the moment, if even for a little while. But almost all humans can't help but lose sleep over the past or the future some of the time, unless something dramatic happens in our lives. For example, take a person who almost dies. From that point on, suddenly the sky is beautiful, the trees are beautiful, his wife is beautiful! Everything is beautiful. Finally, he understands the concept of living in the moment. Animals don't need to learn that lesson, because they are born with that insight.

Human beings, of course, are also the only animals who use language. Though scientists have recently discovered that many animals—including primates, cetaceans (whales and dolphins), birds, and even bees, to name a few—have more intricate and complex communication systems than we ever imagined, humans still remain the only animals who can put together complex words, thoughts, and concepts to create speech. Speech is our number one form of communication, and because we are so reliant on it, we neglect using our other four senses or the "sixth sense" I describe in chapter 2: the universal sense of energy. I'll repeat: All animals communicate using energy, constantly. Energy is beingness. Energy is who you are and what you are doing at *any given moment*. That's how animals see you. That's how your dog sees you. Your energy in that present moment defines who you are.

Species: Dog

Like all other animals, dogs have the inborn need for food and water, sleep, sex, and protection from the elements. Dogs are descended from wolves; in fact, the DNA of dogs and wolves is almost indistinguishable.[7] Dogs can even mate with wolves and produce fertile offspring. Though there are many differences between domesticated dogs and wolves, we can learn much about our dogs' innate natures by observing wolf packs in the wild.

Many North American wolves spend their springs and summers foraging for small game and fish, and their winters in organized hunts, pursuing mammals, sometimes as large as moose. Biologist David L. Mech[8] observed wolves in the wild and noticed that only 5 percent of their hunts were successful. But the wolves still went out every day to hunt. They didn't get together and say, "You know, we've had a run of bad luck. Let's blow off the hunt today." Whether they caught their prey or not, they got up and went hunting. So the need to hunt—to go to work—is hardwired into wolves.

Biologists and other experts think that somewhere between ten and twelve thousand years ago, the first protodogs learned that hanging around humans was an easier route to survival than all those frustrating hunts. They began supplementing their hunting by scavenging from human camps. But early humans did not give these dogs a free ride. They exploited the dogs' natural ability to scent out and capture prey, and later, to keep farm animals in line and pull equipment too heavy for humans. So dogs have been working for thousands of years—whether for us or for themselves. Even if they're not going out to hunt every day, it's natural for them to expect to work for their food. It's what they were built for.

Like all other animals on earth, dogs need jobs. Nature designed them for a purpose, and that inbred desire for purpose does not go away when we bring them into our homes. Neither do the specific tasks humans have selectively bred into them— tasks such as hunting, retrieving, herding, running. But when we domesticate them, we often take their jobs away. We spoil them with comfortable beds, piles of squeaky toys, dishes of free rich food, and tons of affection. We think, "What a life, to be such a dog!" Maybe that would indeed be a nice life for a retired accountant relaxing in a condo complex in Florida after forty years on the job. But the genes of a canine are crying out for her to go out and wander with her pack, explore new territory, roam around, and search for food and water. Imagine how it would feel to have those ancient needs embedded deep inside you, then to have to live your life locked up alone in a two-room apartment all day. Millions of city dogs live like that. Their owners think that taking the dog for a five-minute walk to the corner to poop and pee is enough for them. Imagine how those dogs are feeling in their souls. Their frustration has to go somewhere. That's when they develop issues, and that's one of the ways I get so many clients.

As long as dogs live with humans, their world will be turned upside down in this and countless other ways. It's our responsibility—if we want happy dogs—to try to remember who they are inside, who Mother Nature created them to be. When a dog has a problem, you can't fix it by connecting with the dog's name. You have to see the dog as animal first, dog second, before you can begin to deal with any issues she might have.

The Myth of the "Problem Breed"

When I go to see a first-time client, I sometimes don't know what the problem is that I'll be dealing with. I often don't even know the dog's breed. I like to come in cold and trust my instincts and observations because what the owner tells me is often very far from the source of the real problem. The first thing I'll do is sit down with the owner and listen to his side of the story. I can't count the number of times someone who has read too many books on dog breeds will say, "Well, because she's a Dalmatian, she's naturally nervous," or "He's part border collie, part pit bull, and it's the pit bull that's the problem." Or "Dachshunds are always a problem breed."

I have to explain to these clients that they're making a fundamental mistake by blaming the breed of a dog for its behavior problems. It's the same thing when people make generalizations about human races and ethnicities—that all Latinos are lazy, that all Irish are drunkards, or that all Italians are mobsters. When it comes to trying to understand and correct a dog's conduct, breed always comes third in importance, after animal and dog. In my opinion, there's no such thing as a "problem breed." However, there is no shortage of "problem owners."

Breed is something humans created. Geneticists and biologists believe that the first humans to live with dogs selected stray wolves with the smallest body size and teeth—perhaps because these animals would do less harm to us and be easier to control.[9] Then, hundreds, perhaps thousands, of years ago, we began to mate dogs to create offspring that would excel at certain tasks. Bloodhounds were bred to have heightened scenting abilities. Pit bulls were bred for fighting bulls. Sheepdogs were bred not only to herd sheep but also to look like them. So today we have the

German shepherd, we have the boxer, we have the Chihuahua, we have the Lhasa apso, we have the Doberman. We have hundreds and hundreds of different breeds to choose from.[10] When you are selecting a dog, breed is definitely important to keep in mind, and we'll go more deeply into that later. But it's vital to remember that every breed is still always an animal/dog first. All dogs share the same psychology. The breed is just the outfit that that particular canine is wearing, and sometimes a set of special needs he or she might have. You're not going to be able to understand or control your dog's behavior by considering him or her simply as a "victim" of a breed.

All dogs share the same innate abilities, but certain breeds have been selected to accentuate certain characteristics. We have a tendency to misinterpret those conditioned skills as the dog's personality. One conditioned skill is tracking ability. Because of their breeding, bloodhounds are naturally going to be better at it. They are going to be able to maintain themselves on the ground for longer periods of time. They don't care if they take a break to eat or not, as long as they find that scent! Can all dogs track, can all dogs find things with their noses? Absolutely. They all recognize the world through smells, and all of them use their noses the way we use our eyes, but some of them are going to be better than others at sniffing out a target.

This isn't to say the breed doesn't affect how sensitive a dog is to certain conditions and environments. In fact, the special needs a particular dog might have based on her breed is one of the most important things a new dog owner should be aware of when selecting a breed of dog for a companion. For example, in nature, all dogs travel, but Siberian huskies were bred to travel for longer periods of time. The Siberian husky as a breed can travel for days on end—that's its natural "job." This innate ability, however, makes it harder for a Siberian husky to live in the city because its genes are telling it to range over long distances and take long hikes to work off its excess energy. Without sufficient exercise, it will get frustrated more easily than, say, a dachshund. But when a Siberian husky is frustrated, it will develop the same symptoms and side effects as a dachshund that's frustrated. Or a pit bull that's frustrated. Or a greyhound that's frustrated. Nervousness, fear, aggression, tension, territorial behavior—all these issues and illnesses result when the animal and the dog in her is frustrated. It doesn't matter what breed she is. That's why it's a mistake to obsess about the breed when you're dealing with a problem behavior.

Once again, we come back to *energy* as the source of behavior. All animals, as individuals, are born with a certain level of energy. There are four levels of energy regardless of the breed—low, medium, high, and very high. This is true for all species, including humans. Think of the people you know. Regardless of race, regardless of age or income, don't you know people who are naturally very low energy? Who are "couch potatoes"? What about people who never seem to stop running around, 24-7? Or people who go to the gym for two hours a day, seven days a week? I have two wonderful sons. My eldest, Andre, is medium energy, like my wife—always thoughtful, but when working on a task, focused like a laser beam. My younger son, Calvin, on the other hand, is more like me—very high energy. He's just naturally a ball of fire, and sometimes nothing can slow him down. No energy level is better or worse than any other, but when choosing a dog, it's a good idea to try to match your energy levels with hers, and vice versa. I tell my clients that they should never knowingly choose a dog with an energy level higher than their own. If you are a laid-back kind of person, I wouldn't recommend picking the one dog at the shelter that's jumping around madly in its cage. Choosing an energy level that's compatible between dog and owner is, in my estimation, far more important than choosing a breed—especially if you are looking at a mixed-breed dog or rescuing a dog from a shelter.

A Dog by Any Other Name

So now we're left with everybody's favorite subject: names. This is Billy, this is Max, this is Rex, this is Lisa. Names are something that we—human beings—create. We are the only species that gives its members names. Dogs don't look at a magazine and recognize Will Smith, Halle Berry, Robert De Niro, all those wonderful people. They don't see humans in that way. But we tend to see dogs in that way.

Names go hand in hand with personalities. We're also the only species that identifies its members by their personalities. You can be the charming newscaster or you can be the shifty politician. You can be the teacher who is patient and sweet or the teacher who is stern and strict. Those are personalities. Although dogs don't recognize one another in that way, we tend to project our very human concept of personality onto them.

"What," you say? "My dog, Skipper, has a very definite personality!" In this area, I get a lot of argument, and some resentment, from dog lovers who think their dog is the absolute best, the most unique, original dog that ever lived. I do agree with you that every animal, like every snowflake, is one of a kind. But I challenge you to accept a new way of thinking: that your dog's personality may be something that you have projected onto her. You may be misinterpreting a natural condition, skill, or behavior for what to us humans seems like "personality." You may even be calling a neurosis or problem a "personality quirk"— which isn't necessarily good for your dog.

Let me give you an example. Let's say a man has two terriers. One is named Lady, the other Columbus. The owner named the one Columbus because he loves to explore. Lady is quiet and shy and never explores, so she's "ladylike." That makes sense, doesn't it? A little terrier who pulls on his leash because he loves to explore? And another terrier who stays in the corner and acts like a little lady? According to the owner, the dogs were named after their "personalities." But the truth of the matter is, *all* dogs love to explore. Exploration is part of their nature, and when I see a dog who doesn't seem to like checking out new things—she's unsure, she's fearful—I immediately know she has a problem. What this owner is doing is accentuating elements of his dogs' behavior and labeling those elements as personality. In the animal world, there is dominant and there is submissive (which we'll soon look into more deeply). Lady is clearly the more submissive of the two dogs, and she also probably has a naturally lower energy level. But if we work on her self-esteem, we hope she will turn out to become just as curious as Columbus.

Of course, in the natural world, dogs do recognize one another as individuals, but not in the same way that we do. Their mothers don't give them names. A mother will see her pups as the strong energy, the medium-level energy, or the low energy—those are her kids. Her kids are energy. Her kids are a very distinct and recognizable scent. Later, when they grow up, the other members of the pack will also identify them as scent and energy, and their "personality" and "name" will correspond to where they fall in the group's hierarchy. It's a hard concept for us to get our minds around, but remember the main point of this chapter: dogs see the world completely differently from the way we see it—not better or worse—and owners must learn to appreciate the unique psychology that comes from that disparate worldview.

Most of the time, our pet's personality and name exist because we believe in them. Our wishing makes it so, and it makes us feel better to associate with her in this way. That's a beautiful thing and very therapeutic for us as humans—that is, when it doesn't interfere with the dog's being a dog. But when a dog has issues, you can't begin to solve them by dealing with "Columbus." You have to start with the animal, then the dog, then the breed, and then work your way down to the name stenciled on the food dish.

Don't Analyze This

Unfortunately for us humans, dogs can't lie down on a couch and be analyzed. They can't speak up and tell us what they want or need at any given moment. But in actuality, they are telling us all the time, with energy and body language. And if we understand their psychology, by attending to their instincts, we really can fulfill their deepest needs.

I often have clients who have adopted a dog with issues from a shelter, and have spent months pondering what terrible thing might have happened to it as a puppy to have caused its present-day problems. They'll say about a troubled dog, "He must have been kicked by a woman with high-heeled shoes, because now he's afraid of women with high-heeled shoes." Or "She was scared by the garbage man, so now she goes crazy every time the truck goes by." All these things may be true. But these owners are talking about their dogs' fears and phobias as if they were human fears and phobias. As if the dogs sat and obsessed all day over a traumatic puppyhood, or spent their free time worrying about garbage men and high-heeled shoes. They don't. Dogs don't think the way we do. To put it simplistically, they react. These fears and phobias are conditioned responses. And any conditioned response in a dog can be unconditioned if you understand the basics of dog psychology.

Let me give you an example of a case from the first season of *Dog Whisperer*. Kane is a beautiful, sweet-tempered three-year-old Great Dane who, while running and playing on a linoleum floor, slipped and skidded hard into a glass wall. His owner, Marina, heard the thud and rushed over to him, exclaiming, "Oh my God, Kane, are you all right? Oh, poor baby . . ." and on and on, with a lot of excited, emotional energy. Although Marina meant well and was genuinely concerned for Kane's well-being, what she was doing was reinforcing Kane's natural distress at that moment. In nature, if Kane had been with a balanced dog from his pack and the same kind of accident had occurred, the other dog might have sniffed him and checked him out to make sure everything was okay. Then Kane would have stood up, shaken himself off, and gone on with his day. He would have moved on, and perhaps have become a little more cautious about running on slippery surfaces. But because of his owner's reaction, Kane associated this minor accident with a major trauma. And a phobia was born.

From that day on, Kane was terrified of shiny floors. For over a year, he wouldn't go into the kitchen, and he couldn't be taken to the school where Marina taught and had previously brought him every day. He wouldn't even go to the vet's; Marina always had to bring along a carpet fragment and roll it out in order to get Kane to walk through the veternarian's waiting room. Marina tried coaxing and sweet-talking Kane into walking on lineoleum, to no avail. She tried treats and affection. The more she begged and pleaded, the more she petted and cooed and comforted, the more stubborn—and fearful—Kane became. Plus Kane weighed 160 pounds, so if he didn't want to go somewhere, no amount of pushing or pulling could make him go.

Marina's approach to Kane's phobia might have been appropriate had Kane been a small child. A psychologist with a patient who has been in an airplane crash doesn't insist that the patient get back on an airplane during the first session. Similarly, when our human children have accidents, they do need some comforting and sympathy from us. But most parents realize that even children often react in proportion to *their parents'* reactions to their "boo-boos." That's why we try to comfort our kids without making too much of their mishaps. But unlike human children, dogs don't dream about or obsess over past experiences the way we do. They live in the moment. Kane wasn't spending his days worrying about shiny floors, and he naturally reacted to protect himself when the original accident happened. But since his owner intensified the traumatic experience with her overly excited, emotional energy, then nurtured that fear by giving him affection every time he got near a shiny floor, Kane now saw shiny floors as a very big deal indeed. Whenever an animal isn't allowed to move through its fear, that fear can become a phobia. What Kane needed was a calm-assertive pack leader to recondition him and show him that shiny floors were just business as usual. That's where I came in.

First, I took Kane on a long walk with me, in order to bond with him and ensure my dominant role. Once I was sure he saw me as his leader, I was ready to tackle his phobia. Because Kane is such a large dog—he weighs more than I do!—I had to get a running start with him to get him into the hallway where the original accident had occurred. It took me two tries, but on the second, he ran in right next to me and was on the floor before he knew what was happening or how he'd gotten there. Once on the floor, he reacted as he'd been conditioned—he panicked. He squirmed, he drooled—you could see the terror in his eyes. The difference this time was me. I did nothing but hold him steady.

I stayed calm, strong, and unaffected by his reaction. I didn't comfort him or talk sweetly to him the way Marina always had—that behavior had only reinforced his negative responses. Instead, I sat with him while he went through all the old emotions—and I watched the fear literally drain out of him. In under ten minutes, he was relaxed enough for me to start walking with him—on the shiny floor itself. He tottered next to me, shaky and unsure at first, but after a few passes back and forth, his confidence began to return. Once again, I stayed calm and assertive. I didn't baby him. I offered him the guidance of a strong pack leader and communicated with my energy that this was a normal activity and nothing to be afraid of. In well under twenty minutes, Kane was striding confidently on the same floors he'd been afraid of for more than a year.

The big test came when Marina and her son, Emmet, had to take over for me. Marina expressed to me how difficult it was for her to project calm-assertive energy when she was so worried about how Kane was feeling. It's a natural thing for a human to feel sympathy for another animal who's in distress, but dogs don't need our sympathy. They need our leadership. We are their reference point and their source of energy. They reflect the psychological energy we are communicating to them. It was quite a challenge for Marina to learn how to be Kane's leader when her heart was bleeding for him and she believed her role was to be his "mom." To her credit, however, she worked hard to change— and taught both her husband and son to be better pack leaders as well.

Among animal behaviorists and human psychologists, the technique I used with Kane is sometimes known as "flooding": the prolonged exposure of a patient to fear-arousing stimuli of relatively high intensity. To some animal advocates, this technique is very controversial. I believe that when working with animals, people need to follow their own consciences. In my opinion, the way I worked with Kane was not only humane, it was also instantly effective. Since that day, Kane has had no more problems with shiny floors—or any other phobias, for that matter. He's a wonderfully balanced, calm, peaceful dog.

The beauty of dogs is that, unlike humans with psychological issues, dogs move on right away, and they don't look back. We humans have the blessing and curse of imagination, which allows us to soar to the heights of science and art and literature and philosophy, but which can take us also to all sorts of dark and scary places in our minds. Since dogs live in the now, they don't hold on to the past the way we do. Unlike the Woody Allens of the world, dogs don't need years of therapy or long sessions on a couch struggling to understand what happened to them when they were puppies. When it comes down to it, they are creatures of cause and effect. Once they've been conditioned to react in a new way, they are not only willing but also able to change. As long as we show them strong, consistent leadership, they can move forward and overcome nearly any phobia they've acquired.

"You're leading again."

4

Power of the Pack

There's an aspect of your dog's psychology that I only touched on in the last chapter, but it couldn't be a more important concept when it comes to understanding the relationship between you and the dogs in your life. This is the concept of the *pack*. Your dog's *pack mentality* is one of the greatest natural forces involved in shaping his or her behavior.

A dog's pack is his life force. The pack instinct is his primal instinct. His status in the pack is his self, his identity. The pack is all important to a dog because if anything threatens the pack's harmony, it threatens each individual dog's harmony. If something threatens the pack's survival, it threatens the very survival of every dog in it. The need to keep the pack stable and running smoothly is a powerful motivating force in every dog—even in a pampered poodle that has never met another dog or left the confines of your backyard. Why? It's deeply ingrained in his brain. Evolution and Mother Nature took care of that.

It's vital for you to understand that your dog views all his interactions with other dogs, with you, and even with other animals in your household in the "pack" context. Even though I've spent the last chapter outlining the many differences between how dogs and humans see the world, humans—in fact, all primates—are pack animals, too. In fact, dog packs are really not so different from the human equivalent of packs. We call our packs families. Clubs. Football teams. Churches. Corporations. Governments. Sure, we think of our social groups as infinitely more complicated than dogs' groups, but are they really all that different? When you break it down, the basics are the same: every one of the "packs" I've mentioned has a hierarchy, or it doesn't work. There is a father or mother, a chairman, a quarterback, a minister, a CEO, a president. Then there are varying levels of status for the people under him or her. That's how a pack of canines works, too.

The concept of pack and pack leader is directly related to the way in which dogs interact with us when we bring them into our homes.

The Natural Pack

If you study a wolf pack in the wild, you'll observe a natural rhythm to its days and nights. First, the animals in the pack walk, sometimes up to ten hours a day, to find food and water.[1] Then they eat. If they kill a deer, the pack leader gets the biggest piece, but everyone cooperates in sharing the rest. They'll eat until the entire deer is gone—not just because they don't have Saran Wrap in the wild, but because they don't know when there's going to be another deer again. What they eat today may have to hold them for a long time. That's where the expression "wolfing down" food comes from, and you'll see it in your own dog's behavior much of the time. Wolves don't necessarily eat just when they're hungry; they eat when the food is there. Their bodies are designed to conserve. It's the root of your own dog's often seemingly insatiable appetite.

Only after wolves and wild dogs have finished their daily work do they play. That's when they celebrate. And in nature, they usually go to sleep exhausted. Not once, while watching the dogs on my grandfather's farm, did I ever see a sleeping dog having nightmares, the way domestic dogs in America do. Their ears would twitch, their eyes would move, but there was no whimpering or whining or moaning. They were so completely worn out from their day's work and play that they slept peacefully, every night.

Every pack has its rituals. These include traveling, working for food and water, eating, playing, resting, and mating. Most important, the pack always has a pack leader. The rest of the animals are followers. Within the pack, the animals fall into their own order of status, usually determined by that animal's inborn energy level. The leader determines—and enforces—the rules and boundaries by which the members will live.

I've already explained that a puppy's first pack leader is his mother. From birth, puppies learn how to be cooperative members of a pack-oriented society. At about three or four months, after they're weaned, they fall into the regular pack structure, and take their cues from the pack leader, not their mother. In packs of wolves and wild dogs, the leader is often a male, because the hormone testosterone—present in male puppies from the time they are very small—seems to be a cue to dominance behaviors.[2] You'll see a male puppy mounting both other males and females long before he is sexually mature—and no, that doesn't mean he's bisexual. It means he is acting out in play the dominance and submission behaviors that will be such a big part of his future life as an adult dog.

Though hormones are part of what makes a pack leader, energy plays an even greater role. When humans live in households with more than one dog, the dominant dog can be either male or female. The gender doesn't matter, only the inborn energy level, and who establishes dominance. In many packs, there is an "alpha couple," a male and female pair who seem to run things between them.

In the wild, pack leaders are born, not made. They don't take classes to become leaders; they don't fill out applications and go on interviews. Leaders develop early and they show their dominant qualities quite young. It's that all-important energy we discussed earlier that separates the pack leader from the follower. A pack leader must be born with high or very high energy. The energy must also be dominant energy, as well as calm-assertive energy. Medium- and low-energy dogs do not make natural pack leaders. Most dogs—like most humans—are born to be followers, not leaders. Being a pack leader isn't only about dominance, it's also about responsibility. Think about our own species, and the percentage of people who would like to have the power and perks of the president, or the money and goodies of a Bill Gates. Then tell those people that the trade-off is that they will have to work around the clock, 24-7, almost never see their families, and rarely take weekends off. Tell them they'll be financially responsible for thousands of people, or responsible for the national security of hundreds of millions of people. How many people would choose those leadership roles after being presented with such daunting realities? I believe most people would choose comfortable but simpler lives over great power and wealth—if they truly understood the work and sacrifice that leadership costs.

Similarly, in a dog's world, the pack leader has the responsibility for the survival of all the pack members. The leader leads the pack to food and water. He decides when to hunt; decides who eats, how much, and when; decides when to rest and when to sleep and when to play. The leader sets all the regulations and structures that the other pack members must live by. A pack leader has to have total confidence and know what he's doing. And just as in the human world, most dogs are born to follow rather than do all the work it takes to maintain the position of pack leader. Life is easier and less stressful for them when they live within the rules, boundaries, and limitations that the pack leader has set for them.

For a dog born with a dominant disposition and energy, yes, it is harder and may take a little longer for him to accept a human as his leader. Such animals were not born to be followers; but their instinct for being in a smoothly running pack is stronger than their instinct for being the one and only leader. It is important to remember that a very dominant, high-energy dog should only be with a human who has the energy, skills, and knowledge for being the leader for a dominant, strong-breed dog. The person who chooses a dominant, strong-breed dog also must make a commitment to leadership—and needs to take that commitment seriously.

As we've discussed before, pack leaders project calm-assertive energy. Even if you've never observed a pack of dogs or wolves before, it shouldn't take you long to pick out the leader. He will have a dominant posture—head alert, chest forward, ears up, tail stiff; sometimes he almost swaggers. Pack leaders are clearly very confident dogs, and it comes naturally to them. They aren't faking it, and they couldn't if they tried. Their followers, on the other hand, project the energy known as "calm submission." They walk with their heads in line with their bodies or down, and they stay behind the pack leader while traveling, their ears relaxed or back, their tails wagging but always kept low. If the pack leader challenges them, they might back away, bend down, or even lie down and roll over, exposing their bellies. By doing that, basically they're saying, "You're the boss, and I'm not questioning that. Whatever you say goes."

No Room for Weakness

In nature, if a pack leader shows any weakness at all, he will be attacked and replaced by a stronger member of the pack. This is true across all animal species that live in tiered social systems. Only the strong can lead. In fact, extreme weakness among any member of the pack is not to be tolerated. If there is a dog in the pack that is unusually weak or timid, he will be assaulted by the others. Weakness doesn't cut it among any animal species—except our own. This is one of the most interesting differences between modern human beings and the rest of the animal kingdom. Not only do we accept weakness in some of our pack members, we also actually rescue our "weak" brothers and sisters! We rehabilitate people in wheelchairs; we tend to our sick; we risk our lives to save a "pack member" who might not make it anyway. While what some researchers call "altruistic behavior" has been documented in many other species (especially the other higher primates),[3] compared with most other animals, human beings take this kind of graciousness to an extraordinary level.

Not only do humans rescue our own; we save other animals, too. We are the only species that rescues sea gulls, crocodiles, hyenas, and whales. You'll never see a zebra rescuing an injured elephant. Think about the animal lovers you know—dog lovers, lion lovers, horse lovers. Every animal seems to have its own "fan club" among humans—a group of people with such compassion for a chosen species that they'll rescue even the sorriest specimen of that species. Many of the dogs at my Dog Psychology Center came to me in such bad shape that it was their last chance, and I brought them back from the brink. I've got a dog with three legs, a dog with no ears, a dog with one eye, and a dog who's the product of such severe inbreeding, he's always going to be mentally handicapped. It's because I'm a human and I feel sorry for these dogs that I'll do whatever it takes to give them another chance at a full, happy life. But in their natural habitat, other dogs don't feel sorry for the frail and the feeble. They attack and execute them. There's nothing intentionally cruel about it— remember, we're also the only species with a system of morality, of right and wrong. It's simply that a weak animal endangers the rest of the pack, and nature has ingrained in animals the instinct to breed together the strongest members, so the next generation will have a better chance of surviving to breed again. Nature polices its own.

Our tendency to rescue others comes from our emotional energy. Our compassion and our loving natures are beautiful things, and part of the miracle of being human. But to other animals, emotional energy can be perceived as weakness. Love is a soft energy, so when it comes to pack survival at least, love on its own is indeed a kind of weakness. Animals won't follow soft or weak energy. They won't follow compassionate energy. St. Francis of Assisi and his birds notwithstanding, animals won't follow a spiritual leader. They won't follow a lovable leader. Nor will they follow overly excited energy. We are a pack-oriented species, but as I've said, we are also the only species on the planet that will follow an unstable leader. Animals—whether horses, dogs, cats, or sheep—will follow only a stable leader. That leader's balance is reflected in his consistently calm-assertive energy. So when we project excited or loving or emotional or even overly aggressive energy to the animals in our lives—especially if that is the *only* energy we're projecting—they are much more likely to see us as followers, not as leaders.

To Lead or to Follow?

To dogs, there are only two positions in a relationship: leader and follower. Dominant and submissive. It's either black or white. There is no in-between in their world. When a dog lives with a human, in order for the human to be able to control the dog's behavior, she must make the commitment to take on the role of pack leader, 100 percent of the time. It's that simple.

It doesn't seem that simple, however, for many of my clients. Hundreds of them keep calling me because they are desperate, because their dogs' problem behaviors are totally controlling their lives. Perhaps some of them have a hard time getting their minds around the dominant-submissive paradigm because, in the human world, those words sometimes come with baggage attached. When we hear the word *dominance,* perhaps we think of a wife-beater, a drunk in a bar fight, a playground bully extorting lunch money from the classroom runt, or even a masked man or woman in an S&M club with leather and whips. The word conjures up images of cruelty in our minds. It's important to remember that, in the animal kingdom, the word *cruelty* doesn't exist. And dominance isn't a moral judgment or an emotional experience. It is simply a state of being, a behavior that is as natural in nature as is mating, or eating, or play.

Submissive, as we refer to it here, is not an ethical judgment, either. It doesn't designate an animal or human who is a wimp or overly pliable. Submissive doesn't mean vulnerable or ineffectual. It is merely the energy and the state of mind of a follower.

Among all pack species, there has to be some degree of dominance and submission in order for any hierarchy to function. Think of an office full of workers. What would happen if they all came in and left whenever they felt like it, took four-hour lunches, and argued with one another and with the boss all day? It would be chaos, right? You don't consider an employee who comes to work on time, gets along with her fellow workers, and completes her tasks with a minimum of conflict to be "weak," do you? No. You consider her to be cooperative, a good team player. But in order for there even to be a "team," that employee has to accept a degree of submission in her mind-set. She has to implicitly understand that the boss makes the decisions, and it's her job to follow them.

At the risk of being considered politically incorrect, I still use the terms *dominant* and *submissive*. To me, they accurately describe the natural social structure of dogs. For a dog, there are no judgments attached to the issue of who in a pack is dominant or who is submissive, be it a pack of dogs or a pack consisting of one dog and one human. A dog doesn't take it personally if you take over the leadership position from him. In my experience, most dogs are relieved to know their owners are the ones in charge. Now that we've integrated them into our human world, there are lots of complicated daily decisions to be made that nature hasn't equipped dogs to make. Dogs can't hail a taxi, or push a shopping cart, or get money out of the ATM—at least not without some very specialized training! Dogs can sense this, and I've seen thousands of dogs visibly relax for the first time in their lives once their owners finally committed to a true leadership position. But mark my words—when a dog senses that his owner isn't up to the challenge of pack leadership, he will step in to try to fill the void. It's in his nature to do this, to try to keep the pack functional. The way your dog sees it, somebody has to run the show. And when a dog takes over that role, it often has disastrous results for both dog and human.

The "Powerbroker Paradox"

As I've mentioned before, many of my clients are superpowerful people who are used to calling the shots in every other area of their lives. To the humans around them, they project such strong energy that they can be almost frightening! I've seen some of them give orders and bark commands at their staff, and have watched those workers literally cower at the sound of their boss's voice. Talk about projecting submissive energy! The staff will then scramble all over one another to fulfill their employer's demands—and there's no question of who is in charge. But here's one of the ironies of my work, which I call the "powerbroker paradox." Once these influential people come home, from the moment they open the front door, the only energy they project to their dogs is emotional energy. "Ooooh! Hellooo, Pookey, my little snookums! Give Mommy a kiss! Oh, look at you, you bad dog—that's the second sofa you've eaten this month."

I don't mean to make fun of these clients because I truly empathize with them. Trying to be top dog in the human world is an incredibly stressful experience. I know it feels good to come home to an adorable animal and let your hair down, to hang out with a creature who doesn't seem to judge you and to whom you don't have to prove how great you are every minute. It's such nice therapy for these clients to cuddle with their soft, furry dogs. It's like a long, hot, soothing bath. And in some respects, it's true—their dogs aren't judging them, at least not by the standards by which these people are used to being judged. Dogs

don't care if their owner has a hundred million dollars or a beach
house or a Ferrari. They don't care if their owner's last record
album went platinum or was a flop, or whether she won the
Academy Award this year or had her TV series canceled. They
don't even notice if their owner has gained twenty pounds or just
had plastic surgery. What dogs *do* judge, however, is who is the
leader and who is the follower in the relationship. And when
these powerbrokers come home and let their dogs jump all over
them, when they spend the whole evening feeding the dogs
treats, chasing them around the house, and catering to their
every whim, then it's clear that their dogs have rendered a ver-
dict: that same human who is considered such hot stuff in the
human world has, in the dog's eyes, become a follower.

Oprah and Sophie

Oprah Winfrey—my personal role model for my professional
behavior—is a perfect case study of the phenomenon I've just
described. In the human world, she is not only always in charge,
she is also amazingly calm and even-tempered. In my seminars, I
always use her as the classic example of calm-assertive energy in
action, because she really is the best at it. Oprah doesn't need to
prove she's important; it simply radiates out of her being. She is
also a model for emulating animals in their ability to live in the
moment. Oprah has publicly come out and told the story of her
past, and it clearly wasn't an easy one. She also had to overcome
the obstacle of being an African American woman, which was a
pretty formidable roadblock during the years when she was starting out in her career. But unlike most humans, Oprah has culti-
vated the ability to keep moving forward. Her past has never held
her back. She is, in my opinion, a shining example of human

potential. And she's remained a really nice and generous person on top of it all.

Ever since I came to America, it was my dream to be on the *Oprah* show. To me, that was the very definition of "making it" in this country. And when I did finally get on the show, the encounter exceeded even my wildest expectations. Oprah was gracious, perceptive, inquisitive, and witty, and she even reached out to my wife, Ilusion, sitting in the audience, to include her in the experience. The whole day was like a dream to me. The reason I was on the show, however, was because of Oprah's private nightmare, her hidden weakness. Oprah—my calm-assertive role model—was letting her dog, Sophie, walk all over her!

When I first met Oprah at her forty-two-acre, ocean-view estate outside Santa Barbara in 2005, she had two dogs—Sophie and Solomon, both cocker spaniels. Solomon was the submissive of the two and was very old and feeble. Sophie, however—ten years old at the time—had a problem that was becoming dangerous. When Oprah walked her, if another dog came near them, Sophie would bare her teeth, get into defensive posture, and sometimes even strike out at the other dog. She also had serious separation-anxiety issues, and would howl for hours when Oprah and her partner, Steadman, left her alone. Unlike some of my clients, Oprah was too on the ball to have convinced herself that the problem was all Sophie's fault. She knew that there were things she could be doing differently to help change Sophie's behavior. Still, I'm not sure she was totally prepared for what I had to say to her.

During the consultation—the part of my visit when I sit down and simply listen to the human's side of the story—I could tell simply by the words Oprah used to describe Sophie that Sophie wasn't just her dog, she was her little baby. "She's my daughter!" Oprah told me. "I love her like I gave birth to her myself." To say Oprah had "humanized" Sophie would be an under-statement.

As we talked, I learned that Sophie had been a very insecure little girl from day one. Both Oprah and Steadman described her hiding under the table and having very low self-esteem when they first brought her home. So what did Oprah do? What most dog owners do. She used human psychology and lovingly coaxed Sophie out, petting her and consoling her. Every time Sophie was nervous or fearful, Oprah would reach out and comfort her with affection and emotional energy. Unknowingly, Oprah was doing exactly the same thing Marina had done with Kane after he slipped on the linoleum floor. By applying human psychology to a dog in distress, both women were unintentionally *nurturing* their dogs' insecure behaviors.

I can't emphasize enough that dogs pick up every energy sig-nal we send them. They are reading our emotions every minute of the day. Oprah, who has overcome a painful past by embrac-ing life in the "now," never lived in the moment when it came to Sophie! From the moment she even started thinking about tak-ing Sophie for a walk, she was anticipating the possibility that Sophie might attack another dog. She was playing back in her head past confrontations, and imagining new ones. All that cata-strophizing was making Oprah tense and emotional—energies that Sophie naturally interpreted as weakness. This set the dy-namic between them from the moment Oprah picked up the leash—even *before* the walk.

Oprah would begin the walk by letting Sophie go out the door first—a classic mistake almost all dog owners make. It's important to establish the leadership position on the threshold of the doorway. Whoever walks out first is the leader. Next, Oprah would compound that mistake by letting Sophie lead *her* on the walk. In a pack, the pack leader is always in front, unless he specifically gives "permission" for another dog to walk ahead. With Sophie in front of the leash, the two basically went where Sophie wanted to go. Because of her constant fear that Sophie would get into an altercation, Oprah was unsure of herself and anxious. Meanwhile, Sophie would be plowing ahead. A third-grader could have sussed out who was the leader and who was the follower in that twosome!

I had to remind Oprah that she, the dog owner, was the only one in the relationship who was worrying about what might happen on the walk based on what had happened in the past. Sophie wasn't thinking about those things. Sophie was living in the moment, enjoying the grass, enjoying the trees, enjoying the clean sea air. She wasn't thinking, "I wonder if I'm going to have to attack one of those nasty neighborhood dogs today." None of her earlier confrontations had been premeditated, either. Sophie didn't lie awake nights fantasizing: "I really hate that cockapoo, Shana, and I plan to bite her the first chance I get." Like all dogs, in attacking other dogs, she had merely been reacting to a stimulus that was occurring at that moment.

And what happened when Sophie did encounter another dog and start to show signs of aggression? Oprah would either scoop her up and rescue her from the situation, or become very emotional, plead with her to stop, and apologize to the other dog owner. She didn't act like a pack leader and just correct Sophie's behavior. When a pack leader corrects another dog in a pack, he stops the dog's disagreeable behavior. Calm-submissive dogs always pay attention to their pack leader's instructions.

So what was driving Sophie to these aggressive reactions? Sophie was what I describe as insecure-dominant—she wasn't a naturally aggressive dog, but when she saw another dog that caused a fear reaction in her, she responded by baring her teeth and making threats. Remember, an animal has only four possible responses to any threat—fight, flight, avoidance, or submission. Oprah's reaction to Sophie's aggressive posturing simply intensified the situation. Oprah would tense up and be filled with dread, flashing red lights for Sophie that her owner wasn't in control. After the incident, Oprah would coo at Sophie, pet her, try to comfort her and let her know that everything was all right. Again, plausible psychology for a human child who is scared, but not dog psychology by any means! It's natural for human beings to reach out and comfort other animals in distress in the best way we know how—with gentleness and reassurance. To a dog, however, giving Sophie affection at that moment was like saying, "Good for you, you show that mean other dog who's threatening us." When we show affection to a mind that has developed unstable behavior, that mind doesn't move on. In Sophie's case, it increased her anxiety to the point that, when feeling cornered, she actually lashed out.

I had to communicate to Oprah that she would have to change her entire approach toward Sophie if she wanted her dog to be the balanced and stable pet she was born to be. Because she's so intelligent, Oprah grasped the basics of this concept immediately, but it still wasn't easy to break through the very personal barrier of her thinking of Sophie as "her little girl." At one point I remember saying to her, "You aren't showing her leadership." Oprah was speechless for a second. She turned and looked at Steadman. Then she said to me, very slowly, "You're saying *I'm* not a leader?" That's right. I was telling the same woman who *Forbes* claims is worth over one billion dollars and who currently ranks as the number one most powerful celebrity and the ninth most powerful woman in the world[4] that she was not being a leader to her twenty-pound cocker spaniel.

Like all humans who love their pets, Oprah wanted only the best for her dogs. But her understanding of what was "best" came from a human perspective. She only wanted to love her dogs and give them the most wonderful life possible. But Oprah's dogs hadn't read the *Forbes* list or checked out Oprah's bank balance. They didn't care if her home was furnished by the world's finest decorators or by the Salvation Army. Oprah's dogs would love her just the same if she went broke tomorrow (although, as Oprah dryly observed, both dogs would certainly appreciate the difference if they were suddenly forced to fly in the cargo hold of a commercial airline instead of in the comfort of her private plane). What her dogs wanted most out of life was to feel secure in their places in the "pack" of Oprah's family. And clearly, Sophie wasn't feeling secure.

Oprah needed to learn to become a pack leader. She already was one in the human world. Now she had to practice the kind of leadership a dog would understand.

Rules, Boundaries, and Limitations

In nature, a pack leader makes rules, and sticks to them. A pack couldn't survive without rules, no matter what the species. In many human households, the rules, boundaries, and limitations for dogs are unclear, if they exist at all. Just like children, dogs need rules, boundaries, and limitations in order to be properly socialized. In Oprah's household, for example, Sophie didn't have many rules, and those that did exist weren't always followed. Sometimes, for instance, when Sophie would whine after Oprah left her alone, Oprah would relent, come back, and take Sophie with her. Other times, she'd come back and tell Sophie to "stop it"—but usually, the behavior had already escalated past the point of correction. Both human and animal psychologists call this "intermittent reinforcement," and if you are a parent, you probably know that this type of discipline never works. If you allow your child to sneak a cookie from the jar one day and punish him for it the next, the child will always try again, on the off chance that he'll get away with it. The same goes for dogs. Intermittent reinforcement of rules is a surefire way to raise an unbalanced, unstable dog.

Despite the fact that Sophie had lived in an unbalanced state for ten years, without solid rules, boundaries, or limitations, I stressed to Oprah that it was almost never too late for a dog to be rehabilitated. Even humans can turn their own lives around at age fifty, sixty, or seventy, and we have many more issues than dogs do! Oprah was looking forward to working on the problem, but was shocked when I arrived at her house with five other dogs—Coco, our Chihuahua; Lida and Rex, our Italian greyhound pair; a Lhasa apso named Luigi, who belongs to Will Smith and Jada Pinkett Smith; and the dog that made Oprah the most nervous, Daddy, the burly and very scary-looking pit bull who spends time in my pack when his owner, hip-hop artist Redman, is on the road. Daddy actually has the best energy of all the dogs in the pack. I first met him when he was four months old, when Redman brought him by my newly opened center. It has become a fad among rap artists to have big, tough-looking dogs for status. Redman was different—he was a responsible dog owner. He said, "I want a dog I can take anywhere in the world with me. I don't want a lawsuit." I started working with Daddy that day, and he has never missed a day of being fulfilled as a dog. Everybody who meets him falls in love with him, even though on the outside he's very formidable. Daddy has helped hundreds of dogs become balanced, simply by sharing his own calm-submissive energy. And he's a pit bull—which goes to show you that when it comes to dog behavior, energy and balance can and do overcome the influence of breed. All the dogs I

With the always balanced Daddy

brought with me to Oprah were very balanced dogs. They were there to give Sophie "group therapy."

Sophie's reaction to the other dogs was pretty predictable. When she first saw them, she stood on the doorstep, frozen. Between fight, flight, avoidance, and submission, she was choosing avoidance! I moved her down among the dogs and gave her a slight correction with the leash every time I noticed her lip begin to curl up as she became fearful or anxious. My energy was calm and assertive at all times. At first, I actually had to ask Oprah to remove herself from the situation; she was so terrified that Sophie was picking up on her energy. After about ten minutes, Sophie was able to relax. In about half an hour, she was picking up on the group's calm-submissive energy and seemed actually to be enjoying herself. She was still tentative, but her body language was becoming calm and relaxed. That's the power of the pack at work for you—a group of balanced dogs helping an unstable dog turn around in a matter of minutes. But the energy I was sending Sophie through the leash was vital, too. I was her pack leader, and I was instructing her to get along with the rest of the pack. No ifs, ands, or buts about it. And Sophie got the message.

Oprah and Steadman were amazed to see Sophie interacting calmly with other dogs. Just the fact that it was even possible seemed thrilling to them. I gave them the "homework" of making a regular habit of allowing Sophie around other dogs, while practicing calm-assertive leadership. Like a diet, calm assertive leadership doesn't work unless you practice it every day. It was only through such regular "therapy" that Sophie would permanently change.

....

A dog will usually accept a human as its pack leader if that human projects the correct calm-assertive energy, sets solid rules, boundaries, and limitations, and acts responsibly in the cause of the pack's survival. This doesn't mean that we can't still be uniquely *human* pack leaders. Just as dogs shouldn't have to give up what's unique about them to live with us, we shouldn't have to give up what's so special about being human. We are, for instance, the only pack leaders who are going to love the dogs in the way we humans define love. Their canine pack leader will not buy them squeaky toys or throw birthday parties for them. Their canine pack leader won't directly reward their good behavior. He won't turn around and say, "Gee, guys, thanks for following me ten miles." It's expected that they do that! A mother dog won't say, "You know, you pups have behaved so well today. Let's go to the beach!" In their natural world, the reward is in the process. (That's a concept we humans could sometimes do well to remember.) For a dog there's a reward in simply fitting in with the pack and helping to ensure its survival. Cooperation automatically results in the primal rewards of food, water, play, and sleep. Rewarding our dogs with treats and the things that they love is one way we can bond with them and reinforce good behavior. But if we don't project strong leadership energy before we give rewards, we're never going to have a truly functional "pack."

Homeless Pack Leaders

While the human-dog bond is unique on both sides of the equation, we can't just play the role of best friend, or dog lover. Whether we know it or not, when we play that role, we are automatically fulfilling our own needs first, not our dog's. We're the ones who need the constant affection and the unconditional acceptance.

Who do you think are among the happiest, most emotionally stable dogs in America? This is my observation, and you may find it pretty hard to believe, but I think that dogs that live with homeless people often have the most fulfilling, balanced lives. Go to downtown Los Angeles someday, or to the park overlooking the Santa Monica Pier, and pick out the homeless people who have dogs. Those dogs don't exactly look like American Kennel Club champs, but they're almost always well behaved and nonaggressive. Watch a homeless person walking with a dog and you will witness a good example of pack leader–pack follower body language. Usually, the homeless person doesn't have a leash, but the dog follows either beside the human or just behind her. The dog is migrating with his pack leader, the way nature has ingrained in him.

"Homeless people?" you ask. "How can their dogs be happier?

They can't afford to feed them expensive organic dog food! They can't take them to the groomer twice a month or even to the vet!" How true, but remember, dogs don't know the difference between organic and regular dog food; they don't think about groomers; and in nature, there aren't any vets. Many times, homeless people don't even have goals in their lives—not the way some type A achievers do, anyway. Some of them seem to be content to walk from place to place, pick up cans, and seek a meal and a warm place to sleep. This lifestyle might seem unacceptable to many humans. But for a dog, this is the ideal, natural routine that nature created for him. He is getting the consistent amount of primal exercise that he needs. And he is free to travel. In nature, all animals have "territories"—some large and some small—which they love to traverse, over and over again. Exploration is a natural animal trait, and genetically, it's equated with survival[5] because the more an animal explores, the more likely it is to find food and water, and the more information it will have about the world.[6] In L.A., I've observed that the dogs that live with homeless people really get to know their city far better than a dog that lives in Bel Air. The dog that lives in Bel Air has a giant backyard. But to him, it's just a big kennel. The homeless dog gets to wander for miles and then go to bed tired. The Bel Air dog gets to see the house, the inside of the car, and the groomer's—and then goes to bed with another day's worth of pent-up energy and frustration.

Balance in a dog isn't created by giving them material things. It's created by allowing them to express fully the physical and psychological parts of their being. Living with a homeless person, a dog migrates for food. It usually works for food, and even without a leash, there's a clear leader-follower relationship between the person and the dog.

Many of the people who call me in to help them have trouble

walking their dogs because of all the distractions that cause the dog to pull on the leash or run away or bark—kids, cars, other dogs. They think this is the dog's problem. But check out a dog with a homeless person. The dog has never been to a training academy in his life. He and the homeless person walk along the busy streets passing cats, strollers, scooters, people with yapping little dogs on flexi leashes—yet the dog keeps on moving forward. This is what happens in nature; a dog or wolf pack would never hold together if individual dogs were running off all the time, getting distracted by frogs or butterflies! The homeless person acts as a pack leader does if the dog gets distracted—she only has to send a glance or a grunt the dog's way to remind him of the rules and get him back on track. At the end of the day, the homeless person will reward the dog with food and affection right before settling down to sleep. They share a very elemental existence, probably very much like the earliest relationships between our human ancestors and dogs.

Who's Top Dog in Your House?

Once my clients start to grasp the concept of the pack and the pack leader, they usually ask me, "How can I tell who's the pack leader in my house?" The answer is very simple: who controls the dynamics of your relationship?

There are dozens and dozens of different ways in which your dog will tell you, loud and clear, who's the dominant one between the two of you. If he jumps on you when you come home from work in the evening, he's not just happy to see you. He is the pack leader. If you open door to go for a walk and he exits ahead of you, it's not just because he loves his walks so much. He is the pack leader. If he barks at you and then you feed him, it's not "cute." He is the pack leader. If you are sleeping and he wakes you up at five in the morning pawing you to say "Let me out; I gotta pee," then he's showing you even before the sun comes up who's running the house. Whenever he makes you do anything, he is the pack leader. Simple as that.

Most of the time dogs are the pack leaders of the human world because the human will say, "Isn't that adorable? He's trying to tell me something." There it is, that old *Lassie* syndrome again, "What's that, Lassie? Gramps fell down the well?" Yes, in this case, human, your dog *is* trying to tell you something—he's trying to remind you that he is the leader and you are his follower.

So, when you wake up on your own terms, you are the pack leader. When you open the door on own your terms, you are the pack leader. When you exit the house ahead of your dog, you are the pack leader. When you are the one who makes the decisions in the household, then you are the pack leader. And I'm not talking about 80 percent of the time. I'm talking about 100 percent of the time. If you give only 80 percent leadership, your dog will give you 80 percent following. And the other 20 percent of the time he will run the show. If you give your dog any opportunity for him to lead you, he will take it.

Pepper and the Perils of Partial Leadership

What happens when we give only partial leadership to our dogs? I've seen many situations where the human asserted the correct leadership energy and behaviors in all but certain situations. This is a great formula for an unbalanced dog because even more confusing for him than having to be a leader over a human is not knowing when he has to lead and when he has to follow.

Take another case from the first season of *Dog Whisperer*. Christopher, a photographer, had adopted an adorable eight-year-old Wheaton terrier mix named Pepper, and the two of them had bonded deeply. Every day Chris walked from home to the studio he shared with another photographer, and he had trained Pepper to walk there with him. Pepper was such a good dog on their walks that Chris no longer even needed to use a leash with her for their "commute." To see the two of them together was to witness the same correct leader-follower body language seen in homeless people and their dogs. Traffic could pass, kids on skateboards could whiz by, horns could honk, and Pepper kept right on trotting beside Chris, head down, tail wagging. One little word from him was enough to correct her if she got distracted. It was clear Pepper loved their walking time together; she always arrived at the studio refreshed and relaxed.

Once inside the studio, however, another side of Pepper would rear its head.

The studio where Chris and his business partner, Scott, worked was also the space where they took pictures of clients. This meant that new people came in and out of the place several times a day. Pepper didn't seem to like anyone coming in to the studio. She'd run to the door, bark, growl, and nip at the new person's heels, "herding" him into the center of the room.

While Chris and Scott set up their lights and props, clients would usually be invited to sit in a designated waiting area. Unfortunately, Pepper had decided that the big vinyl couch in the waiting area was "her" couch. Clients who sat there would be met with fearsome growling and barking, and even threatened with bites.

Pepper wreaks havoc on the photography studios

Pepper on "her" couch

This clearly wasn't the kind of behavior that could be tolerated. It wasn't harmless—Pepper had torn the hem off someone's pant leg once, and if she kept on threatening Chris and Scott's clients, it could be very damaging to their business. Chris was afraid he'd have to get rid of her—for many dogs whose owners can't find substitute homes for them (and how many people will take on a dog that they know has problems?), this means being given back to a shelter. Unfortunately, 56 percent of dogs who go to shelters—especially dogs who've been returned multiple times—end up being euthanized, simply because they can't find a human who can get along with them.[7]

Chris called me in as a last resort. He was seriously thinking about giving Pepper away. In talking with him and Scott, it was clear to me that the two of them were giving Pepper no leadership whatsoever in the studio. From the moment she walked in, the place was hers—no rules, boundaries, or limitations. Chris would walk in the door and immediately start concentrating on his work, and Pepper would be left to fend for herself. Since neither Chris nor Scott was acting like the "leader" in the environment of the studio—at least, not in dog terms—Pepper assumed that it was all up to her. She was the queen, and she neurotically protected her territory in the only ways she knew how.

It was in the course of our conversation that I found out that Chris had been perfectly successful in walking Pepper out in the street—even off-leash. It's much more difficult to get a dog to obey you in the great outdoors, with all its distractions, than it is inside the boundaries of home. I have many more cases of dogs that are compliant in the house but that misbehave on walks than the other way around, so I found this case intriguing. I asked Chris to demonstrate for me how he walked to work with Pepper, and I saw a completely different animal. I also saw a completely different Chris! He was focused, in control, and clearly looking out for Pepper, and they seemed to be emotionally in tune with each other. Why was the situation so radically different in the studio?

Basically when Chris came to work, he shifted into a different mind-set. All the great discipline that he had instilled in Pepper went out the window the minute the two of them came through the studio door. Chris had reneged on his leadership obligations, partly out of lack of information about dog psychology, but also partly because being a leader is hard work. It does take a certain amount of energy and concentration to be one all the time, and Chris was often so busy and harried at work that he couldn't be bothered with setting proper rules for Pepper. Once they left work, he redirected his energy to being her leader again, and everything was fine. But now, because the situation had gotten so far out of control, he'd have to go back to the drawing board if he was ever to get her to respect him within the walls of the studio.

We rehearsed several scenarios of people coming to the door, and I observed how Chris allowed Pepper to go berserk every time the bell rang. I showed him how to make her sit quietly, in a submissive state, even before the door opened. You can tell a submissive posture in a dog from the position of the ears and the look in the eyes, but you must also be attuned to sensing submissive energy. Chris had taught Pepper to respond to commands, and I watched him telling her (not very convincingly) to "lie down" over and over. Her body went down, but it was clear her mind was still active and agitated. Her ears were twitching and her eyes were fixated on the door. When it opened and the visitor entered, she went wild again.

I showed Chris that it was less important that Pepper be lying down when the door opened than it was that her mind be submissive and relaxed. I also showed him how to give her a command that meant business. Basically, Chris was being a pushover, and he couldn't fool Pepper about this. Remember, energy doesn't lie. He wasn't yet committed to the hard work it would take to split his concentration at the office between being Pepper's leader and being a full-time photographer. It seemed overwhelming to him to have to do both at once. Chris really wanted to keep Pepper, and I helped him to realize that salvaging this dire situation was his responsibility alone.

When I finally saw him really mean it when he gave Pepper a command, he didn't use words at all. He did what I do. He just made a sound: shhhhh. It wasn't the specific kind of the sound that was important—in fact, I chose that sound because it was the sound my mother used to use to keep me and my brothers and sisters in line! What mattered was the energy behind the sound. The key, I told Chris, was in correcting Pepper *before* her mind got caught up in its excited, aggressive state. That would mean correcting her—shhhhhing her—again and again, until she became conditioned to remaining calm and submissive at all times while she was with him at the studio.

The case of "Picture Perfect Pepper" shows an extreme outcome of giving our dogs only partial leadership. With lower-energy, naturally happy-go-lucky dogs, the consequences might not be so serious, but in the case of Chris and Pepper, the stakes were high indeed. Chris risked lawsuits, losing clients, and ultimately losing his business if he couldn't control Pepper—and Pepper risked losing her home, her owner, and very possibly her life (if Chris failed at finding a permanent home for her). Fortunately, once he understood the gravity of the problem, Chris took his responsibility seriously, and stepped up to the plate. There is no need for a dog like Pepper to live such an unbalanced life. All the elements she needed to be happy and stable were inside of her. However, she needed Chris, as her pack leader, to help her bring them to the surface.

Leading Is a Full-time Job

Dogs need leadership, from the day they're born to the day they die. They instinctively need to know what their position is in regard to us. Usually owners have a position for their dogs in their hearts but not in their "packs." That's when the dogs take over. They take advantage of a human who loves them but offers no leadership. Dogs don't reason. They don't think, "Gee, it's so great that this person loves me. It makes me feel so good, I'll never attack another dog again." You can't say to a dog like you'd say to a child, "Unless you behave, you're not going to the dog park tomorrow." A dog can't make that connection. Any show of leadership you give dogs must be given at the moment of the behavior that needs correction.

In your household, anybody can be a pack leader. In fact, it is vital that all the humans in the house be the dog's pack leader—from the smallest infant to the oldest adult. Male or female. Everybody must get with the program. I go to many households where the dog respects one person, but runs roughshod over the rest of the family. This can be another recipe for disaster. In my family, I am the dogs' pack leader, but so are my wife and two sons. Andre and Calvin can walk through my pack dogs at the Dog Psychology Center without the dogs so much as blinking an eye. The boys learned pack leadership from watching me, but all children can be taught how to assert leadership with animals.

Pack leadership doesn't hinge on size or weight or gender or age. Jada Pinkett Smith weighs maybe 110 pounds soaking wet, but she was able to handle four Rottweilers at once even better than her husband was. Will Smith was good with the dogs and they respected him, but Jada really put in the time and energy needed to be a strong pack leader. She's gone with me to the beach and the mountains, where I take the pack out for off-leash walks.

Leading a dog on a walk—as evidenced by the dogs who live with the homeless—is the best way to establish pack leadership. It's a primal activity that creates and cements those pack leader–follower bonds. I'll go into more details about mastering the walk in a later chapter, but as simple as it sounds, it's one of the keys to creating stability in the mind of your dog.

In dogs that are trained for specific jobs, the pack leader doesn't even need to be out in front. In Siberian husky dogsled teams, though the human pack leader is at the back of the sled, it's she who is running the sled. Dogs who live with handicapped people—people in wheelchairs, the blind, people with special needs—often have to take the physical lead in some situations. But the person they are helping is always the one in control. It's a beautiful thing to watch a service dog who lives with a handicapped person. Often, the two seem to have a kind of supernatural connection between them—a sixth sense. They are so in tune with each other that the dog can often sense what that person needs before being given a command. That's the kind of bond dogs in packs have with one another. Their communication is unspoken, and it comes from the security they have within the pack structure.

With the proper calm-assertive energy, pack leadership, and discipline, you, too, can have this sort of deep connection with your dog. In order to accomplish this, however, it's important to be aware of the things you may be inadvertently doing that are contributing to your dog's problems.

"He has a few dominance issues."

5

Issues

How We Screw Up Our Dogs

Almost all dogs are born naturally balanced. If they live as they do in nature—in stable packs—they spend their days in peace and fulfillment. If any dog in a pack becomes unstable, that dog will be forced to leave the pack or will be taken out by the other pack members. It sounds harsh, but it is nature's way of ensuring that the pack survive and continue for future generations.

When humans adopt dogs and bring them into our lives and homes, most of the time we have the dogs best interests at heart. We try to give them what it is we think they need. The problem is that we are making assumptions based not on what canines need but on what humans need. By humanizing dogs, we damage them psychologically.

When we humanize dogs, we create what I call "issues"— which are pretty much the same things a human psychiatrist calls "issues" when referring to his patients' problems. "Issues" are negative adaptations in dealing with the world. As human beings, our issues range far and wide and can be as simple as a fear of spiders or as complex as obsessive-compulsive disorder or foot fetishes. For dogs, issues are much simpler. But like human issues, dog issues are caused by an imbalance.

In this chapter, I want to address the most common canine issues that I'm called in to help correct. I hope you'll learn not only how to address these issues once they've formed but, more important, how to prevent them from forming in the first place.

Aggression

Aggression is the reason that I'm most commonly called in on a case. I am sometimes considered a dog's "last hope" before he or she is given away or even put down. Aggression isn't really an *issue* at all. It's the *outcome* of an issue.

Aggression in a dog isn't natural. Even wolves in the wild are rarely aggressive toward their own kind, or even toward humans[1]—unless there is a clear, specific reason such as threat or starvation. Aggression develops when a dog's issues aren't dealt with, when frustrated energy has no release. Unfortunately, such aggression always escalates if left unchecked. The sad truth is that when I am called in to treat an aggressive dog, I usually find a dog that could easily have been saved from having this problem. She could've been stopped before she got this messed up. Dog owners are sometimes motivated to seek out help only when their dog bites someone and they suddenly find themselves with a lawsuit on their hands. They'll say things like "She's a sweetie around the house with the children," or "He only acts this way when the doorbell rings." I wish every person with a dog would take more seriously early signs of aggressive behavior, and seek a professional's help before their neighbors drag them into court—or worse, before somebody gets hurt.

Dominance Aggression

While aggression isn't a natural state for a dog, dominance is natural for some dogs. Your dog may be a naturally dominant, high-energy animal. Does that mean she's bound to be aggressive or dangerous? No. It does mean, however, that you need to play the role of an even more reliable, calm-assertive pack leader with her. I mean that you have to play that role 24-7. Because that's what leadership means to a dog. A leader is a leader around the clock. No matter how tired you are, no matter whether you

Dominance aggression: ears up, tail up,
chest forward, teeth bared

want to concentrate on a ball game or your magazine, you still send her the same calm-assertive leadership energy.

Remember, naturally dominant dogs, pack leaders, are few and far between. Just as in the human world there are only a few Oprah Winfreys and a few Bill Gateses, there are a corresponding number of born pack leaders in the dog world. These dogs, if they don't get enough physical and psychological challenges, can indeed become very dangerous animals. They can and might become problem dogs. We owe it to these dogs—if we bring them into our lives—to provide the stimulation and the challenges they need.

Contrary to what many people believe, there is no such thing as a "dominant breed." Think about it—in a litter of puppies, one will stand out as the most dominant, and will grow up to run the pack. The others will be followers. Same litter. Same breed. There are *powerful* breeds—pit bulls, Rottweilers, German shepherds, Cane corsos—but it's up to the pack leader in the breed to direct that energy into healthy outlets. If you have a powerful breed dog, you'd better make sure you're the pack leader.

In the wild, the most naturally dominant animal becomes the pack leader. As I've said before, leaders are born, not made. But what if something happens to that leader? Number two will step in—often, the female companion of the male leader. Then an outside male might challenge her for pack leadership. If she feels that he's not powerful enough to take over, she'll chase him away or kill him. But if the new guy is indeed the most powerful, the whole pack will surrender to him right away—without a fight. Mother Nature does the "voting" for them—the new leader's energy automatically gets him elected. But once that hierarchy is determined, the dogs who are in the number two and three slots don't take it personally. They're not "ambitious" the way a human might be—the way a vice president is just waiting for his turn to be president, or the junior executive is just waiting to take over the company. Dogs are instinctually programmed to accept that the most dominant animal leads the pack. If another dog's more powerful than they are, they'll happily fall in line. Your dog will not take it personally if you establish your dominance over her. If she could, she would probably thank you for it.

If you have a naturally dominant dog, you need to establish your authority early, often, and convincingly. Think of your dog as having come into your life for a reason—to make you a stronger, more confident, more calm-assertive person. Who among us could not benefit from a little more calm-assertive energy in our lives—whether we're at work, with our family, or even while sitting in a traffic jam? It's best if you raise the dog from puppyhood to see you as leader, but you can become pack leader to a dominant dog at anytime in its life. It's all about the energy you project. You could be absolutely blind, have one leg, one arm, be in a wheelchair—but if your energy is more powerful than a 165-pound Rottweiler's, you own her. Automatically. I'm not a big guy, but at the Dog Psychology Center, I handle thirty to forty dogs at once. Often, all it takes is a glance from me to short-circuit a dog's forbidden behavior. It's not my size, it's my intensity.

When a person owns a powerful breed or has a dog with a dominant mind, if his level of energy is lower than the dog's energy, then he'll have to work on himself psychologically. Remember, this is natural. Your dog does not want to be your equal. Her world is made up of leaders and followers, and it's up to you, the owner, to choose which role you will play. If you're not willing to do this, or you simply cannot do it, you may not have the right dog for you. In a later chapter, I'll talk about red-zone aggression, which is serious business. Powerful dogs in the red zone have caused severe bites and even deaths. Most of the time, these are dominant dogs whose owners can't handle them. So think long and hard about the dog you are living with. If you can't handle her at all times and in all situations, it's bad news for you, for the dog, and for society.

Here's an example of a client who let a dominant dog get out of control to the point where his aggression was heading toward the danger zone. Let's call the client Sue. I worked with Sue for six months, trying to teach her how to manage her dog, Tommy, an Irish setter/German shepherd mix. From the beginning, Sue had done everything wrong with Tommy, who was a naturally dominant dog. It started with her letting him jump all over her. This progressed to the point where she would let the dog mount her and stay still until he finished mounting. Tommy was out of control, highly territorial, overly protective of Sue, and clearly the dominant one in the household. It was a very sick relationship. He had bitten some neighborhood kids and attacked the pool man, and animal control had been alerted. I tried to teach Sue to master the walk, to project calm-assertive energy, but she simply couldn't do it. She was dealing with psychological issues of her own, and for whatever reason, she could not follow up on rules and discipline. I finally broke it to her. I said, "I've done whatever I could to help you. But at this point, the only thing that is going to keep Tommy alive is if we place him in another home."

Of course it was heartbreaking for Sue. But it did save Tommy's life. Not only is he very much alive, Tommy is now a cadaver dog for the LAPD and is also performing in a movie for DreamWorks. He finally has healthier outlets for channeling all his intense, dominant energy. And he has no problem following commands from his handlers. It was a simple situation of the wrong dog with the wrong person, but a bad match can make for some dangerous problems.

Humans can exacerbate dominant aggression in a number of ways. The first is by allowing dominance in the first place. Remember, if you don't set the agenda for the things you do with and for your dog, then she's the pack leader. Another way is by playing "dominance games" with a dog and letting her win. Even if you play tug-of-war with your puppy, if she gets used to winning, she may begin to see this as a sign of her dominance over you. Roughhousing with dogs, even if they're just puppies, can lay the groundwork for aggression problems later on. If your dog starts to get possessive or growls during a play fight, you could be creating a monster.

Fearful Aggression

Much aggression is caused by fear, especially in little dogs with a Napoleon complex. When I worked at the groomer's in San Diego, I noticed right away that the meanest dogs were often the smallest. Often, fearful aggression will begin with just a snarl or a showing of teeth. If your dog shows these signs when you take her to the groomer's or when you try to get her out from under a table, now is the time to get help! Like all forms of aggression, fear aggression always escalates. The dog learns it can keep people away by showing her teeth, and pretty soon, the teeth baring becomes a nipping. The good news is that fear-biters at this stage usually don't dig in when they bite. They usually just nip, and then retreat. Their goal is for you—or the offending party—to just go away and leave them alone. But any aggression can escalate into something worse. Your dog isn't cute when she snarls or snaps. That's not "just her personality." She's unbalanced, and she needs help.

Pinky shows extreme fear

Fear aggression can be caused by abuse. If a dog has been hurt and discovers that she can stop the pain by lashing out, then of course that's what she will do. Most cases of fear aggression that I'm called in on, however, result not from cruelty but from the owners *giving love*—at the wrong time. Oprah's dog, Sophie, is a prime example. When Sophie lashed out at another dog, Oprah would scoop her up and comfort her, thus reinforcing the behavior.

I have a dog at my center now, a female pit bull mix named Pinky, that is an extreme case of fear aggression. When a human approaches her, she rolls up her lip in a snarl, tucks her tail between her legs, crouches down, and starts to shake. And I mean *shake*. Her legs tremble so much she can barely stand up. She is immobilized by fear. Pinky's owner felt sorry for her. He felt so sorry for her that he was always soothing her, giving her affection, nurturing her behavior and her mind at its most unstable. When you see an extreme case like Pinky, you realize how truly debilitating fearful aggression can be to a dog.

Give Affection—but at the Right Time!

This is as good a time as any to stop and remind you—yet again—of one of the most common ways we screw up our dogs and give them issues. We share affection, but at the wrong times. We give affection when the dog's mind is the most unstable. This is often the hardest advice for my clients to hear. "Hold back affection? It's not natural!" Please don't misunderstand me. Love is a beautiful thing, and one of the greatest gifts we can share with our dogs. But it's not the most important thing they need—especially if they have issues. If you're unstable, you can't really experience love; you aren't able to feel it. Love doesn't help an unstable dog. Aggressive dogs are not healed because their owners love them, any more than an abusive husband will be healed if his wife, his victim, simply loves him more. Those parents on *Nanny 911*—of course they love their children! But love's the only thing they're giving. They're not giving their kids exercise. They're not giving them psychological stimulation. There are no rules. Are those kids having a good time? No. That's why their parents called the nanny. Unstable dogs aren't having a good time either, even though they're often much loved by their owners. That's why their owners call me.

Love is not meant to enhance instability. Love is meant to reward stability, to take us to a higher level of communication. Just like in the human world, in the dog world love means something only if it is earned. I would never tell people to stop loving their dogs, or to love them "less," or in any way to measure the love they give them. Give your dog as much love as you have. Give as much love as your heart can handle and then some! But please, give it at the right time. Share affection to help your dog, not just to fulfill your own needs. Giving love at the right time and only the right time is a way you can truly *prove* your love for your dog. Actions speak louder than words.

Fearful aggression doesn't come out of nowhere. It is carefully tended like a garden by unknowing, and well-meaning, owners. Another example of a fearful-aggressive dog is Josh, whom the writers on my television show nicknamed the "Grooming Gremlin," for his long eye-concealing hair. Josh was a shelter dog that no one would adopt. He would bare his teeth at anyone who passed by his cage. Everybody who came into the shelter felt sorry for Josh—everybody. "Feeling sorry" for an animal in a shelter is something most people do. Sympathy is only human. But when fifty people go to a shelter and all of them send that soft, sympathetic "oh, the poor dog!" energy to an animal, that energy eventually becomes who that animal is. It defines him.

Ronette, a nurse, felt so sorry for Josh that she adopted him on the spot. Then she proceeded to continue to feel sorry for him every day. When he snarled at her daughter for approaching his food dish, Ronette would scoop him up and comfort him, as if her daughter were the offending party. When he attacked the professional groomers so often that he was banned from the place, she'd spend hours grooming the crotchety little fellow, who would not allow scissors near his eyes.

Believe it or not, I've been bitten by very few dogs in my career. Josh turned out to be one of them! He bit me while I was grooming him—but I continued on as if nothing had happened. He had to learn that a human was not going to back down, no matter how aggressive he became. Being a little dog, he was more snarl than nip and more nip than bite. He surrendered, and today Josh can go to the groomer's without drawing blood.

I use both Pinky and Josh as examples because I want to stress that "feeling sorry" for a dog is not doing that dog a favor. It is actually hurting her chances of becoming balanced in the future. Imagine if someone "felt sorry" for you all the time. How would that make you feel about yourself? Dogs need leadership before they need love. Let love reward balance. That's how balance is maintained.

How do you deal with fearful aggression? You don't give in. You have a choice—either wait out the dog and let her come to you, or go in and get her. If you go in and get her, you have to follow through. You simply cannot let her win. You must remain calm and assertive, and you can't get angry. Remember at all times that you are doing this for the good of the animal. Patience is the key. Waiting it out. Man is the only animal that doesn't seem to understand patience. Wolves wait for their prey. Crocodiles wait. Tigers wait. But, especially here in America, we're used to drive-thrus, FedEx, and high-speed Internet. You cannot rush the rehabilitation of a dog with fearful aggression. You may have to go in and get that dog fifty, one hundred times before it sinks in. I have a couple of fearful dogs at the Center that I know I'll be getting out of corners again and again and again until they finally come to understand that only calm submission will be rewarded.

With Pinky, the fearful-aggressive pit bull, the moment I put my thirty-five-cent leash on her, she relaxes. That's the nature of a follower—she wants to be told what to do. If I walk with her only a few feet, she begins to show all the physical signs of calm submission. She relaxes and calms down. If I wait too long before telling her what I want her to do next, the body language changes again—the tail goes between the legs, the shaking

Once I walk Pinky on her leash, she begins to relax

Giving Pinky affection—*after* she is calm-submissive

starts. No amount of affection is going to help this dog—in this case, affection contributed greatly to her problem. When do I give Pinky affection? The moment I see her relax when we walk with the leash. I will continue to do that until she is rehabilitated.

Dogs can become aggressive as a result of fear, dominance, possessiveness, territoriality, and a slew of other reasons—and aggression varies in degrees. In the next chapter, we'll talk about what I call the "red zone." Red-zone cases—extreme, chronic aggression—should always be referred immediately to a professional. Never attempt to handle a dog like this yourself. But you need to gauge your own degree of comfort. If your dog is only as aggressive as Josh, but you don't trust yourself to handle the situation, please err on the side of safety. Call in a professional dog trainer or animal behaviorist, for the good of both you and your dog.

Hyperactive Energy

Does your dog jump all over you when you come home? Do you think it's just because your dog is happy to see you and has "spirit"? Do you look at this behavior as your dog's "personality"? It's not spirit or personality. Hyperactive energy—overexcitement—isn't natural for a dog. It's not healthy.

In dogs' natural state, they do get excited and do play with one another, but excitement has a time and place. After a hunt, or after they've eaten, they have what is like a celebration, which we interpret as affection. They can and do "play rough" with one another, becoming excited-submissive or excited-dominant. But they don't practice excited behavior for a long time, and they don't practice excitement with that hyperactive "panting" sound you get with an overexcited domestic dog. That is a different type of excitement, a kind of crazy excitement. Some dogs in America seem to be in a state of hyperexcitement all the time. And it's not good for them.

I've noticed that my clients often interpret the words *happiness* and *excitement* as the same thing: "She's just happy to see me!" The two aren't the same. A happy dog is alert; her ears are up, her head is up, and her tail is wagging. An overexcited dog is jumping up, panting, and can't stop moving around. This is pent-up energy. Hyperactively energetic dogs are often among the hardest cases to rehabilitate. Hyperactive energy fosters other issues as well, such as fixation and obsession.

When their dogs jump on them at the door when they come home, many of my clients greet them with lots of affection. First of all, if your dog is jumping on you, that's an act of dominance. Don't allow it. Dogs are naturally curious, and they'll obviously be interested when someone comes to the door of your house. But they need manners to greet visitors with. Dogs don't greet other dogs by jumping all over them. They greet one another by sniffing. If that etiquette is good enough for the dog world, it's certainly good enough for your home.

Keep your dog leashed when visitors come to your home while you are teaching her how to greet visitors politely. Once you feel you are making visible progress, ask your guests to help you out. Instruct them not to acknowledge your jumping, overexcited dog—no talk, no touch, no eye contact—until she has calmed down. When a dog is being ignored, it sometimes calms down in mere seconds.

Hyperactive dogs need exercise, and a lot of it. And they need it before they get affection. When you come home, take your dog for a long walk. Then feed her. You have provided her with a physical and psychological challenge, followed by a reward of food. Then later, when her mind is calm, give her affection. Don't encourage the crazy jumping behavior, even if it seems fun for you and makes you feel loved. I'm sorry, but all that fuss is not because your dog is "happy to see you." It's because she has too much pent-up energy and she's got to release it somehow.

Anxiety/Separation Anxiety

Anxiety can contribute to hyperactive energy. You don't see a lot of anxiety in nature. Fear, yes; anxiety, no. It's only when we bring animals into the home or cage them up that we create anxiety in them. Anxiety can cause the kind of whimpering, whining, howling, separation anxiety that Oprah's dog Sophie used to experience every time Oprah went away. For dogs to be concerned about separation from you is normal. It is instinctual for them to worry or be sad if the pack is broken up, even if that "pack" consists of only you and your dog. And it's not natural for a dog to be shut up in a house or apartment alone all day with nothing to do. Your dog can't read a book or do a crossword puzzle—or watch my television show. Her energy has nowhere to go while you're gone. No wonder so many American dogs experience separation anxiety—and end up with all that built-up, hyperactive energy when their owners return home.

By the way, when you return home to find that your dog has eaten your favorite pair of shoes, it's not because she's "mad at you" for leaving and "knew" you loved those shoes! There you go, humanizing your dog again! Your dog ate your shoes because of her bottled-up energy. First, she smelled your shoes; they smelled familiar, like you. Smelling the shoes and reacting to your familiar scent, she got excited. Once she got excited, she had to release all that energy and anxiety. So she unleashed it all on your unlucky shoes.

I find that owners often don't recognize symptoms of anxiety in their dogs. They think that the separation anxiety begins when they leave the house—but in reality, it starts with unreleased energy that has been building since the moment their dog woke up. An owner wakes up, brushes his teeth, drinks a cup a coffee, and makes breakfast—and all the while his dog is in the background, following him room to room, pacing. The owner thinks, "Oh, she just loves to be with me; she has to make sure I'm fine all the time." All this is a fiction the human creates in his mind in order to feel good. That dog is showing you not how much she loves you, but how anxious she is. If you leave the house without giving her some way to release that energy, of course she'll have separation-anxiety issues.

I tell my clients to take their dogs for a good long walk, run, or even a Rollerblade session first thing in the morning; that's good for the human's health, too. If you absolutely can't do that, put the dog on a treadmill while you're eating breakfast or putting on your makeup. Really tire her out. Then it's feeding time. By the time you leave the house, your dog will be tired and full, and in a naturally resting state. The mind will be calm-submissive, and it will make much more sense for her to be quiet for the rest of the day. You'll also be less likely to have a hyperactive dog greet you at the door. Another piece of advice is not to make a big deal out of coming and going. If you share excited energy when you come and go, it only feeds an anxious mind.

Obsessions/Fixations

Another possible outcome for a dog's unreleased energy results in the dog's becoming fixated on or obsessed with something. It

could be anything from a tennis ball to the cat, but it's not natural and it's not good for your dog.

A fixation is wasted energy. A dog needs to channel her energy
into something in order to be balanced and calm-submissive.
A dog living with a homeless person walks all day, so that's
where the energy goes. A dog that lives with a disabled person
has the physical-psychological challenge of keeping her owner
safe, which is another way the dog releases her energy. Owners
who run and walk with their dogs on a regular basis help their
dogs drain energy.

Many owners feel that if they open the back door of their
house, their dog will get enough of a workout by following a squirrel around the yard—a squirrel that, 99 percent of the time, the
dog will never catch. So the dog spends all day just looking up at
the squirrel in the tree, becoming fixated on a squirrel that doesn't
give a damn about the dog. (Have you ever seen an anxious squirrel?) The only one who is going nuts is the dog. All her energy is
concentrated on the squirrel. That's one way of creating a fixation.

Another way is allowing a dog simply to sit and stare at a cat
or a bird or any other animal in the house. Because the dog is not
biting, barking, or growling, the owner thinks it's okay. But being
in a fixated mode is not normal for a dog. The dog's eyes will be
focused, her pupils will be dilated, and sometimes the dog will
drool. The body language will be tense. If the owner gives the
dog a command when it is in this fixated mode, the dog won't respond. Her ears won't even twitch in recognition of her owner's
voice. When the owner takes a dog to the dog park and it runs
back and forth, back and forth, compulsively chasing smaller
dogs, it's not playing. That's not a game. That's fixation. Even if
it doesn't come to a bite this time, a fixation like this is serious
because it can escalate into the red zone.

Another kind of fixation is when a dog obsesses or fixates on a toy or activity. Ever meet a dog who goes insane over a tennis ball, begging you to throw the ball again and again and again, until you want to pull your hair out? Many owners think they can substitute taking a dog out to play fetch for giving him regular walks. That doesn't work. Yes, it's exercise, but not the kind of primal activity that migrating with a pack leader provides. I like to compare it to taking the kids to Chuck E. Cheese's versus taking them to piano lessons. Chuck E. Cheese's will have them bouncing off the walls. That's excitement. Piano lessons will be a psychological challenge. That's calm submission. Playing catch is excitement; a walk is calm submission. If an owner skips the walk and just plays with the dog, the dog will have to use that playtime as the only way to totally drain her energy. The dog is being given that activity while her mind is anxious and excited. She'll play until he drops, which will be long after the owner does. At the same time, she'll go into the kind of high gear she would never reach naturally. When wolves or feral dogs hunt, they're very organized. They're calm. They're not fixated on what they're hunting. Focused, yes. Fixated, no. One is a natural state. The other is not.

The problem is, owners often see fixations as "cute" or "funny." Or they describe them as love. "She just *loves* that Frisbee!" "He just *adores* playing with that ball." That's not a healthy kind of love. A fixation is just like an addiction in a human, and can be just as dangerous. Think of a gambling addict in Las Vegas, sitting there all night, pouring coins into a slot, and pulling that one-armed bandit, for hours on end. That's a fixation. Smoking, drinking—anything that you can't control and where there are no limits, then you're in a fixated mode. You're not in control anymore. In this case, the ball controls the dog. Or the cat controls the dog. Or the squirrel controls the dog. Some dogs can become so fixated on an object that they will bite or attack another dog or a person who tries to take that object away from them. If you don't watch out, you're heading for the red zone.

At the Dog Psychology Center, if we're going to play with a ball, I make sure that before we do, everybody's quiet. If I'm going to feed the dogs dinner, first, everybody's quiet. If I'm going to give affection, first, everybody's quiet. I never give anything to the dogs if their minds are not calm-submissive. That's how I make a fixated dog become normal. Because he never gets anything if he's in that state. That's how I can have fifty dogs playing with the same ball without anybody getting hurt. We also never play or eat without doing some sort of vigorous exercise—walking, running, or Rollerblading—first. Draining energy is vital.

Dogs with fixations try our patience. Most people try to reason with their dogs verbally when they're fixated on an object such as a favorite toy or a tennis ball. Then this escalates to orders: "No, leave it. Leave it. Leave it. Leave it. Leave it." That only creates more excited and unstable energy for the animal. By this time, the human is already frustrated and angry at the dog because the dog hasn't heard a word he's been saying for the past ten minutes. Then the owner makes the decision to grab the dog physically and pull the object away. Now he's projecting so much unstable, frustrated energy that the dog's fixation only gets worse.

Uncrossing Jordan

The most physically exhausting case I handled in the first season of my television show was that of Jordan the bulldog and his multiple obsessions. Jordan's owner, Bill, had specifically wanted a calm, low-energy, lazy bulldog. Jordan certainly seemed quiet when Bill picked him out of the litter, but he grew up to be a hy-

peractive, dominant, and obsessive-fixated dog. He would fixate
on a skateboard, a basketball, a garden hose—really, pretty
much any object that was within reach. He'd take that object in
his mouth and never let go. Bill and his family did the number
one worst thing to do with an animal that's got an object of fixation in its mouth: they played tug-of-war with Jordan. By trying
to pull the ball or the skateboard away from the dog, they were
activating his prey instinct, making him go even crazier. Bill's energy didn't help much, either. Patience is a virtue when it comes
to a fixated mind. Of course, so is calm-assertive energy. Bill
seemed like a laid-back, easy-going guy on the surface, but un-
derneath he was actually very tense and easily frustrated. Remember when I said that energy doesn't lie? Bill wasn't fooling
Jordan. His passive-aggressive, frustrated energy was mirrored in
Jordan's obsessions.

When rehabilitating dogs, it's usually easier for me to remove
a dominant, aggressive state of mind than a hyperactive-fixated
state of mind. Jordan was no exception. I started with the skateboard. Because bulldogs usually get hot and worn out easily, I
figured it wouldn't take much for me to drain Jordan's energy. He
would prove me very wrong. That bulldog was one determined
little fellow. With each object, instead of pulling the object away
from him, I challenged him to back away from it, thus claiming
the object for myself. Every time he moved forward, I corrected
him with a tug. This eventually sends a signal to the brain that
what I want is submission. I went forward instead of moving
away from him. And I stayed with that same calm-assertive energy until Jordan finally got it, but because he had been living in
that fixated state for so long, it wasn't easy. I was dripping with
sweat by the end of the session.

Working with Jordan's owner, Bill, was my next task. I had to
get Bill to understand his part of the equation. He needed to be-

"Uncrossing Jordan"

come more patient and to practice being calmer and more assertive. I truly believe, and it has been my experience, that animals are put into our lives for a purpose: to teach us lessons and to
help us become better people. Jordan was certainly pushing all of
Bill's buttons. Perhaps if Bill had found himself a lower-energy,
mellower dog, he wouldn't have been challenged to change. Bill
loved Jordan, and he was motivated to become a more balanced
person so that Jordan could be a more balanced bulldog.

A fixated or obsessive dog needs an outlet for her pent-up energy, which begins with the walk. She also needs an owner who
will be there to "snap her out of it" the moment she begins to fixate. You can't wait until she's already into the fixated mode. And

you'll know that mode when you see it. Her body language will change, and she'll stiffen. Her pupils will dilate. When this happens, she needs to be brought back to a calm, relaxed state immediately, with an appropriate correction. I advised Bill to go for a good long walk to tire Jordan out, then to put the object in front of him and make sure he didn't go for it. If a dog's problem has been going on a long time, you're going to need to do this again and again and again—perhaps for months if the fixation is really bad. It's as they say in AA: one day at a time. If you've been consistently been doing negative things in your life—smoking, drinking, overeating—you have to practice consistency in replacing those things with positive activities. Rehabilitating a fixated-obsessive dog may seem like a lot of work, and it can be. But we owe it to our dogs to put in this kind of effort in order for them to become balanced.

Phobias

You remember Kane, the Great Dane who was afraid of shiny floors? That's a classic example of a phobia. A dog can develop a phobia for just about anything, from a certain pair of boots to another animal to an entire gender of people! Phobias are, very simply, fears that the dog has not been able to move beyond. If a dog's mind isn't allowed to move forward after a fear-inspiring incident, that fear can become a phobia. In the natural world, an animal learns from fear. A wolf learns to avoid traps. A cat learns not to play with snakes. But animals don't make a big deal out of the things that scare them. They don't lose sleep over them. They experience the emotion, learn from it, and then move on with their lives. We humans create phobias for them by the way we react to their fears. We keep them stuck. Marina, Kane's owner, made a huge fuss when Kane slipped on the shiny floor that first time. Then she made the mistake of comforting him whenever he was near the object of his phobia.

Even if we don't know the cause of a dog's phobia, guess what will either cause or intensify any phobia there is? You guessed it—once again, it's giving affection at the wrong time. When a child is afraid and we comfort him and give him affection and love, that's human psychology. When a dog is afraid and we comfort her and give her affection and love, that's also human psychology—not dog psychology. A dog wouldn't show affection to another dog that was afraid! The correct response to a dog's phobia is to show leadership. First, drain the dog's energy—since a phobia is a kind of reverse obsession, the same principles apply. If a dog is tired and relaxed, she's much less likely to be phobic—and much more responsive to a strong pack leader who will help her move past her fears.

Low Self-Esteem

Self-esteem isn't an issue, but it does play a part in many of the dog problems that I come across. When I refer to self-esteem in a dog, I'm not talking about what the dog thinks about how he looks or whether he's popular or not. Self-esteem in a dog, to me, relates to energy, dominance, and submission. Dogs with low self-esteem are submissive, weak-energy, weak-minded dogs who may suffer from fears, panic, or phobias. They often exhibit anxiety. They may show fear-aggressive behavior (like Josh or Pinky), or they may simply be terminally shy.

Dogs with low self-esteem can also develop obsessions, but in a different way than the way a dominant, energetic dog like Jordan developed his. Take Brooks, an Entlebucher. When Brooks

Brooks goes crazy chasing light and shadows

was a puppy, he was very timid. After being bitten by a neighbor's dog, he became even more afraid. He would cower and
slink away whenever anyone tried to pet him. Having low self-
esteem, he felt as if everyone were coming after him, and he was
afraid. Then one day, someone played a game of "chase" with
him using a laser pointer—one of those pen-shaped tools that
send a beam of light across the room. This became a game
Brooks really loved because he had a chance to chase something.
Something was running away from *him* for a change! He felt a
little bit dominant over something and good about himself, and
all the energy that he had stored up in his insecurities could be
released while he chased after the light. From that point on,
Brooks became obsessed with light. He was constantly being dis-

tracted by rays of sunlight, by reflections, by patterns of light and shade on the ground. His owners, Lorain and Chuck, couldn't even take him on a walk without Brooks running off and chasing after whatever stray reflection came along. In Brooks's mind, light became his only way to release pent-up energy. To insecure Brooks, the light was something that he could try to control. It never chased after him. It always moved away from him. This was an obsession created directly by both lack of physical exercise and by Brooks's low self-esteem.

Unlike high-level-energy and dominant Jordan, Brooks was a weak-minded, submissive dog, so snapping him out of his obsession took me less than five minutes. I only had to tug on his leash a handful of times before he got it. Of course, his owners would have to continue correcting him—consistently—each time he began to go into fixated mode, but it wasn't long before his obsession became a distant memory.

There are dogs whose self-esteem is at what I call rock bottom—dogs like Pinky. They are stuck in their insecurity. Instead of fight or flight, they freeze up. They'll hide, they won't move, they'll shake—they simply can't move forward in whatever they need to do. They won't get better on their own; they need a human to help them.

Dogs with low self-esteem are desperately looking for a pack leader! They *want* to be told what to do—that's sometimes the only time they'll relax, as in Pinky's case. Such dogs respond well to rules, boundaries, and limitations. The "power of the pack" will help them get better faster—being around her own kind is powerful therapy for a dog with low self-esteem—but her time in the pack must be closely supervised at first because of all dogs' natural instinct for attacking weakness. Little by little, these dogs get better, but they need strong guidance from their human pack leader.

One last word about self-esteem. A domestic dog's self-esteem shouldn't be too high, either. In nature, only the pack leader gets to strut around with his tail up and chest forward, projecting dominant energy to the others. If you're the pack leader with your dog, then only you get to do that in your house! When I come to a house where all the humans are tiptoeing around the dog, where the dog is the bully and everybody answers to her, then I know that that dog should feel a little less proud of herself. Becoming pack leader over a dominant dog means taking her down a peg. That definitely doesn't mean physical abuse or humiliating her in any way. And remember, she's not going to resent you for taking the lead. She might resist a little at first—to see how much she can get away with—but she won't take offense once you prove to her that your energy is more powerful than hers.

Prevention

All of the issues I've presented here can be prevented if you remember to treat your dog like a dog, not a human—and you make it a priority to work to fulfill your dog's life as much as she fulfills yours. In chapter 7, I'll share with you my simple method for creating a happy, balanced dog. But first, I want to address the most serious cases I'm called in to help rehabilitate—cases of "red-zone" aggression.

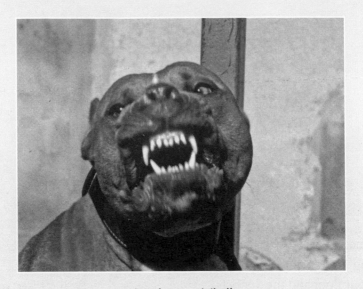

A red-zone pit bull

6

Dogs in the Red Zone

Dangerous Aggression

Imagine this—you come home to your upscale apartment building after doing a little grocery shopping. The elevator stops at your floor and the door slides open. The first, and last, things you see are two snarling 120-pound Presa Canario/mastiffs breaking away from their owner's leash and charging straight toward you.

That's how life ended for Diane Whipple, a thirty-three-year-old lacrosse coach in San Francisco, in January of 2001. The dogs' owners were both convicted of involuntary manslaughter and served four-year prison terms. This was perhaps the most notorious dog-attack death in the United States, but it's not the only one by far. Eighteen people on average die each year in this country from dog attacks.[1] We spend more than $165 million treating the nearly one million serious dog bites that occur every year.[2] Dog bites result in approximately forty-four thousand facial injuries in U.S. hospitals.[3] And tragically, 60 percent of facial dog-bite victims are children.[4] Most of the dogs responsible for

171

these bites will end up as statistics—just part of the 2.7 million animals put to death in shelters every year.[5]

Remember, these animals did not "premeditate" their attacks. They weren't "born killers," nor did they suddenly turn into killing machines. Unlike a human murderer sentenced to death for his crimes, none of these dogs had a sense of right or wrong about taking a life—whether human or animal. As I've said before, there is no morality in the animal kingdom; there is only survival. If dogs lash out in violence, they are acting on their fight-or-flight survival instincts. Dangerous aggression is not the cause; it's the outcome of a dog's serious behavioral issues. And more often than not, a violent dog's aggressive behavior has been deliberately exacerbated—or even nurtured—by the very human beings who are allegedly its caretakers.

In the wild, dogs are natural predators. They are also hard-wired to physically defend their territories. But aggression against humans—or other dogs—should never be permitted in the domestic dogs that live with us. Never. If we are to be our dogs' pack leaders, the first rule of the pack should be "No violent aggression!"

I made my reputation as a specialist in dog behavior by reha-bilitating some of the most formidable dog breeds out there—pit bulls, Rottweilers, boxers, and German shepherds. I love these brawny breeds, but they are definitely not appropriate for all owners. Unfortunately, when a dog owner can't handle his high-energy, powerful breed dog, the owner, the dog, and sometimes, innocent bystanders suffer.

I believe that more than 90 percent of the time what I call red-zone aggression is preventable. The majority of cases where I'm called in to help involve some kind of aggressive behavior. And in more than twenty years of working with dogs, I've met only two red-zone cases that I believed could not be rehabilitated as social animals that could live safely with humans. Based on my own experience, maybe 1 percent of all the dogs who've come to me with aggression issues have a mental imbalance, or are so deeply damaged by humans that they can't safely be returned to society. The upshot of this is we're putting a lot of animals to death who don't deserve to die. The only "crimes" these dogs committed were ending up with the wrong human caretakers.

Defining the "Red Zone"

I never encountered a dog in the red zone until I came to the United States. I'd seen rabid dogs and dogs physically fighting with each other, but once one dog had established dominance by putting the other to the ground, usually the contest ended right there. In nature, threatening behavior usually serves to deter outright aggression. Unless an animal is weak and must be executed by the pack, it is in the pack's best interest to keep aggression to a minimum. Before I arrived here, I'd never seen a dog that didn't stop his aggressive behavior—pinning another dog to the ground or chasing or scaring a person away—after getting a warning bite. But the red zone was something else entirely. The red zone means killing—be it another animal or a human being. It's not a dominant or territorial thing. The intention of that dog is to assault its target until he exhausts it. Until there is no life left in it.

A red-zone case won't listen to you, even if you are holding on to him. It doesn't matter if this dog is your lifelong companion who sleeps in the same bed with you. Once that red light goes on, it's as if you didn't exist. The dog will struggle against you, and would rather die than cease his attack. You can hit him, yell at him—he won't hear you, he's that focused. His mission to kill overpowers any pain you might inflict, and in fact, striking or screaming at a dog in the red zone will only accelerate or intensify his lethal state of mind. He's a dog with a fixation—but a deadly one.

A red-zone case is never something that happens overnight. That's why it is so tragically preventable.

"Ticking Time Bombs"

"I had no idea that he would ever do anything like that. How could you anticipate something like that? A totally bizarre event? How can you anticipate that a dog that you know, that is gentle and loving and affectionate, can do something so horrible and brutal and disgusting and gruesome?"[6]

Those were the words owner Marjorie Knoller spoke in her own defense at the Diane Whipple murder trial. Ironically, Knoller and her partner, Robert Noel, seemed to be the only ones in their San Francisco neighborhood who hadn't "anticipated" such a "bizarre" reaction from their Presa Canario/mastiff mix pair, Bane and Hera. These dogs were already in the red zone by the time the two lawyers adopted them, and in the words of a veterinarian who sent Knoller and Noel a warning letter about the dogs, they were "ticking time bombs" just waiting to go off.

The story of this senseless and preventable death began with a Folsom Prison inmate whom attorneys Knoller and Noel were representing and whom—for whatever reason—they ended up adopting as their son. This inmate was trying to start an illegal Presa Canario breeding business from his cell. Powerful dog breeds like Presas, Cane corsos, and pit bulls are exploited because of their extreme strength and territorial tendencies, and, unfortunately, are often condemned to lives as "gladiators" in illegal dogfights or as guards for crack houses, meth labs, and other criminal activities.

In the San Francisco case, the two Presas, Bane and Hera, had been kept for the inmate by a woman who had a farm near Folsom Prison. After they attacked and killed some chickens, sheep, and a cat, the woman decided she didn't want anything more to do with them. While she and the other people on the farm cowered in fear, the two dogs were kept chained up in a remote corner of the property, which only served to increase their frustration and aggression. Eventually, the inmate persuaded his two city-dwelling lawyers to adopt the dogs.

Once they had experienced killing the weak farm animals, Bane and Hera were already deep into the red zone. No one on the farm corrected them after they killed; they just banished them to their corner. Then the dogs were brought to the city and taken in by inexperienced owners, to live in a one-bedroom apartment, where their pent-up frustration continued to build. They got lots of affection from the two lawyers, but the way they reciprocated the affection was by jumping all over their owners—by dominating them. The lawyers did seem to walk them frequently, but the dogs were always out in front, dragging the owners along and dominating them during the walk. After the tragedy occurred, several witnesses came forward to describe having seen Marjorie Knoller chasing after the dogs as they pulled her on their leashes, totally out of control.

In the city, there were no goats or chickens for these dogs to target. Most of the weak energy they sensed there came from human beings. When the dogs were in the apartment building elevator, all they had to do was snarl, and people would back away from the elevator and refuse to enter it. People shrank back in fear whenever they saw these two formidable dogs on the street. This cause-and-effect intensified both dogs' dominant states of mind. To them, a human projecting fear was no different from a chicken or a goat projecting fear. Fear is fear. It's weak energy. No one had blocked their dominant, aggressive behavior when they attacked the animals on the farm. And no one was blocking it now. The dogs had no idea why the woman at the farm had gotten rid of them. They knew only that dominant, aggressive behavior was how they had learned to survive and gotten their way. So why should they change their behavior now?

I wish I could turn back the clock and start this terrible story over. I'd begin by conditioning these dogs from day one that aggression is not acceptable. Period. To do this with such a powerful breed of dog, however, requires an enormous amount of work and energy. Ideally, these dogs should have been getting four to eight hours of primal activities and exercise every day. They should have been socialized from the time they were puppies to accept other animals and other dogs as members of their pack, and humans and especially children as pack leaders. Humans should not have been conditioning them to engage in dominance "games" such as tug-of-war and wrestling. As the dogs got older, they were always going to win such games, thus increasing their perception of their own dominance. Their owners should never have used pain to inflict punishment. These dogs needed exceptionally strong, consistent, calm-assertive humans as their pack leaders.

For those who would argue that the dogs' breed was at fault, it is indeed true that Presas, Cane corsos, pit bulls, and Rottweilers were all originally bred to be canine "gladiators." But they are animals and dogs first, before breed. That same powerful energy can be redirected and channeled into other activities. Humans were gladiators in the past, too, but today we redirect that energy into basketball, baseball, soccer, football, and hockey. Presa

Canarios were originally bred to be guard dogs, but they were also used by the Spanish to herd. Herd dogs don't kill their flock. Presas and their relatives have in the recent past made excellent show dogs. Their physical and psychological energy has been redirected into their performance in the ring.

Breed doesn't necessarily have to shape a dog's behavior, but powerful breed dogs have special needs and require special people to care for them—dedicated and responsible people. Unfortunately, these two lawyers were not equipped to deal with these powerful animals. They took the dogs to obedience training, but as you know by now, learning to respond to commands does nothing to take away an unbalanced dog's fear, anxiety, nervousness, dominance, or aggression.

The owners said they "loved" the dogs, but once again, affection isn't the most important thing our dogs need from us. They also need rules, boundaries, and limitations—and from what witnesses later said at the trial, it looks as if these dogs' owners were at worst negligent or at best inconsistent with rules. One neighbor who was bitten by one of the dogs said that Robert Noel's only comment after the incident was, "Hmm, that's interesting." Other witnesses described seeing the dogs threaten and attack other dogs as early as two days before the killing. A professional dog walker testified that when she asked Noel to muzzle his dogs, he told her to shut up and called her offensive names.

Diane Whipple, the innocent victim, had also been bitten by one of the dogs, and since that day had been deathly afraid of them, going out of her way to avoid them in the building. The dogs' owners not only didn't apologize to her after that incident, but more important, they also never sought professional help to see to it that the dogs would be comfortable with Whipple and safe for her to be around them in the future. The owners did absolutely nothing, thus ensuring that the next time the dogs encountered Whipple's fearful energy, she would again be a target.

The attack on Whipple was the stuff that horror movies are made of. It lasted from five to ten minutes, and the medical examiner said that only the soles of Whipple's feet and the top of her scalp were left intact. She died at the hospital within four hours of the attack. Two more unnecessary deaths resulted from the tragedy—both Bane and Hera were put down. Bane, the male, was euthanized on the day of the attack. I offered my services to try to rehabilitate Hera. These dogs were not born killers; humans taught them to be that way. But even though I believe Hera might have had a chance at rehabilitation, by that point public outcry had sealed her fate. Even if I had been able to turn her behavior around, no one would have trusted her again.

Creating a Monster

I've said before that pack leaders are born, not made. Red-zone dogs are just the opposite—made, not born. Humans create dogs to be red-zone monsters. We started thousands of years ago by breeding dogs to be fighters, selecting them for certain characteristics and matching them up with a similar mate. Pit bulls and bull terriers were bred in the Victorian era for combat in the ruthless sports of dogfighting and bull-baiting. They were selected for their ability to clamp onto a foe with powerful jaws, holding on with relentless pressure. Rottweilers are descendants of ancient Roman drover dogs. They traveled with the Roman army as it fought its way across the European continent, guarding the army's gigantic herds of cattle by fighting off wolves and other predators.[7] During his invasion of Britain in 55 B.C., Julius Caesar described the ancestors of the mastiff breeds fighting alongside their masters. These dogs showed such bravery that they were brought back to Rome and pitted against other dogs, bulls, bears, lions, tigers, and even human gladiators in the Circus Maximus.[8] These ancient mastiffs were the ancestors of Bane and Hera, the Presa Canarios that killed Diane Whipple.

We breed these dogs to be warriors, but under their armor, they're simply dogs with more powerful weapons than other dogs. They don't begin life as dangerously aggressive; we can socialize them as puppies to get along with kids, humans, even cats and other animals. Though fighting is in their genes, they need guidance to bring this instinct out. In modern America, dogfighting is illegal, but it is much more common than you might think. "Dogmen," pit bull breeders, believe that the only way to preserve the line of "pure" American pit bull terriers is to prove their "gameness": their ability to fight to the death. These men engage in a sport known as "game testing," throwing their dogs into a ring with another dog and culling out the ones that manage to survive but that don't perform to the breeder's standards. These losing dogs are either killed by their owners or abandoned, left to wander the streets. Sometimes they're lucky and are picked up by a rescue organization. Usually, they're picked up by animal control and eventually put down if a home can't be found for them—usually for the simple reason that they happen to be wearing the outfit of a pit bull, a Presa, or a Rottie. And sometimes they attack and kill other dogs—or people.

It has also become fashionable and macho for gang members to have big, tough dogs at their sides—which they wield like four-legged artillery. Illegal dogfighting has grown to become a popular activity for some gangs. Betting on which dog will make it out of the pit alive is a thriving form of gambling. Dogfighting isn't confined to gangs and criminals, however. According to the *New York Daily News,* in the United States, an upscale dogfight underground exists in which thousands of dollars change hands. "We're like a secret society in the last sport that's Out There," boasts an unnamed source quoted in the article. "We've got all walks of life involved, celebrities, Wall Street brokers, ordinary people."[9] No matter where these dog fighters come from, what's scary is that those who get off on this blood sport sometimes bring their kids along to watch, creating a vicious circle of brutality. They're desensitizing a new generation to cruelty to animals, and to violence in general.

People who raise pit bulls, Presa Canarios, Cane corsos, or other dogs for fighting turn these innocent dogs into killers by abusing them. When they're young, the dogs are never allowed to be puppies; they have to be warriors all the time. The owners will start smacking the dog in the head at an early age, putting hot sauce on his food, teasing him, letting him be attacked by a bigger dog—all because they believe that this treatment will make the dog tough. They will punch him and pinch him repeatedly until he bares his teeth, at which point they'll stop pinching him. In this way he learns to bare his teeth for self-preservation. They'll buy chickens and let the dog chase one while praising him. Then they'll tie the chicken up so the dog can learn to kill. The dog has absolutely no choice in the matter. When the dog is no longer useful to the owner, they'll discard him like trash—often dumping him in a vacant lot or leaving him by the side of the road. That's why you'll see so many powerful breeds—pit bulls and pit bull mixes, boxers, Rottweilers, mastiffs, and German shepherds—in shelters. Many times they are considered "unadoptable" and will eventually be put to sleep. My Dog Psychology Center is home to many such dogs that were judged "lost causes" before they came to me for rehabilitation. Some of these "lost causes" are now living happily with human families, or have productive jobs with police or search-and-rescue organizations.

For people who raise pit bulls or other dogs for illegal activities, it's all about looking good. They feel that if they walk around with a very muscular dog with scars and cropped ears and a chain around his neck, they're going to look rough and tough, and have status immediately as a real bad guy. Fortunately for their dogs—or at least the ones who survive to get a chance at rehabilitation—these "bad guys" are also bad dog trainers and handlers. First of all, they start the abuse at an early age, making the dog more traumatized about fighting than desiring to fight. The dogs actually become very fearful, anxious, and tense about fighting. They fight only out of fear—out of fight-or-flight response.

Their owners' ineffectiveness is why I have such great success rehabilitating such dogs. First, I invite the dogs to go into a calm state of mind. The animal in them immediately recognizes that this is a far better situation than the one they've been living in. Unlike humans, who have the power (or curse) of denial to keep them in an abusive situation, animals will always move toward balance. Automatically, the brain says, "Hey, finally I get a rest." They are relieved to be out of that state of constant tension. Yes, they're still pit bulls, but before that they're dogs. And dogs aren't supposed to kill one another. So once I block those pit bull genes, the true colors of the dog inside are allowed to surface. The brain is no longer sending pit bull signals; it's sending only dog signals.

Breed and Aggression

Though there is no such thing as a red-zone breed, statistically, pit bulls cause the most bites in the United States, accounting for 41 of the 144 fatalities since 2000, according to the National Canine Research Foundation. Rottweilers ranked second, with twenty-three attacks. Those numbers are the reason why pit bulls are banned in two hundred cities and towns across the United States, including Miami, Cincinnati, and Pawtucket, Rhode Island.[10] In some states, homeowners can't get home owners insurance, or have to pay hefty premiums if they own certain breeds. For instance, Allstate won't insure homes where people own pit bulls, akitas, boxers, chow chows, Dobermans, Rottweilers, Presa Canarios, or wolf hybrids.[11] While higher insurance premiums may be one way to encourage more responsible ownership, I believe that the outright banning of breeds is not the answer. (Interestingly, the American Kennel Club doesn't even recognize the pit bull per se as an official "breed.") Branding dog breeds as outlaws is a quick, easy Band-Aid, but it's not the cure for dog bites or attacks in America.

The truth is, any breed of dog can become a red-zone case—it's the power of the dog and the physical size of the victim that determines the extent of the damage. Other breeds, too, have killed people. For instance, in 2000, a little Pomeranian mix killed a six-week-old girl in Southern California. In 2005, a Siberian husky—usually considered a "mild-mannered breed"—fatally attacked a seven-day-old Rhode Island girl.[12] The owner most often is responsible—not the breed, and not the dog. By the same token, almost any individual dog may become a good, obedient companion, even though he comes from a breed that is considered naturally "aggressive." Remember, aggression is not a natural state—it is the outcome of instability. It's all about the bond and relationship between the dog and his calm-assertive pack leader.

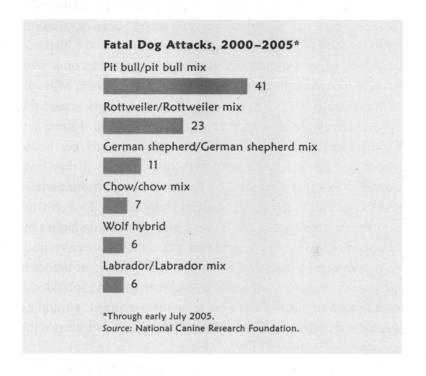

Fatal Dog Attacks, 2000–2005*

Pit bull/pit bull mix
41

Rottweiler/Rottweiler mix
23

German shepherd/German shepherd mix
11

Chow/chow mix
7

Wolf hybrid
6

Labrador/Labrador mix
6

*Through early July 2005.
Source: National Canine Research Foundation.

Emily in the Red Zone

One of the most powerful episodes of *Dog Whisperer* covered the red-zone case of a six-year-old pit bull named Emily. This case illustrated, among many other things, that when we stereotype a breed of dog by our worst expectations of its behavior, we often create what we fear most.

You couldn't imagine a more appealing puppy than Emily. Even from birth, she was petite for her breed, sporting a milky white coat with cocoa-brown spots. When teenaged Jessica saw that one of Emily's spots was shaped like a perfect heart, she knew that Emily was special. It's a charming feature like this that endears us to a dog and prompts us to bring it to live with us, often without really understanding the extent of our responsibility to that animal.

Jessica fell in love with Emily at first sight, and impulsively brought her home. Jessica lived with her father, Dave, who had let his daughter get away with everything while she was growing up. He didn't want her to have a dog—and when he learned that the dog she'd chosen was a pit bull, he was even more averse. He had always heard that pit bulls were dangerous, uncontrollable dogs. But Emily as a puppy was the cutest thing he'd ever seen, so as usual, he caved in to his daughter's wishes.

It turned out that just as Dave never gave Jessica any rules, boundaries, or limitations, so Jessica didn't give Emily any, either. At the same time, Dave watched with dread as Emily grew up, unfortunately, regarding her with an undercurrent of fear. "One day she's going to be dangerous," he believed, consciously or unconsciously. As much as he loved the dog, he couldn't keep these thoughts out of his mind. As I've tried to illustrate in this book, the thoughts we have about animals become energy—energy they pick up. Our impressions of them become who they are. It's not magic mumbo-jumbo; energy comes out in myriad physical ways. The way we pet a dog. The way we handle a dog. The scents and emotions we transmit to the dog. During her whole puppyhood, Emily was living with an owner who was preparing to be afraid of her. He tiptoed around her, worrying that she'd grow up to be a big, bad pit bull, and all the while letting her run roughshod over the house, bark wildly at other dogs on walks, and totally dominate him and his daughter in every activity, in every way.

Emily was also raised in a household where she wasn't exposed to others of her kind. This happens to many dogs. Some

dogs—mellow, medium or low-energy, happy-go-lucky dogs—
are not affected by this. They can be five years old when they go
to their first dog park, and act as if they've known the other dogs
all their lives. But many dogs are not happy-go-lucky dogs.
Many—especially shelter dogs—are like Emily. They are sensitive, reactive . . . and extremely receptive to their owner's energy.
The first time Emily was taken for a walk, she reacted aggressively to dogs that approached her. And Jessica and Dave always
pampered and comforted her after such displays of aggression.
Emily therefore inferred that it was her job to protect her family.

By the time I met Emily, she was six years old and a sweet dog
with her human companions—provided they never asked her to
do anything. With other dogs, however, she was as far into the
red zone as she could get. If she so much as scented another dog
nearby on a walk, she'd go crazy. She'd bark, struggle against the
leash, and try to attack. She'd pull so hard on her leash, she'd
come close to choking herself, but was oblivious to the pain—a
classic sign of a dog in the red zone. Red-zone dogs will indeed
hurt themselves in their frenzy to kill. Dave was afraid that Emily
would hurt not only another dog but also any person who got
between her and that dog. So, worried about Emily's temperament, Dave and Jessica stopped walking her altogether. For years,
they left her to run around their medium-size backyard, where
her aggression and frustration continued to build. Dave and Jessica had created the very monster they had feared—a very dangerous pit bull.

Emily's dog aggression was so severe that I brought her to the
Dog Psychology Center for six weeks of intensive therapy I call
Boot Camp. She was definitely in touch with that part of her
mind that was pit bull. I needed her to be with the pack so she
could reconnect with the deeper parts of her mind that were animal and dog.

Being with others of their own kind is powerfully therapeutic for dogs. Although they readily accept us as members of a pack, we'll forever be speaking to them in a foreign language. Dogs speak one another's language instinctually. In order to achieve full balance, they need to be around other dogs with balanced energies. Emily needed to be around dogs in order to relearn how to be a dog.

When she first arrived at the Center and got a look at my pack of forty dogs staring at her from behind the fence, her tough-girl demeanor evaporated. It was like a canine version of *Scared Straight*. Would she fight, flee, avoid, or submit? The usually aggressive Emily actually froze. She was under so much stress she vomited three times before she made it behind the gates. I walked her through the crowd, where she let other dogs smell her for the first time. She was terrified. But when I put her alone in a fenced-off area, she relaxed. She gave me calm submission so readily that I knew she would leave the Center a different girl.

During her six weeks at the Center, I worked with Emily daily. I kept her isolated at first, letting her watch the pack interact with each other. Dogs learn a great deal from watching other dogs and picking up their energies. Then, after a vigorous run or Rollerblading session to drain her energy, I began putting her out with the pack first for an hour a day, then two, then three, and so on. During her first weeks, I always supervised her when she was in the pack, so I could break up a fight in case one began. She instigated one small scuffle early on, after which I lay her on her side and asked her to submit to the other dog. After that, she started to get used to the routine. Whenever I worked with her, I'd exercise her first—a tired mind is more ready to submit. Emily was an extremely high-energy dog and had years of pent-up energy fueling her aggression. We did extra Rollerblading and running on the treadmill. By the end of the second

Emily the pit bull

week, she was beginning to relax around the other members of the pack.

Midway through Emily's program, I invited Dave and Jessica to come visit her. I wanted to observe what effect their presence had on her progress. I could tell they were tense by the way they walked through the pack. Then, sure enough, while Dave was walking her, Emily suddenly attacked Oliver, one of two springer spaniels in the pack. I broke the fight up in seconds, but it confirmed what I had been concerned about from the start. Dave's tentative energy, the way he tiptoed around Emily, and Jessica's extreme anxiety over Emily's aggressive tendencies sent Emily right back into the dominant state she had always experienced when she was around them. Emily would need more work and patience from me, and her owners would need some serious work, too. I had to communicate to them how much they were contributing to Emily's instability. It was hard for them to hear because they truly loved her, and their initial instinct was to feel guilty for the past. For Emily's sake, I asked them to let go of the past and try to live in the present—the only place where Emily was living! Their homework was to prepare for the calm-assertive leadership positions they'd have to take on once Emily came home to them.

Before I brought Emily to the Center, there had been a very real danger that she could attack and kill another dog. She was in a constant state of hyped-up tension. When I brought her home to Dave and Jessica six weeks later, they barely recognized the calm, relaxed pit bull walking alongside of me. The hardest part for them was not being able to greet her with an effusive "Welcome back!" and shower her with affection from the start. I tried to get them to see that by holding back their emotions, they were giving her the gift of a new, calmer way of being. Emily wasn't thinking, "Hey, I wonder why they're not all excited I'm home?" Remember, dogs sense when we are happy, and especially when we are happy with them. The kind of emotional, excited energy Jessica and Dave had been used to sharing with Emily needed to be tempered because it had only created more excitement for her—and excitement in a high-energy dog creates excess energy that needs to be released. Once Emily was used to being home and was calm-submissive, then Dave and Jessica were welcome to share affection to their heart's content. I gave them as daily homework to walk Emily by the home of her old enemy, the Doberman next door. It would take patience and a strict routine. They needed to get used to correcting Emily properly if she ever started going into aggression mode again.

The good news about Emily is that not only is she doing well, but she has also come back to the Center to stay while her owners are out of town. It has done my heart good to see her here again. She was welcomed back by everybody as an old familiar member of the pack.

Too Far Gone

Though some trainers and behaviorists disagree with me, I believe there are very few dogs that can't be rehabilitated, even if they've reached the red zone. To me, the dogs in my pack are walking proof that if a dog's needs are being fulfilled every day, its natural instincts incline it toward balance. Still, of the thousands of dogs I've worked with, there were two cases that came to me where I couldn't in good conscience allow the dogs to go back into society. I'll never forget those dogs, or stop wishing I could have done more for them. Working with those dogs was a lesson to me that it is possible for an animal to be too far gone for me to help it. It also showed me the terrible, unforgivable damage human beings can inflict upon the animals that trust us to care for them.

The first dog was Cedar, a two-year-old female purebred pit bull. Cedar was not a fighting pit bull, but she had been terribly abused by whoever had raised her. There was a lot of whipping and physical cruelty, and her aggression had obviously been nurtured and encouraged. She had also been trained or conditioned by humans to attack humans. She didn't just go for the legs or arms; she went for the neck. She went in for the kill. This isn't natural—the pit bull breed was not bred to attack humans, period. Cats, goats, other dogs, yes—but it's in a pit bull's nature to run away from a human or to attack only when crowded or cornered. Clearly, a human had redirected Cedar's aggression toward attacking people, and had done this to a point where Cedar wanted nothing to do with any other human being, ever. Her previous owners obviously saw her as a weapon, not a living creature. Then, for whatever reason, they abandoned her.

A kind man from a rescue organization found Cedar roaming around the street. Cedar became very fond of this man. Even dogs that are human-aggressive have the need to form a pack, and will often bond closely with one person. However, if anyone else gets near the dog, watch out. It soon became clear that Cedar saw all other humans as enemies. She attacked anyone else who came around her. The man who'd rescued her meant well, but he did what everybody always does—he nurtured the aggression with affection and sympathy. He would say, "But she loves me. She doesn't do that to me." Unfortunately, she did attack everybody else. The shelter approached me and asked if I could rehabilitate Cedar.

From the moment I reached into Cedar's crate, I could see the look in her eye as she growled and started staring at my neck. I managed to get a leash on her and worked with her for hours, every single day—over and over, to the point where both of us were exhausted. After a little over two weeks, I was able to get her to accomplish calm submission with me, but with no one else but me. If one of my assistants approached her, Cedar would start the attack behavior over again, aiming right for the neck. At that point, the shelter asked me for a progress report. I had to tell them that I didn't believe Cedar was safe to return to society. She was just too damaged, and posed a real life-threatening danger. Cedar is still alive today, but she's kept confined with the one man she trusts. No other human can even be in the same room with her. She was my first "failure." In a lifetime of living and working with dogs, I'd never seen a case like this. Cedar truly opened my eyes to how deeply a dog can be damaged.

The second dog I couldn't rehabilitate was a five-year-old male chow/golden retriever mix I'll call Brutus. He had been rescued by a woman and had become unnaturally possessive toward her. After he attacked and tried to kill her husband, the woman came to me. I had Brutus for a long time, and for a while it seemed that he was doing well. But every once in a while, if I corrected him, he would wait until my back was turned and try to attack me. Unlike Cedar, who went for the jugular, Brutus would attack low, but he went at it full force. He wouldn't let go, he wouldn't surrender, and he was never predictable. When his rescuer returned, I told her that although he was calmer than when he arrived, I didn't feel that he was fully rehabilitated. I couldn't predict this dog's reactions, and after all the time I had had with him, I still wasn't comfortable with his progress. Despite my warnings, the woman still wanted to take him back. A week later, I called her to check up on him, and the woman raved about how much better he was doing. About a month after that, he attacked another man.

Brutus will have to live out his life under close supervision at a no-kill shelter. And like Cedar, he was condemned to this life by humans who mistreated him.

I would like to see sanctuaries created for any dogs who can't achieve rehabilitation and who can't safely be around humans. In my wildest dreams, I imagine golf courses being turned into dog sanctuaries, with professionally trained people to care for the dogs—and to study them as well. These damaged dogs can definitely teach us a lot. They can teach us about the abuses that create killer dogs. They can show us how detrimental it is for them to live unstable lives, and they can help us differentiate between unstable dogs that can't let go and dogs that have the ability to become balanced. We can begin to learn what signs to look for in a dog that can't be turned around. In my opinion, we shouldn't be putting them down. These dogs are dying from what we humans have done to them. I think we should be creative enough to find a way in which they can live out the rest of their lives as comfortably as possible.

A Dog Is Not a Weapon

In this modern world, everybody's concerned about crime and how it can affect their families. For thousands of years, humans have been using dogs as guards and as weapons, both against animals and against other humans. Today, it seems we're mostly afraid of one another. Dogs, especially the powerful breeds, can indeed make good guards for your family. They certainly serve as a powerful deterrent. Statistics show that 75 percent of dog owners want their dogs to play a protective role in their households.[13] But when we insist that a dog be both our loyal, loving companion *and* a weapon for our protection, we may be asking too much.

Some of the red-zone dogs I've described were chained and confined to small areas as "guard dogs," and even if they underwent no other form of abuse, the frustration that built up in them was potentially lethal for any intruder—including a mailman, a relative, or an innocent child who just happened to wander by. If your dog attacks someone, you can be sued for everything you own, and as in the Diane Whipple case, you can even be charged with a crime and go to prison. And think of your dog's welfare. Most dogs that attack people are put down by law enforcement or animal control. These agencies don't want to take a risk as far as the general public's safety—or public opinion—is concerned. If you are using your dog as a defensive weapon, this could very well happen to you.

Although most of my work is now in dog rehabilitation, I have been and still am involved in the training of guard dogs, police dogs, and attack dogs. There is an art to training these animals, and doing it responsibly takes a professional. If you decide you want a powerful breed dog to serve as protection for your house, you need to go about doing it the right way. You need experienced guidance and must learn to share the strongest form of calm-assertive leadership with your dog. However, you should first weigh carefully all the pros and cons of having your dog lead a double life—of being both guardian and friend.

Training a Rottweiler to be an attack dog

Our Responsibility

As dog owners, we have a responsibility both to our dogs and to our fellow humans to manage our dog's behavior. If we have a dog who hasn't been properly socialized or rehabilitated, and is in any way dangerous to our neighbors or their dogs, then we are behaving recklessly by letting that dog out in society. There are some dog behaviorists and veterinarians who believe that positive reinforcement and approval techniques alone are appropriate for any dog, any time, in any situation. In my opinion, if a dog's behavior can be conditioned using treats and positive reinforcement, that's an ideal situation. It's always best for humans to approach dog behavior and training with a positive and compassionate outlook, and it's never, ever right to punish a dog out of anger. Dogs—and all animals—must always be treated humanely. But we must also remember that red-zone dogs will often escalate in their aggression until they kill or maim either another dog or, in a worst-case scenario, a human being. A red-zone dog is dangerously out of balance, and no amount of loving or praise or cookies will stop him from doing serious harm.

If you are the owner of a powerful breed of dog, you can do nothing to control the energy of the people around you. You can't expect someone not to be fearful of your dog—even if your dog has never hurt a flea. The only thing you can control is your dog. And you owe it to the other people and animals around you to do so.

Red-zone dogs need to know we're in control. That doesn't mean we should be aggressive with them. Punishing a dog does not cure aggression—usually, if a dog is in the red zone, it exacerbates it. But as that dog's caretaker, we must be strong and assertive, and we must consistently *correct* unwanted and dangerous behavior. Dogs have to know our power and that we are the pack leaders. As much of this is accomplished through our mind-set as it is our physical discipline. That said, many aggressive dogs can only be helped by qualified experts, who are advanced and experienced in handling dangerous red-zone cases. If you have the slightest doubt about your ability to handle your dog—or if you think the dog could pose a threat to you or your family's safety—you owe it to yourself and your dog to find an accomplished expert whose techniques and philosophy you can live with.

Finally, it's my personal opinion that no red-zone dog should lose its life unless every possible avenue of rehabilitation or placement for that dog has been exhausted. There are far too few no-kill shelters in the world—and those that exist are always filled to the brim and hurting for money. The dedicated people running these centers, however, share my conviction that it is wrong to commit an animal to a death sentence when it had no moral awareness or intellectual control over what it was doing. We should not be condemning dogs to death for having become the monsters their humans owners created—and that the dogs were never born to be.

With Coach

7

Cesar's Fulfillment Formula for a Balanced and Healthy Dog

This book isn't a "how-to" manual. As I mentioned in the introduction, I'm not here to teach you how to get your dog to recognize voice commands or hand signals; I'm not here to teach you how to properly make your dog "heel" or do tricks. There are plenty of guides and books related to dog training, and many qualified specialists out there who can do that. But although my primary mission is simply to help you understand your dog's psychology better, I also have some practical advice to offer you. This advice applies to all dogs, no matter the breed, no matter the age or size, no matter the temperament, or whether the dog is dominant or submissive. This is my three-part formula for fulfilling your dog's life. Be reminded—this isn't a one-time fix for a troubled dog. Dogs aren't appliances; you can't simply send them out to be repaired once and that's it. If you expect this formula to work, you have to practice it every day of your dog's life.

The formula is simple: in order to have a balanced dog, you must provide three things:

exercise
discipline
affection

. . . in that order!

Why is the order important? Because it's the natural order of your dog's inborn needs. The problem in the United States is that most dogs receive only part of the formula from their owners—affection, affection, affection. Some people do better, giving their dogs half affection, half exercise. Others practice all three, but put affection first. As I've stressed again and again in this book, that is a recipe for an unbalanced dog. Yes, our dogs crave our affection. But they need exercise and leadership first. Especially exercise, as you'll soon see.

1. Exercise

This is the first part of your dog's formula for happiness and it is absolutely the one thing you cannot skip. Ironically, it's the first thing most owners in the United States fail at doing. Perhaps it's because Americans in general seem to have problems with getting enough exercise for themselves, and don't recognize that all animals, even humans, have an inborn need to be active. Just getting out and being physical, moving our bodies, seems to have taken a backseat to everything else in our society these days. Our modern lives are so busy that it seems overwhelming to have to add in daily walks with our dogs on top of everything else. But if

Exercise

This should be the first and most important activity between dog and significant other

Discipline

This should be done as setting rules, boundaries, and limits between dog and significant other. Discipline also means consistency with the given jobs and activities.

Affection

This should be the last activity done with a dog by the significant other. Affection can also be used as a reward for good behavior (preferably with no verbal sound).

you are going to take on the responsibility of living with a dog, this is the contract you sign. You need to walk with your dog. Every day. Preferably at least twice a day. And for a *minimum* of thirty minutes at a time.

Walking with your dog is a primal activity. It is hardwired into her brain to migrate with her pack. Dogs don't simply enjoy walks because they get to pee and poop and get some fresh air— although shockingly, this seems to be the perception of many owners. To some dog owners, "walking the dog" means letting her out in the yard to do her business, then letting her back in the house. This is torture for a dog. Every cell in your dog's body is crying out for a walk. In nature, dogs will spend up to twelve

Affection

Affection

Affection

Affection | **Exercise**
Half of the quality time is spent exchanging affection between human and dog. | The other half of the time is spent exercising the dog.

Exercise

Affection

Discipline

Wrong Ways

hours migrating for food. Wolves—dogs' living ancestors—have been known to range over hundreds of miles and hunt for ten hours in their natural habitat.[1] Dogs naturally have different energy levels, and some dogs need to walk more often than others. Some breeds have genes that tell them to walk longer, or faster, or farther. But all dogs walk. All animals travel. Fish need to swim, birds need to fly . . . and dogs need to walk!

Walking with your dog is the single most powerful tool I can offer you to help you connect with all the aspects of your dog's mind—animal, dog, breed, and name—all at the same time. By mastering the walk, you have the ability to truly bond with your dog as her pack leader. The walk is the foundation of your relationship. It is also where a dog learns to be a dog. She learns about her environment, about the other animals and humans in it; about dangers such as cars and things to be avoided such as bikes and skateboards. She gets to pee on trees and really get to know her territory.

Animals need to connect with the world and be out in it. It's not natural for them to spend all their time indoors or behind walls. Another part of the "powerbroker paradox" that I spoke of—the tendency for very powerful people to have very messed-up dogs—is that these people often have huge, luxurious homes with enormous backyards. They think letting their dog roam in their estate's backyard is enough exercise for her. Never think you can substitute having a big backyard for going on a primal walk with your dog! Sure, it could be several acres of property, but to your dog it's a just very big kennel behind walls. Also, allowing your dog simply to roam around all day by herself isn't providing her with the structure she gets when she migrates with her pack leader. A structured, regular walking schedule is vital, especially for dogs with behavior problems and issues.

MASTER THE WALK

Every once in a while, after I've visited new clients and worked with their dogs, the clients will say to me, "We paid three hundred and fifty dollars for this consultation, and all you're going to tell us is to walk our dog more?" In some cases, yes, it is that simple. However, it's all about what I call "mastering the walk." There is one right way to walk with your dog and a million wrong ways to do it. I'd say that 90 percent of Americans do it the wrong way. Think I'm exaggerating? Here's an exercise for you: Go to a big-city park, such as Central Park in New York or Griffith Park in Los Angeles, and watch all the dog owners walking their pets. Observe ten of them. Count how many of them have their dogs out in front of them, on a long leash or a flexi leash. Note how many of them are being pulled by their dogs. Add up the numbers of walkers who are standing by waiting patiently while their dogs sniff the ground, the trees, everything around them, completely oblivious to their owners' presence. None of these dog owners has correctly mastered the walk.

Now, out of the ten dog and owner groupings you saw, how many had their dogs obediently walking next to them or behind them? Not many? Now check out the other side of the tracks—the part of town where the homeless live. See any difference in the body language of both the person and the dog? Ironically, the homeless seem to have the art of walking with a dog down pat. They aren't being dragged behind by their dogs; their dogs don't set the agenda of where they're going or what they're going to do. Why? Number one, because they travel together for so many miles a day, every day. And second, because the dogs see the homeless owners as their pack leaders. The homeless owners aren't pampering their dogs, giving them treats, or petting them all day—although the dogs can sense that their homeless owners are happy about having them around. The owners are providing leadership—someone to follow, who'll eventually lead the dogs to food and water and a place to rest. Their lives are simple but structured. A proper walk should be just that—simple, but structured.

THE LEASH

First of all, I usually recommend a very simple, short leash. The leashes that I use are nothing more than fifteen-cent cords of nylon that I loop into collars myself. Of course, if you are concerned about fashion, you don't have to go as down and dirty as I do, but I recommend—especially for problem dogs—that you fasten the collar over the top part of the dog's head, not around her neck (see photographs on page 204). Most collars rest on the strongest part of a dog's neck, which allows her to have full control over her head and sometimes, if she's a strong-breed dog, full control over you, too! If you want to see an example of how my style of leash looks, take a look at an American Kennel Club dog show. This is how handlers of show dogs leash their animals. You'll see handler and dog running around the ring together, with the handler lightly holding the leash and using it to gently lift the dog's head up. Dogs in dog shows look so proud of themselves with their heads up, and considering the relationship between energy and body language, that's probably how they feel. No, they're not proud of their haircut or their blue ribbon. They don't care about those things. In the dog world, a head held high is positive body language, a sign of healthy self-esteem. By holding the leash in this position, you also have maximum control over your dog—she can go only where you want her to go.

Many people in the United States seem to like flexi leashes

How to hold a leash

because they believe their dog needs "freedom" during a walk. There will be a time to share freedom later in the walk, but it will be the kind of freedom that you control. I'm not a fan of flexi leashes except for the mellowest, most happy-go-lucky dogs. Still, ultimately the choice of leash is up to you. Whatever you choose, don't let your dog's excitement over seeing you get the leash and put it on her control the whole experience. I had one client from *Dog Whisperer,* Liz, whose Dalmatian, Lola, would go wild and jump all over her the moment Liz took the flexi leash off the coatrack. Then Lola would charge out the door, pulling the flexi leash to its maximum length—and sometimes right out of Liz's hands. Needless to say, this is entirely the wrong way to leave the house with your dog.

LEAVING THE HOUSE

Yes, believe it or not, there is a right way and a wrong way of going out the door. First of all, never let your dog control the activity, the way Liz did with Lola. Your leadership must start before the walk. Don't allow your dog to wear the leash until she is in a calm-submissive state. Once your dog is calm, put the leash on and proceed toward the door. Don't let your dog get overexcited again while you're standing at the door or in the doorway. Even if you have to wait, once again make sure your dog is in a calm-submissive state. Then open the door. You go out the door first. This really does matter. By going out the door first, you are saying to your dog, "I am the pack leader, inside and outside of the home."

When you walk your dog, make sure she is beside you or behind you. When someone's dog is way out in front of them or pulling them, the dog is walking the human, the dog is leading the pack. You're probably used to your dog wanting to sniff every bush, tree, plant, and patch of grass she sees. That's normal for a dog, but when you are in "migrating" mode, the dog should not stop until you tell her to stop. Imagine if a wolf pack needed to migrate ten miles and every dog was doing its own thing, sniffing trees and grass instead of moving forward? The pack would never get to the food. The walk is first to bond the two of you and show your leadership, second, for exercise, and third, for your dog to explore. You should hold the leash firmly but with a relaxed arm, as if you were carrying a briefcase. And most important, remember your calm-assertive energy. Think Oprah! Think Cleopatra! Think John Wayne! Think about an experience where you felt strong and in control. Straighten your posture. Lift your shoulders high and stick your chest forward. Do whatever it takes to really own that calm-assertive energy and project it through the leash and to your dog, who picks up on every signal you send. Many of my clients have been amazed at how simply increasing their calm-assertive energy and projecting it on a walk has calmed their dogs down. It's not magic. It's nature at work. Dogs naturally want to follow a calm-assertive leader. Once you claim that role, they naturally fall in line.

Now that you've established a rhythm and you've been walking uninterrupted for a few minutes, now is the time to let your dog go ahead of you—a little bit. Release the tension on your leash and let your dog pee, sniff the grass, whatever she wants to do. Remember, she's doing it when you say so. That's the key. Ironically, when you give a dog permission to do this, she'll probably spend less time on it than if she were allowed to do it on her own from the beginning. When I walk my pack of forty to fifty dogs off-leash in the mountains, we'll go for thirty, forty minutes with them behind me, and then the pack is allowed to be in front of me for five minutes. That's the kind of "freedom" your dogs need—but with rules, boundaries, and limitations. I allow them to go only thirty, forty feet away from me. If they cross the line, a quick sound from me will remind them to fall back.

Personally, my favorite exercise to do with my pack, one that really gets their energy drained, is to go Rollerblading with them. I put on my in-line skates and skate with as many as ten dogs at a time down the streets of South Los Angeles—on leash, of course. Sometimes I get funny looks; people can't believe their eyes. But the dogs love this. Sometimes I pull them, sometimes they pull me, but I am always in charge. By the end of a three-hour session, everybody's tired and more than happy to be calm-submissive for the rest of the day!

Rollerblading with the pack

TREADMILLS

If you're not able to walk your dog as much as her level of energy requires, then a treadmill is a viable option. The treadmill should not be the only walking your dog does—remember, she needs to walk with *you*. But it's a great way to give added stress relief to a dog that has a lot of energy to burn. It becomes both a physical and a psychological challenge for her. Dogs are like men in the human world—we both can concentrate on only one thing at a time! And when a dog's on a treadmill, she's going to have to concentrate. She's going to get "in the zone."

Many of my clients are skeptical about putting a dog on a treadmill. They think the dog will hurt herself, especially if she's on a leash. Proper supervision is required at first, but any dog has the ability to do this. Dogs using treadmills are nothing new. This isn't something I invented. Back in 1576, Doctor Johannes Caius of Cambridge University described a mongrel breed of dog he called a "turnspit."[2] These dogs were specifically trained to walk on treadmills that mechanically turned the spits on which people roasted their meat. This breed of dog is now extinct—since the popularity of the oven took off, no doubt!—but if dogs could be trained to walk on the manual treadmills of the fifteenth and sixteenth centuries, how much more difficult could it be for them to be trained to walk on the electric ones of the twenty-first century?

One of my clients was the CEO of a sixty-billion-dollar company, and a household name. His dog, a powerful male German shepherd, was out of control, attacking and biting people, but the owner was in total denial about it. It was his wife who called me in. I worked with her husband for several hours, and could see that he was completely defensive: It wasn't his fault. It was his wife and kid's fault. He was a busy guy. He didn't have time to

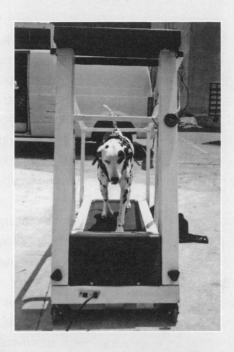

Training dogs to walk on a treadmill

walk the dog. I said, "Well, since you insist you can't walk your dog, can you put him on a treadmill?" And he said, "No. No way. This dog would never in a million years go on a treadmill." I just stayed quiet. When he had finished, I asked him, "Are you ready to see him on the treadmill?" He started getting angry with me. "I'm telling you, this dog will never, ever be on a treadmill." It took me five seconds to put that dog on the treadmill, and he took to it right away. The dog was right at home in a matter of seconds. My client was speechless. He's not the kind of guy many people prove wrong—or dare to tell he's wrong. But I was there for the good of the dog, not his owner's ego. I'm afraid this powerful man may not put in the energy to follow through on my advice—until he's slapped with a lawsuit. Unfortunately, that's the only thing that will get some of my clients to take their dog's behavior seriously.

I recommend that you first hire a professional to teach you the safety basics about putting a dog on a treadmill. For a dog, the first two weeks on a treadmill are a mental challenge, because the floor is moving, and the dog's instinct tells her to run away when the floor is moving! After two weeks, you'll see your dog scratching at the treadmill, begging you to turn it on. Dogs become addicted to it—a healthy kind of addiction. If you start at a very low speed and you supervise your dog closely until you're sure she's completely comfortable, you should be able to put her on the treadmill and go about your business, as long as you're not too far away. Never leave her there too long without checking on her, of course. But treadmill walking at a reasonable speed—while not a substitute for a walk outdoors—can be a safe and healthy contribution to your active dog's exercise regimen. It's especially important for powerful breed dogs that need extra workouts to help control their dominance or aggression.

DOGGIE BACKPACKS

Another technique I use for high-energy dogs that need more of a workout is a doggie backpack. Adding weight to a dog during her walk—or even during her treadmill walk—makes her work harder. It also gives her something to focus on, a job to do. Dogs love having jobs, and as I've already mentioned, they can't do more than one thing at a time. If they're focused on walking and carrying, they are much less likely to be thinking about chasing after every cat that walks by, or yelping at bicyclists. Have you ever watched a Boy Scout troop on a hike? No matter how hyperactive they may be back at camp, they are always calm and submissive when they're hiking with backpacks on! Wearing a backpack almost always calms a dog down; it's like Prozac—without the side effects. The backpacks are made in various sizes and styles; look up "dog backpack" on the Internet to find one that's right for your pet. The ballast you put inside the pack should weigh between 10 and 20 percent of your dog's body weight, depending on her energy level and needs.

Backpacks have helped work miracles in many of the dogs I've rehabilitated. Coach, an aggressive and overly protective boxer, exhibited behavior that was so out of control that he was scheduled to be put to sleep the very day I came to work with him. Although he had been to obedience classes, his family had not been walking him, at all. With regular walks and new rules, boundaries, and limitations from the entire family, Coach is so well behaved now that he walks to school with his eight-year-old owner and carries the boy's books in his doggie backpack. There's nothing more therapeutic for a dog than giving him a job to do, and carrying a backpack is a job. Coach is a dog who went from death row to being a companion dog worthy of *The Little Rascals*—in a matter of weeks.

DOG WALKERS

Finally, if you absolutely cannot walk your dog—if you are injured or ill or incapacitated in some way—I suggest you hire a professional dog walker. It's not an ideal situation for forming that pack leader–pack follower bond that you want with your dog, but it does help her get used to having a human leader. Some committed dog owners I know walk their dogs in the mornings and evenings, and hire a walker to make sure their dog is properly exercised at noon. Not everyone can afford such a luxury, but for those who can, I'll bet it's a lot less expensive than the legal fees you'd be paying if your underexercised dog's behavior problem got you into a lawsuit. You should check out the references of any dog walker, of course, and make sure to observe him when he's out for a walk. Is he in control of the dogs? Are they dragging him around, or are they showing him respect? Make sure you're comfortable with anyone you're leaving your pet with. Your dog can't complain to you when you bring her home, so you'll have to rely on your own judgment.

DOGS NEED JOBS

From the beginning of creation, dogs were made to have jobs. In the wild, the pack functions like a well-oiled hunting machine, and when we first domesticated dogs, we specifically bred them to take advantage of their innate working abilities. We started creating the breeds based on how we thought we could best use them for our own needs. We like the way one dog jumps over obstacles. We like the way another dog digs in the ground. We like the way this dog retrieves, and that one herds sheep. Ninety-five percent of dog breeds around the world today were origi-

nally working breeds. No more than 5 percent of today's dogs were bred to be lapdogs. Dogs, both wild and domestic, were born to work. But in modern-day America, we don't always have legitimate work for our dogs with special talents.

Therefore, the walk is the most important job you can give a dog. Walking with you, the owner, is both a physical and a mental activity for your dog. After she has accomplished this primal form of exercise, then it's fine to do the other things you enjoy doing together—playing fetch, swimming in the pool, and doing tricks, the more exciting kinds of activities. Just as you wouldn't leave your kids at Chuck E. Cheese's all day, you also set a time limit for these more frenetic activities with your dog. But like the big backyard, these games are not substitutes for the walk. You cannot skip the walk. After the walk, your dog will naturally go into the deepest form of resting mode—humans would call it meditation mode. When she is in this mode, you can leave the house and go on with your day, secure in the knowledge that your dog knows you're the pack leader, and that all that boundless energy inside her is being channeled properly and constructively.

2. Discipline

When it comes to dog behavior, the word *discipline* has gotten a very bad rap lately. The people who refuse even to allow that word to pass their lips usually define *discipline* as *punishment*. To me, the word has a different meaning altogether. Of course it means rules, boundaries, and limitations. But it also has a much more profound meaning for me—with regard to my dogs and also to my own life.

Discipline makes you a better person, makes you fit, makes you healthy, and helps you have a healthy relationship because you are disciplined to do what is best for the relationship. This doesn't mean I "discipline" my wife by telling her when she has done something wrong—in my household, it would probably be the other way around, anyway! Discipline in our relationship means I'm part of a couple, part of a structure that tells me what my boundaries are. Because I'm disciplined, I'm going to live up to my commitment. When I promise my wife I'll do something, I'm going to do it. When she promises me she'll do something, she's going to do it. Every single day. To me *discipline* is a word that helps me to stay on target, to reach my goals and dreams. It's a word that allows me to stay balanced, to be a respectful human being, an honest human being, someone who wants the best for himself and for everything around him—from trees, to animals, to human beings. Without discipline, you can't really be a good role model. If you're not a disciplined person, you become negative energy or negative source.

Running my Dog Psychology Center, I have to be disciplined. I have to be disciplined with planning each day. I have to keep to a schedule. I have to make sure every day that the dogs have water, that they have food, that they have exercise. I have to watch their health closely and take them to the veterinarian if they get sick. I have to clean up after them. If I were not disciplined about these things, not only would my business fail, but my precious dogs could become ill and even die. Discipline to me is serious business.

Mother Nature responds to discipline. Discipline—rules, boundaries, and limitations—exists in every species on the planet. Bees are disciplined. Ants are disciplined. Birds are disciplined. Dolphins are very disciplined. If you've ever seen dolphins hunting a school of anchovies, you've seen how orderly they are in working together to herd their prey. Wolves are disciplined not only when they hunt but also when they travel, when they play, and when they eat. They don't question discipline. Nature doesn't view discipline as a negative thing. Discipline is DNA. Discipline is survival.

Think about how discipline figures in your life. If you're Lance Armstrong, discipline means keeping in shape, training, eating the right foods, and riding for so many miles a week. If you work at Starbucks, discipline means getting to the job on time, memorizing all the endless names of coffee drinks, knowing how much foam to put in a cappuccino and a latte, and knowing how to be polite even when there's a long line of impatient customers. That's discipline. To succeed at anything, you must practice discipline. If you're taking a Tae Bo class with Billy Blank, you'd better be disciplined when he tells you to lift your leg. And he's not being mean about it. He simply knows you can't accomplish what you went there to accomplish without practicing discipline.

That's how I share discipline when it comes to dogs. It's my job to tell them when to wake up, when to eat, and how to interact with one another. I set rules, boundaries, and limitations about where to go and at what pace, when to rest, when to pee, whom to chase, whom not to chase, where to dig a hole, where to roll over. All that is part of discipline. To me, discipline is not punishment. It's the rules, boundaries, and limitations that exist for the good of the dogs and for my relationship with them.

CORRECTIONS

In nature, dogs correct one another all the time. Mothers correct their pups constantly. Pack leaders correct pack followers. Natural dog packs are filled with rules, boundaries, and limitations. There are dozens of unspoken rules of etiquette in a wild dog or wolf pack, sometimes communicated by energy, sometimes by body language, sometimes by a physical touch or a bite. A *correction*—what some people might call a "punishment"—is simply a consequence of a dog's breaking the rules. With dogs, there's always a consequence to breaking rules. No exceptions. If the pack members could talk, they'd say to an offender, "You're not being disciplined like us; you're not part of our pack. We're going to give you one chance. You do it again, and you're out of here. Either we'll kill you or we'll kick you out of the pack." Dogs don't resent other dogs for correcting them, and dogs don't hold grudges against dogs that make mistakes. They correct and then move right on with their lives. It's all very simple and natural to them.

In nature, setting limits isn't "cruel," and in order to set limits, all animals sometimes need corrections. We all know human parents who don't set limits. It's *their* kids who are running around the restaurant screaming and throwing food, and disturbing your nice quiet dinner. They're the parents calling for *Nanny 911* when their house is in chaos.

Think about how humans learn. We often need to make mistakes and be corrected before we know what the rules are. If you're in an unfamiliar state where you don't know the traffic laws and you make a right turn on red, a policeman stops you and tells you there's no right turn on red in that state. Now you know the rules, but he's going to give you a ticket anyway. That's your punishment. That's your correction. And it will probably work. After paying a $250 ticket, you can bet you'll never make a right on red in that state again.

Like humans and all other animals, dogs need to be corrected when they break a rule. The reason I like the word *correction* rather than *punishment* is that the latter word has human connotations—and too many people correct their dogs the way they would punish a child. With a child they'll take away a privilege— "You didn't clean up your room so you can't go to the ballgame tomorrow"—or, after yelling at the child, send the child to his room. Dogs don't have a clue what you're saying when you're yelling at them. All they hear is your excited, unbalanced energy, which will either scare or confuse them, or which they'll simply ignore. Dogs don't have a concept of "tomorrow," so you can't threaten them by withholding a trip to the dog park. If you send them to another room or put them outside, they probably won't make the connection between the banishment and the bad behavior. Dogs live in a world of cause and effect. They don't think, they *react*, so they need to be corrected the instant the unwanted behavior occurs. You can't even wait five minutes before correcting a dog, because chances are she's already moved on to another state of mind. Remember, dogs live in the now. Corrections have to happen in the now—and be repeated every time the rule is

broken—before a dog will understand what aspects of her behavior are unwanted by you.

How we go about correcting our dogs is also the subject of
much debate. There is an influential school of thought right now
that argues that positive reinforcement and positive training
technique alone should be used with dogs, or with any animal. In
my opinion, positive reinforcement is to be desired and is wonderful—when it works. It works for happy-go-lucky dogs and
for the dogs we raise as puppies. If you can get the behavior you
desire out of feeding your dog treats, by all means, go for it. But
the dogs that come to me are often ones whose behavior is way
out of control. They're rescued dogs who've had terrible pasts
filled with abuse, deprivation, and cruelty. Or they're dogs who've
lived their whole lives without any rules, boundaries, or limitations whatsoever. Then there are the red-zone dogs that we've
discussed. These dogs are too far gone to be rehabilitated simply
by using treats.

Abuse, on the other hand, is never acceptable. Hitting a dog
isn't acceptable. You cannot use fear as a means of making an animal behave; it doesn't work. Showing an animal strong leadership and giving it rules is not the same thing as instilling fear and
punishing it.

The distinction is in how and when you use corrections. You
never, ever correct an animal out of anger or frustration. This is
when animal abuse—or child abuse, or spousal abuse—occurs.
When you try to correct your dog out of anger, you are usually
more out of control than your dog is. You are fulfilling your own
needs, not the animal's—who will sense your unstable energy
and often escalate the unwanted behavior. You can never let an
animal push your buttons. You are there to teach her and show
leadership, and if you're going to correct her, you must always
remain in your calm-assertive state of mind. This may be a chal-

lenge for you—as it was for Jordan the bulldog's owner, David. But perhaps that is why this animal came into your life—so that both of you could learn a healthier way of behaving.

That said, when you correct your dog, it's your energy, mindset, and the timing of the correction that matter more than the method, as long as the method isn't abusive. Never strike a dog. A quick, assertive touch can snap a dog out of an unwanted state. I curl my hand into a claw shape so that when I quickly touch a dog's neck or just under its chin, my curled fingers feel like the teeth of another dog or of the dog's mother. Dogs often correct one another with gentle nips, and touch is one of the most common ways with which they communicate. A touch is more effective than a strike could ever be. Use the least forceful technique possible to snap a dog out of an unwanted behavior or state of mind. Your purpose is to redirect the dog's attention back on you, as the pack leader. Correction can be anything from a sound, a word, a snap of the fingers—whatever works best for you and doesn't do physical or mental harm to the dog. What works for me in correcting dogs is to practice what they do with one another—eye contact, energy, body language, and forward motion toward each other. Remember, dogs are always reading your energy, and they'll know what you mean when you're energy tells them, "It's not okay to do that." When I have a dog on a leash, I'll give a little tug upward to snap the dog out of unwanted behavior. It's a short little jerk that barely lasts a moment, and doesn't hurt the dog—but the timing of it is vital. Whatever the correction method, it has to happen the split second the dog begins the unwanted behavior. This is where knowing your dog comes in. You need to learn to read your dog's body language and energy almost as well as she's already reading yours.

For example, all dogs love to roll in the carcasses of dead animals. It's how they disguise their scent in the wild when they hunt—and it's one of Mother Nature's most ingenious inventions, a behavior that's embedded deep in the dogs' genes. However, when dogs live with us, having them come home covered with dead skunk or squirrel isn't only unpleasant, it's also unsanitary. I like dogs to live as naturally as possible, but as pack leader and the one who's paying the bills, I think it's within my right to try to limit this aspect of my dogs' behavior. So if I see a dog begin to sniff something unusual, I've got to correct her instantly, before she begins to run toward the scent. Remember, dogs are much faster than we are. If you miss "reading her mind" and therefore miss the opportunity to give correction, you're going to be washing dead skunk out of her fur when you get home.

THE DOMINANCE RITUAL

Another controversial aspect of correction is the dominance ritual—what most trainers and behaviorists call the "alpha roll." It's a replica of what dogs or wolves do with each other in the wild: the dominant dog puts another on his side until that dog signals submission. It's basically a wolf asking another wolf to cry "Uncle!" and admit that he's been one-upped. This is the way a pack leader keeps order without having to resort to all-out violence against other pack members. To hear some behaviorists talk, putting a dog into an alpha roll is as cruel as lighting him on fire. I have been criticized by many in the positive-only school of behavior, and called inhumane and barbaric, for using this technique. I respect those critics' opinions, and agree that this technique is appropriate only for certain cases, and to be used by experienced dog handlers. If you feel, as they do, that this method is cruel, then you should regard my advice with that in mind.

I believe that, when it comes to how we relate to animals, it is always a matter of personal conscience.

In my opinion, asking a dog to submit to me by lying on her side is a very natural thing to do. Within my own pack, a stern look, a sound, or a gesture from me will almost always send an errant dog into a submissive state—sitting or lying—without my ever having to touch her or, in some cases, even come near her (see the three-part sequence that follows). It goes without saying that I'd always rather get the behavior I want with simply a look or a sound than with a touch. However, with extremely dominant dogs, with dogs that attack people or other dogs, or with two dogs that are fighting with each other, I sometimes have to physically put the dog or dogs on their side. A dominant dog will put up a fight—wouldn't you, if you were used to being boss?—and will struggle against me. This is natural. If you've gotten away with a certain kind of behavior all your life, you're going to rebel against someone who finally tells you, "No!" In this case I have to hold on firmly until that dog stops resisting. I started using this technique with my first pack of Rottweilers, and still use it whenever necessary. It elicits a primal response in the dog that I am the pack leader.

When outsiders see a dog lying on her side, ears back, eyes forward, they assume the dog is responding to me that way out of fear. This isn't a fearful position. (See the section on body language again.) It is a totally submissive position, as submissive as you can get. In the dog world, this is the ultimate sign of respect. Of surrender. *Submission* and *surrender* don't have negative connotations in the dog world. There's no such thing as *humiliation* because a dog doesn't dwell on the past. A dog isn't going to hold it against me. Although many of the dogs in my pack at some time in their lives have had to submit after misbehaving, they still

Cesar achieves total submission without any physical contact

love me and follow me every day. With forty dogs in one place, not a day goes by without someone getting into mischief. But mischief can escalate into more disruptive and dangerous behavior, and like any good pack leader, it's my job to stop it before it goes that far.

When it comes to the dominance ritual, however, please take note: although I personally practice it in my work rehabilitating severely unbalanced and aggressive dogs, I caution anyone who isn't a professional—or at least extremely experienced in dog behavior and aggression—*never, ever* to forcibly put a dog on its side. With a dominant or aggressive dog, someone who is inexperienced could easily be bitten, mauled, or attacked. This is serious stuff, life-threatening stuff. If your dog is exhibiting the kind of behavior problems that require this kind of correction, then you should be consulting a professional, anyway. You should not be on your own in attempting to restore discipline to a dog that's this far gone in terms of dominance or aggression.

RULES, BOUNDARIES, AND LIMITATIONS

You have "house rules" for your children. Why shouldn't you have the same for your dog? So many of my clients come to me after they've hit rock bottom. Their dog is literally running the household, and the family is thrown into chaos. Many of my clients admit to me in shame that they're "isolating" themselves— they don't see their friends anymore because they fear what their dog might do when a new person comes to the house. Their lives have become unmanageable—almost as if they were living with an alcoholic or a drug addict in the family! Some beautiful people I was fortunate to meet during the first season of my television series, the Francescos, had been a boisterous, outgoing, very social Italian American family, until a tiny bichon frise named Bella came into their lives. By the time I met them, they had stopped inviting the rest of the family over to their house, for fear that Bella might attack them. This tiny ball of fluff didn't even weigh ten pounds, but she controlled the entire family. She would bark nonstop at anyone who entered the house, and never stop barking until that person left. The Francescos loved Bella—it had been the dying wish of a beloved aunt that the Francescos have a puppy for her orphaned daughter and niece to love. Bella represented something spiritual to them—a person they loved very much but had lost—so they tiptoed around her, never giving her any rules, boundaries, or limitations. They didn't realize that they weren't doing Bella any favors by pampering her. She was a very unbalanced dog, always on edge because she was trying so hard to be a pack leader and not doing a very good job of it. She wasn't having a good time in life. Most dogs instinctively know that they're not meant to run your household. They don't *want* to run your household! But if you're not doing it, they sense they have no choice but to try to take over.

It's instinctual for a dog to crave rules and structure in her life. Nature is all about rules and rituals of behavior. Now that domestic dogs live with us, it's up to us to set the rules. What you allow and you don't allow in your own household is up to you— whether the dog sleeps on the bed with you, whether she's allowed on your furniture, whether she can dig in the backyard, whether she is permitted to beg for food at the dinner table. But there are certain behaviors of hers that I recommend you always block, because by allowing them, you could be encouraging dominance. You should not allow the dog to jump on you—or anyone else, for that matter—when you walk in the door. You should not allow your dog to whine when separated from you. No possessiveness over toys. No snapping or biting. No jumping on you in bed to wake you up. No aggressiveness toward people or other dogs or household animals. No incessant barking.

Some of the behaviors that you'll want to block may be instinctual ones. This is why you must be much more than just your dog's owner. You must be the pack leader. A pack leader controls both a dog's instincts and her genetics. As a dog owner, you can control only affection and genetics. A dog trainer can control only genetics. A dog handler can control only genetics. You can send your dog to obedience school and teach her how to sit, stay, come, and heel. You can teach her how to catch a Frisbee or run an obstacle course. That's genetics. But just because a person goes to Harvard doesn't mean he's balanced when he graduates, and just because a dog knows how to obey doesn't mean she's balanced, either. When you train a dog, you don't get access to that dog's mind, you get access only to conditioning. And conditioning doesn't mean anything in the dog world. Dogs don't care about winning the Westminster. They don't care about winning the prize for catching the most Frisbees. A dog may be able to follow commands, or retrieve, or track, or do any number of things that her breed, her genetics, programs her to do. But can she play happily with other dogs without a fight? Can she travel in a pack? Can she eat her dinner without being protective over her food? That's instinct. A pack leader controls both.

For example, you may have had this experience with your dog. She loves to play ball. In your backyard, you play catch and retrieve all day long. That's your dog's genetics. That's the breed in her. You control your dog's behavior, but with the ball. Her motivation to be with you is the ball, because you have the ball. But let's say your dog loses interest in the ball. Her new motivation is the cat. She starts chasing the cat. That's her instinct calling her. Can you control her now? Can you block that behavior? Or, without the ball, outside of the backyard, can you control your dog during a walk? Can you keep her from chasing squir-rels while you're walking? You can't block her from chasing the cat or the squirrel with a tennis ball. The only way you can block these behaviors is with leadership. Unless you are in control of her instinctual side, you cannot predict or control what your dog may or may not do.

As pack leader to thirty to forty dogs at the Dog Psychology Center, I often have to block instinctual behaviors in order to keep the pack running smoothly. It's instinctual for dogs to mount one another, but sometimes I have to block them be-cause if that behavior gets too intense, it could escalate into a fight. I don't allow the dogs to fight over food, or over a tennis ball. No fighting or aggression is allowed in my pack—none is tolerated. No bigger dogs are allowed to go after smaller dogs—that's how our teacup Chihuahua, Coco, can live happily in the same pack with two giant German shepherds, seven pit bulls, and a Doberman. I have to block the stronger dogs from going after the weaker ones or the ones who have unstable energy. It's natural for dogs to try to get rid of unstable energy in a pack member, but I have to teach my pack to accept weaker members and not harass them. That's how the pack helps rehabilitate un-stable dogs—showing them *by example* what balanced, calm-submissive energy looks and feels like. I also block the dogs from chewing on or digging in the greenery or rolling in each other's poop. Those rules are my choices because they suit me as a hu-man being. As pack leaders to our dogs, we have the right and responsibility to choose the rules they live by.

However, whenever I block any instinctual behavior, I must replace it with another activity to redirect the energy. You can't just take something away and give nothing in return. The energy that drove the dog to the undesirable behavior doesn't just van-ish because you blocked it! You must replace an undesirable

Gordon is fixated on his shadow—which, in nature,
is perceived as instability

Munchkin naturally attacks Gordon's instability—
a behavior that must be blocked or corrected

activity with a desirable one. That's why I have obstacle courses,
swimming pools, treadmills, tennis balls, and other distractions
for the dogs at the Center. That's why they spend from five to
eight hours every day in vigorous exercise, and why I make every
activity—from walking to taking a bath to eating—a psychological challenge for them. If you don't give your dog ways to drain
her energy and exercise her mind, it will be a lot more difficult
for her to stick to the rules and boundaries that you set for her.
If you are a good, responsible pack leader, you will provide not

Playing with dogs in the pool at the Dog Psychology Center

only the structure for her life, but plenty of outlets for her natural energy as well.

3. Affection

Dogs in the United States may be lacking in the amount of exercise and discipline they get every day, but they certainly aren't lacking in affection. That is why many people here choose to bring dogs into their lives—for that amazing, unconditional, canine love and affection they share. And dogs are affectionate animals. They are very physical animals, and touch means a lot to them, both in their natural world and when they come to live with us. But as I've said before, affection that hasn't been earned can be detrimental to a dog. Especially affection that is shared at the wrong time.

When is the right time to share affection? After a dog has exercised and eaten. After a dog has changed his unwanted behavior into a behavior that you asked for. After a dog has responded to a rule or a command. If your dog jumps up on you demanding to be petted, it's probably your instinct to oblige her. This behavior sends her the signal that she is in charge. Share your affection only with a mind that is calm and submissive. Ask your dog to sit down and calm down. Then you share affection, on your terms. Your dog will quickly come to realize that there is only one correct behavior to get her the things she wants.

When is the wrong time to give affection? When your dog is fearful, anxious, possessive, dominant, aggressive, whining, begging, barking—or breaking any rule of your household. The owners of Bane and Hera, the killer dogs in San Francisco, were always giving affection to the dogs after the dogs had been terrorizing people all day. Anytime you give affection, you reinforce the behavior that preceded it. You cannot "love" a dog out of her bad behavior, just as you can't "love" a criminal into stopping his crimes. When I was first married to my wife, Ilusion, she gave me all the love in the world, but it wasn't that love that snapped me out of the bad behavior that I was used to getting away with. What got me to change and become a good husband and partner was when she finally drew a line in the sand. I could shape up, or she was shipping out. I have to admit, it wasn't love that changed me. It was rules, boundaries, and limitations!

You can find excellent examples of the proper way to give affection when you observe dogs that have jobs. Handicapped people with service dogs must understand that the dog isn't there just to be their friend. They have to learn to play the leadership role before they can expect the dog to turn on the lights, open the doors, or lead them to the bus stop. Even though these dogs have been trained by professionals, they won't respond to the handicapped person until that person learns to share calm-assertive energy. If you've seen these dogs in action, you've noticed they wear a sign that says not to give them affection while they're at work. By law, you can't touch those dogs. Affection will only create excitement, and a dog can't do its job when she's excited. When does the handicapped person share affection? After the dog has performed a task, and at home, at the end of a hard working day. Dogs in search-and-rescue and police dogs don't receive affection while they're working, unless it's immediately after they have completed an important task. Drug enforcement officers don't play with their dogs all day and then expect them to calmly search out packages for illegal substances. To have to work for affection is a very natural thing for a dog. It's only we humans who believe that if we're not giving affection to the dog 24-7, we're somehow depriving it of something.

FULFILLMENT

When I talk about "fulfilling" our dogs, I mean fulfillment in the same way we think about fulfillment in our own lives. Are we happy? Are we living each day to the fullest? Are we reaching our potential, exercising all the talents and abilities we were born with? It's the same thing for dogs. A dog's life is fulfilled if it can live comfortably in a pack, feeling safe and secure under the guidance of its pack leader. A dog is fulfilled if it has frequent primal exercise and, in some way, feels that it is working for food and water. A dog is fulfilled when it trusts its pack leader to set consistent rules and boundaries for it to live by. Dogs love routine, ritual, and consistency. They also love new experiences and the chance to explore—especially when they feel they have a reliable bond with their pack leaders.

Dogs fulfill us in so many ways. They fill in for human companions when we're lonely. They keep us company on our morning walks. They give us something living, soft, and warm to cuddle with. They serve as alarm clocks, burglar alarms, and sentries. They win us money in competitions. We don't ask them to do these things, but they do. They can't speak and ask us for what they need. Giving them these simple things—exercise, discipline, and affection, in that order—will go a long way toward thanking our dogs for everything they bring to our lives.

Affection time at the Dog Psychology Center

8

"Can't We All Just Get Along?"

Simple Tips for Living Happily
with Your Dog

Human beings and dogs have coexisted interdependently for thousands of years. In developing countries and in primitive societies, dogs are not always treated with the degree of love and kindness we give them in the United States. However, dogs in those places don't seem to have all the issues and neuroses that they have here, either. How can we share our love with our dogs without giving them "issues"? How can we be strong pack leaders without losing the compassion and humanity that made us want to bond with dogs in the first place?

These are questions that have no simple answers. However, I offer you some practical tips from my experience with clients that I hope will help you and your dog live a stress-free life, and thus move you toward the highest levels of connection between two species.

Choosing a Dog

As I've mentioned before, choosing the right dog is the corner-stone of a long, fulfilling relationship between the two of you. Before you even commit to having a dog, however, please ask yourself what your motivation is for bringing that dog into your life. You don't need to share these musings with anybody else, but you need to be absolutely honest with yourself because, I promise you, you won't be able to fool a dog. Are you miserable and lonely and intending to use the dog as a surrogate for human companionship? Do you want the dog to play the role of the child you never had, or become a substitute for the kids who have just left your "empty nest"? Are you bringing the dog into a household to fill the emptiness in your heart after another dog has passed away? Do you want to have a tough-looking dog by your side for status, or a cute dog you can walk in the park to at-tract girls? Do you want the dog to be a protector and weapon and little else? If these are your primary reasons for wanting a dog, I ask you to remember that a dog is a living being with pow-erful feelings and needs and desires that are different from—but not lesser than—your own. A dog is not a doll, a child, a purse, a status symbol, or a weapon. In choosing a dog to share your life, you have an incredible opportunity to form a powerful bond with a member of another species. But that opportunity comes at a price—the price of responsibility.

Know yourself before you know your dog. Before you take the plunge in becoming a dog owner, I recommend that you be able to answer yes to the first part of each of these important ques-tions, and no to the part of the question in parentheses:

1. Am I committed to walking my dog for at least one and a half hours *every* day? (Or will I simply let the dog out in

the backyard and rationalize that he is getting plenty of "outdoor exercise"?)

2. Am I committed to learning how to become a calm-assertive pack leader with my dog? (Or will I let my dog walk all over me because it's easier?)

3. Am I committed to setting clear rules, boundaries, and limitations in my household? (Or will I let my dog do anything he wants, whenever he wants?)

4. Am I committed to providing regular food and water for my dog? (Or will I feed him only when I remember to?)

5. Am I committed to giving affection only at appropriate times and when my dog is calm-submissive? (Or will I hug and kiss the dog when he's fearful or aggressive, or whenever the mood strikes me?)

6. Will I commit to taking my dog to the veterinarian on a regular basis, making sure he is spayed and neutered and has all his proper checkups and shots? (Or will I only go to the vet when my dog is sick or injured?)

7. Will I make sure my dog is socialized and/or trained properly so he is never a danger to other animals or people? (Or will I hope for the best and warn people to stay out of my dog's way?)

8. Am I willing to clean up after my dog whenever I walk him? (Or will I consider my dog's poop to be someone else's problem?)

9. Am I willing to educate myself on dog psychology in general and any specific needs my dog's breed has in particular? (Or will I just lead by instinct?)

10. Am I willing to put some money away in case I have to call in a professional for a behavior problem or rush to the vet for a medical emergency? (Or will the dog only get what I can afford at the moment?)

Did you pass? If you did, congratulations. You're ready for a dog. If not, you might want to rethink your choice of pet. There are plenty of homeless cats out there who need rescuing, too, and their needs are very different and not as burdensome as a dog's.

Now, which dog to choose? As I've said before, breed is one important factor, and there are many excellent guides you can pick up that will educate you about the hundreds of dog breeds out there. I recommend the American Kennel Club's Guide to Dog Breeds, with its beautiful color pictures and fascinating genetic histories of the purebred breeds. Bash Dibra's *Your Dream Dog* is another book packed with information about choosing a breed that works for you. *Mutts: America's Dogs,* by Michael Capuzzo and Brian Kilcommons, takes a unique look at "classifying" mixed breeds. The story of dogs is a fascinating one, and you can never do too much reading about it.

Still, when it comes to matching a human with his or her perfect dog, I believe that *compatible energy* is much more important than breed. Throughout this book you've seen examples of dogs whose energy outmatched that of their owners. Jordan the bulldog is the first to come to mind. Emily the pit bull was another example. If you are a laid-back, mellow kind of person, a high-energy Chinese crested that jumps around in the kennel will only cause heartache, or headaches, for both you and the dog. If you're a runner who wants to jog with your dog, a lethargic, short-legged bulldog will not be your ideal choice.

First, be honest about your own energy level. Then assess the energy of the particular dog you are thinking about getting. And take your time doing this. If you have the opportunity, return to see the dog on a second day, at a different time of day, to determine if there is any variation in behavior. Many people nowadays don't select purebreds from breeders but instead go to the local shelter or rescue organization to adopt a dog that's been lost or abandoned. Since most of the dogs at my Dog Psychology Center have rescues in their backgrounds, I applaud the altruism of those gestures. But too often a person will "fall in love" with a cute dog at the pound, or a dog they "feel so sorry for," and decide on the spot to adopt it. They will bring it home without thinking, and end up in the kind of hell so many of my clients experience. This is unfair to the dog because very often it gets returned to the shelter. And dogs that have histories of multiple returns run a higher risk of being euthanized. They also often develop new and often more serious issues, courtesy of every human who adopts and then rejects them. So taking your time in choosing a dog is serious business. If you can afford to, bring a professional along with you when you make your final decision. You can also bring this person along to help you introduce the dog to your home.

Bringing a Dog Home

When you bring a dog from a breeder or a shelter into your new home, remember that to that dog, you are simply transporting him from one kennel to another. You may have a six-million-dollar, fifty-acre, fourteen-bathroom kennel with a pool, hot tub, guesthouse and tennis court, but to the dog, it's just a bigger kennel. Walls are not natural to animals, period—no matter which famous architect designed them. Therefore, you need to create the experience of migration for your dog before you bring him home. The very first thing you do once you reach your home is go for a long, long walk with your dog—at least an hour walk—through his new neighborhood. Take as long a walk as you can possibly afford, then add in an extra twenty minutes on top of that. During this walk, you are both building a bond of trust with your new companion and establishing your position as pack leader. The rules of your entire relationship are being established in those first important moments. Your dog is also getting the feeling of his new neighborhood. You are creating for him what it might feel like to migrate to a new home with his pack leader. And, of course, you are tiring him out so he'll be more amenable to conditioning once you enter the house.

Entering the house for the first time is as important as that first walk together. You have only one chance to make this first impression. If you do it right, you will save yourself a lot of heartache. If you do it wrong, you're going to have to rehabilitate your dog from day one.

Make sure you enter the house first. Then "invite" the dog in. Don't let your husband and kids come running out to shower the dog with affection and welcome him home. As hard as it will be for them, tell them to stand where they are. Bring the dog to them and let him approach them and learn their scents. By now of course, you've taught everybody how to project calm-assertive energy, so that's all the dog will be feeling in the room, right? Most people give in to the temptation to let the dog roam the house and property, delighting at watching him sniff and suss out every new room and object. If you do this—especially if you are trailing around after him—you are allowing him to claim the entire property for his own. For the first two weeks, you must give him "permission" to do everything. The first night, dedicate a room for him and a sleeping place, possibly his crate or kennel. I often recommend that families hold off on affection for a week or two, until the dog has learned the rules of the house and become accustomed to his new "pack." For most people, this is an impossible request, which I totally understand. Once your dog is quiet, in his kennel, and ready for sleep, then you can share affection and begin your heart-to-heart bonding. But remember, it's not loving energy but the energy of your leadership that will make your dog feel safe and secure in your home.

The next day, begin what will become your dog's regular routine. A long walk first thing in the morning, then food, then affection, then rest. Introduce the dog gradually to one room at a time, always making it clear that *you* are the one giving *him* permission to enter. Establish early on what is off-limits and what is okay. Don't waffle or change the rules, no matter how sad his brown eyes look. Remind yourself that your consistency and strength during this early phase are gifts you are giving the dog—every bit as important gifts as the food and shelter you share with him. You are giving him the gift of a solid, reliable pack—one in which he will soon be able to relax and become his calm-submissive self.

The Rules of the House

The rules you make for the dogs in your household are completely up to you. But there are some overall rules that I strongly recommend you follow in order to keep your pack leader status intact.

• Wake up on your terms, not his. Your dog is not your alarm clock. If your dog sleeps in your bed, condition him to get quietly off the bed if he wakes before you do and needs water or to stretch his legs. Then he needs to wait calmly for you to get up and start the structure of his day.

• Start the day with very little touch or talk—saving affection for after the walk. The walk is your bonding time together. If you walk, then try to walk for an *hour* every morning. If you are a runner, you run, if you are a biker or Rollerblader, you bike or blade. Ideally, you have chosen a dog that is fit enough for whatever your preferred activity may be, and if it's a very active sport, you can shorten its duration. But walking at a brisk pace is the best overall exercise for both human and dog—both on a physical and on a psychological-primal level. If you absolutely, positively don't have a full hour to walk, add a backpack to make it a better workout for your dog, or put the dog on a treadmill for a half hour while you're getting ready for work.

• Feed your dog calmly and quietly, never giving him food when he is jumping up and down. He gets fed only when he's sitting down, calm-submissive. He never gets fed as a response to a bark. At the Dog Psychology Center, the calmest, mellowest dog always gets to eat first. Can you imagine what an incentive this is for the rest of the pack to act calm and submissive?

• Your dog doesn't beg for scraps or interrupt your mealtime. When the pack leader is eating, no one interrupts him. You set the distance your dog is allowed to be from the human dining table, and you stick to it. Don't buy your dog's pleading looks— his wolf forefathers never competed with their pack leaders for food and neither should he.

• After exercise and food comes affection time. Instruct your dog to be in a calm submissive position, and then love him till its time to go to work. By doing this, you are conditioning your dog to have a beautiful, balanced, satisfying morning, every day of the week!

• Never make a big deal about leaving the house—or coming home, for that matter. If you must leave a dog at home all day, practice going in and out of the house many times before the first few times you actually leave him alone. Make sure he is in a calm, submissive state whenever you leave or enter the house. Once he's in the position you desire, don't talk, touch, or make eye contact while you're leaving. As difficult as it may be for you, act cool toward your dog while projecting your calm-assertive energy. If you've properly exercised your dog and not nurtured his fear or anxiety, his natural body clock will tell him this is time for him to rest and be quiet for a while. Do not allow howling or whining when you leave. You may have to wait several minutes before your dog is calm enough for you to leave, but be patient, and make sure this routine sinks in for him. Don't worry; you'll be able to love him again when you come home.

• Once you return home, hold back as much affection as you can at first. Do not encourage overexcitement. Change your clothes, grab a snack to tide you over, and take your dog out again. This walk can be a bit shorter—a half hour—since you're going to be in for the evening together. After the walk, once again reinforce your mealtime rules, and then allow your calm submissive dog to be your best friend after dinner.

• Sleeping arrangements for a dog should be clear and unambiguous. A dog should have a regular place to sleep, and should not be able to choose it on his own. When your dog first comes to live with you, put him in his crate or kennel every night for the first week. This will get him accustomed to the new surroundings while providing limits. After the first week, replace the kennel with a pillow or dog bed. That is now his resting place. If you're a person who wants your dog to sleep in bed with you, fine. It's natural for dogs to sleep with other members of the pack, and it's a powerful way to bond with your animal. But don't let the dog take over the bed. Keep the rules clear. You invite the dog into the bedroom. Get in the bed for a few minutes, and then signal that your dog can come up. You choose the portion of the bed that the dog sleeps on. Sweet dreams.

• Every human in the household needs to be a pack leader. From your toddler to your elderly grandparents, your dog needs to respect everyone in the household as higher up on the dominance ladder than he is. This means that every human in the house has to live by the same set of rules, boundaries, and limitations. Discuss these together and make sure everybody considers them law. Remember, intermittent reinforcement creates an unpredictable dog that's much harder to condition in the long run. So your ten-year-old can't sneak Max treats under the table if the family rule is no begging. You can't allow your dog to jump on the furniture when you're at home but not when your husband is in the house. Inconsistent leadership leads to an inconsistently obedient dog.

• Scheduling playtime with your dog every week is a great way to add extra physical exercise to your walk routine. (Although by now you know it is never a substitute for the walk!) It is also a way to let your dog express the special needs and abilities of his breed. You can play fetch, swim in the pool, play with the Frisbee, and run an obstacle course—whatever your pleasure or your dog's special talent. Just make sure your dog has had at least one of his major walks before you play—don't do it first thing in the morning!—and set strict limits on the time you spend. Don't let your dog "talk" you into spending three hours throwing the tennis ball when you have set aside only one.

• Don't avoid or postpone bathing your dog just because he hates it. Though your dog probably doesn't care how clean he is, you deserve to have a dog you like to be near. There are many ways you can make bathtime a more pleasant experience for both of you. First, let your dog get to know the tub or sink in a relaxed, pleasant way, before you try to bathe him. Next, remember that in nature dogs don't wash themselves. They go in the water or roll in the mud in order to cool off when it's hot; that's a natural instinct. Use that instinct to your advantage and give your dog a good workout—a brisk walk, a run, a treadmill or Rollerblade session—before the bath. Get him good and hot (this is easier in the summer). Make the water lukewarm and appealing. You can also associate bathtime with treats, but don't rely on them. A tired, relaxed dog that's just worked up a sweat is your best bet for a happy bath.

• Don't allow possessiveness over toys and food! Make sure your dog knows that his toys are your toys first; make sure he is calm-submissive or active-submissive before you feed him and that he doesn't growl if you come near him when feeding.

• Don't allow out-of-control barking. If your dog has an excessive barking problem, most of the time it will be due to physical and psychological frustration. This is a dog desperate for more physical activities and a more proactive pack leader. Your dog is trying to tell you something with his bark. Listen to him!

Dogs and Kids

The subject of dogs and children could be a book unto itself. As someone who grew up around animals and is raising his own kids among a pack of dogs, I can attest to the fact that living with dogs can be one of the most rewarding and memorable experiences of a child's life. Dogs teach children empathy; they teach them responsibility and caretaking; they teach them to be in tune with Mother Nature; they teach them balance; they teach them unconditional love. I wouldn't dream of raising Andre and Calvin without the joy of having dogs in their lives. However, we must always remember that when we keep a dog, we are inviting a carnivorous predator to live with us in our home. As close as we are to dogs, human and dog are separate species. It is our responsibility as parents and pet owners to protect our most precious family members—our children—and to make sure both our kids and our dogs know how to coexist safely and happily.

More than half of serious dog bites and fatalities in the United States happen to children from five to nine years of age, but babies are especially vulnerable. As I write this, Southern California is still reeling over the tragic death of a Glendale newborn, snatched from her mother's arms by the grandparent's Rottweiler.[1] Invariably in such cases, the owners are in denial. "He was always such a gentle dog," they say. Then usually a neighbor comes forward and indicates that there may have been warning signs that were missed or ignored.

A baby can be confusing for any dog who has never seen one before. Babies smell different from adult humans. They are shaped differently from adult humans. They sound and move differently from adult humans. For dogs with strong prey instincts, just the tiny size and weakness of a baby may trigger an attack. In addition, the family will naturally be fawning over the baby and not paying as much attention to the dog. If your dog has a problem with dominance, or is obsessive over you, you may be heading for trouble.

Families who are expecting a baby and have a dog in the house must first sit down and honestly evaluate the situation. What is their dog's temperament? What is the dog-owner relationship? If the parents are weak pack leaders and are letting a dominant dog run their household, especially if it is a powerful breed of dog that has shown aggression in the past; if the dog is used to constant attention and is territorial or possessive, I would seriously recommend the family find a new home for the dog long before the baby arrives. As important as dogs are in my life, I know that as a father I would never put my kids' lives in danger. There are some household situations where dogs and babies should not mix, though this is more often due to the owner's relationship with the dog than with the dog itself. If socialized properly, not only can most dogs live peacefully with babies, but they can also become their devoted protectors.

But if there is even the slightest doubt in your mind about your ability to handle your dog in all situations, I suggest you take the nine months you have to find your dog a suitable new home. This may be heartbreaking for you, but the good news is, dogs do move on much faster than humans. The dog will feel disoriented at first when he moves to a new pack, but in nature, wolves do change packs when the need arises. If a pack gets too big for the resources in the environment, wolves will split off and find or form new groups. If you find the right home for him, your dog will adjust after a day or two. It's his instinct to adjust and try to fit in. He'll recognize you if he sees or smells you again, but he won't spend his time pining for you. Remember, dogs live in the moment.

PREPARING DOGS FOR THE BLESSED EVENT

Assuming you are not in the situation I describe in the previous paragraphs, there are many things you can do to prepare your dog for the baby's arrival and, most important, to condition him to respect the baby as another pack leader. You need to start early. Any potential weakness in your pack leader–pack follower bond should be corrected *now*. If your dog is overly dependent, anxious, or has separation-anxiety issues, he may react strongly to a change in the pack structure. As difficult as it seems, you may need to desensitize your dog by beginning to act a bit cooler toward him, long before the baby comes home. Don't let him nervously shadow you as you walk around the house. Stop allowing him to sleep with you. Set new rules about the furniture he is allowed to sit on. Let him know that the baby's room is off-limits. Practice walking him with a stroller or carriage, always making sure he is behind the carriage. Encourage and reward calm submission during these sessions.

Once the baby is born, bring home a blanket or piece of baby clothing with the baby's scent on it, and introduce it to your dog. This is a way to have your dog "meet" your baby before they ever come face to face. Don't stick the item into your dog's nose and have him sniff. Set boundaries at first. Make him sniff from the other side of the room, then instruct him to come slightly closer, but not any closer than you would allow him near the baby. (This isn't an unnatural thing for you to request of your dog—remember, in nature, the mother dog initially keeps her pups away from the others in the pack.) The dog must always be calm-submissive around the baby's scent. Correct any anxious or fixated behavior. Reward only calm-submissive behavior.

When the baby comes home, don't introduce your dog to her outside the house. Make sure the baby is in the house, and then invite the dog in afterward. Make it clear that it's the *baby's* house, not the dog's. Introduce your dog to the baby in stages. Start by letting him know the baby from across the room. Then little by little you can let him get closer. Your calm-assertive energy is vital. Once Ilusion was comfortable with me bringing my sons around the pack, I would walk through the pack carrying them while projecting my most assertive form of calm-assertive energy. I held my sons with pride. I was communicating to the pack that these babies were a part of *me—the pack leader*. They were to be respected in the same way the pack leader was respected. My boys then learned their behavior from me. They watched how I interacted with the dogs, and imitated that way of being.

At the same time as you are sensitizing dog to kid, you need to teach your child as she grows how to respect the dog while remaining a pack leader. That's why supervision is so important. Dogs should never be around kids who are learning how to walk and are too full of physical energy. Kids need to learn not to pull on ears and tails, and must be taught never to play tug-of-war with a dog. If a child is becoming too rough, that's when you hold her and redirect her, or show her a different way to touch. The more repetitions you do, the more she learns the correct way to approach the dog. Eventually, the dog sees that the child means no harm. I taught Andre and Calvin early on how to recognize cues from a dog's body language to learn when it was and wasn't an appropriate time to touch the dog. I had them help me feed the dogs, and taught them never to give the dogs the food dish until they were sitting and calm-submissive. Instruct your children on the correct way to meet any new dog—no talk, touch, or eye contact until the dog is comfortable and calm-submissive around you. As soon as my boys could walk, they were toddling through that pack and owning the place. Do as I did. Condition your children to be pack leaders from birth. A generation of dogs will thank you for it!

Visitors

How to treat visitors coming to your home can be a difficult issue for a dog. Most people want their dogs to be, if not their protectors, then their alarm systems. If a stranger comes to the house late at night, owners naturally want their dogs to alert them to this. At the same time, they want their dogs to behave and be docile when friends or the mailman comes to the door. It's tough to have it both ways. How is the dog supposed to know the difference if the person is on the other side of the door? It's up to the dog's owner to teach him polite doorway manners and enforce those manners when necessary.

When a new visitor comes to the door, make sure your dog stops barking right away and is in a calm-submissive seated position when the new person enters. Do not allow any jumping up on the guest. At the same time, instruct any new person who comes into your home never to greet your dog in the traditional—but wrong!—way. No getting down to the dog's level and petting and talking to it! Your guest must learn the rules I use for visitors to the Dog Psychology Center: no touch, no talk, and no eye contact at first. Your dog must be allowed to *politely* get used to your guest's scent before your guest gives any affection. Your dog has the ability to remember thousands upon thousands of different scents, so after one or two visits, your guest will be familiar to your dog. But with every new person your dog meets, repeat this mannerly ritual.

The dreaded mailman can also become an issue for a dog. Since dogs live in a cause-and-effect world, if your dog becomes accustomed to barking when the mailman comes, this is how it works in his canine mind: "The mailman comes. I bark and growl. The mailman goes away. I scared him away." In some dominant-aggressive dogs, this can revive their predator instinct, and potentially incite aggression toward the mailman. For you the owner, this can translate into having to go pick up your mail from the post office, or, in a worst-case scenario, into a lawsuit. The U.S. Postal Service takes the safety of its carriers extremely seriously these days. In the case of one dog featured on *Dog Whisperer,* not only the owner of the offending dog but the entire neighborhood lost its mail privileges! (As you can imagine, this didn't make the owner very popular with her neighbors!) We dealt with this issue by conditioning the dog not to bark at all when a stranger approached the door. Once we had made progress in this area, I dressed up in a postal uniform and came to the door again and again and again, until the dog had lost its desire to bark at me. This was a trade-off for the owner—she chose to give up her "intruder warning system" in order to get her mail privileges back. Remember, you can always get a burglar alarm to replace your dog as an alert system. But you can never replace your mail carrier!

Going to the Groomer and the Vet

Anytime we bring a dog into a new and unfamiliar situation, it's important that we prepare him for the environment he's going to be entering. Most people will bring along cookies to try to calm their dog, but if the dog is already in a panicked mode, that's probably not going to work. Remember, dogs have no concept of what a groomer is. They don't understand why they have to have veterinary checkups. Very few dogs do not protest when they're being groomed or taken to the vet for the first time. Very few do not become tense or nervous. These are very unnatural situations for them. This makes it necessary for the groomer and the vet to act as behaviorists as well as do the jobs they are there to perform—and some are not capable of doing this. It is not their job. It's up to you to help make it a more comfortable experience for your dog.

Before going to the vet's office, it's important that you hold your dog and touch him in the same ways the doctor will hold him. This is something you should do gradually but on a regular basis long before the visit. The brain needs to get conditioned to be touched in some areas that the dog wouldn't normally be touched. Most of us touch our dogs while giving affection, touching their heads, stroking them, scratching their bellies and backs. A doctor will open your dog's mouth, check his ears and eyes, check his behind. You can increase your dog's likelihood of success by "playing doctor" at home. Get everyone involved, even the kids. Have someone wear the same kind of coat your vet wears. Let your dog get comfortable around some of the tools your vet uses—even if you're only using toy versions. Get him accustomed to and comfortable with the alcohol smells. You can give your dog massages or treats during these sessions to create a positive association.

It's the same thing when it comes to the groomer. The only dogs that are naturally comfortable around groomers are those that are from a lineage of show dogs. Somehow, they seem to inherit their parents' calmness with regard to the process of grooming. For other dogs, it can be a nightmare. Remember Josh, the "Grooming Gremlin"? I can't tell you the number of clients I have who dread going to their dogs' groomers more than they dread going to their own dentists!

Because I'm a very competitive human being, I've always

loved a challenge. For me, it's a thrill to work with an unstable dog and try to help him become balanced. So when I worked as a groomer in San Diego and was handed a dog like Josh, it was a pleasure for me. It's no different from a cowboy whose job it is to ride a bull or a wild horse. We get a thrill from it. We don't want to harm the animals; we just want to tame them. What I saw was an opportunity to tame the animal in these dogs, while also making them look good on the outside. If the dog was easy, then great, I'd do it faster. But a difficult dog wasn't anything negative for me. Of course, the dogs picked up on my positive energy, so I was able to make it a very pleasant experience for them. However, I understand why most groomers dread these dogs. They hate being handed a dog that might bite them, and they unconsciously blame the dog. The dogs pick up on this negative energy, and it exacerbates their anxiety. The truth of the matter is, dogs act this way because their owners never properly prime them for the situation.

Just like preparing for the vet, you can set up scenarios to condition your dog gradually to be more comfortable at the groomer's. Buy some clippers or scissors and try them on your dog to gauge his reaction well ahead of time. If the dog is nervous, wait until he's hungry. Feed him, and then while he's eating, try snipping the scissors or clippers near him. Do this a few times. He'll begin to associate these tools with eating time, which will make for a more pleasant experience at the groomer's.

Most important—and I can't stress this enough—before you take your dog to the vet's office or the groomer's, or before the mobile grooming service arrives at your home, *take your dog for a long, vigorous walk!* Ideally, you should walk your dog as usual before you leave the house, and then once you arrive at the vet's or groomer's, take him for another, shorter walk around the block. If your dog arrives at a new location having exercised, he'll have less pent-up energy and will be more receptive to a new, possibly fear-inducing situation. If your dog associates going to any off-site location with more walking and bonding time with you, he'll begin to look forward to it. Adding treats that your dog enjoys will help, too, but spending quality time walking with his pack leader will taste better to him than any doggie biscuit on the market!

Going to the Dog Park

Dog parks—especially off-leash parks—are hotbed issues in many American communities. For your dog, a dog park can be a welcome break from his routine. The dog park can be used to help your dog increase or maintain his social skills, and perhaps give him some fun running and playing with members of his own kind. But that's all you should expect from a dog park. It is *not* a place for your dog to work off his excess energy. It is *never, ever* to be used as a substitution for a walk. Because whenever you put a number of unfamiliar dogs together, you run the risk of conflict. The "power of the pack" is strong in a dog—but remember, at the Dog Psychology Center, it sometimes takes me weeks to successfully introduce a new dog to the pack, and my pack is made up of already balanced and stable dogs! Do you honestly know that all the dogs at your neighborhood dog park are balanced and stable? Are you absolutely certain that your dog is? A dog park is an environment that is behind walls. And every time you incarcerate many animals in one place, you're going to see scuffles.

Does this routine sound familiar to you? You're tired. It's been a long day. You don't feel like walking your dog. So you throw your dog in the car. Your dog is overexcited. You say, "It's okay, Rex, we're going to the dog park!" Your dog picks up on your energy and your signals. He recognizes scents and landmarks and figures out where you're going. He starts to get excited and jump up and down in the car. You think, "Oh, he's so happy, he's going to the dog park!" No, that's not happiness. That's excitement. And you should know by this point in the book that excitement for a dog does not equal happiness. It usually equals unexpressed, frustrated energy. So what are you doing? You're bringing a frustrated, overexcited dog to a dog park. Depending on the dog, that can be a recipe for disaster.

When a dog with excited, frustrated, anxious, or dominant energy gets to a dog park, the dogs there are going to sense his energy immediately. This energy will be interpreted as unstable, and remember, dogs don't naturally nurture instability. So the other dogs will either approach him, challenge him, or run away from him, because he's too packed with a very explosive, negative energy. Seeing those other dogs move away from him can send the unstable dog into predator or charge mode, because that's the easiest way for him to release frustration. A dog in this mode can get in trouble, attacking another dog, and then all the other dog owners will start judging him. Some owners will start figuring out when this dog usually comes to the park and will try to bring their dogs thirty minutes before or after that. When the dog does encounter these owners, they will send him negative energy, which he'll pick up on. The dog park is no longer a positive experience for him.

Of course you already know my recommendation for what you should do before taking your dog to the dog park, don't you? Walk him! Take at least a thirty-minute walk at home, then, when you've parked your car near the dog park, walk him around the neighborhood there. If he's a high-energy dog, use a backpack. Remember, he's supposed to be using the dog park to work on his social skills, not as a substitute for regular exercise. Drain as much of his excited energy as you can, then take him to the dog park when his energy level is close to zero. That way, when he gets to the dog park, he'll be relaxed but will still move forward and engage with the other dogs. This will encourage more healthy social interaction.

Compare it to going to meet your friend at a Starbucks. You're not going to sit and chat at Starbucks when you're all hyped up, ready to go dancing or jogging around the block, are you? No. You're going to go after the gym, after work, after going out at night, when you're calm and ready to relax. That's when you engage your friend on a healthy social level. Dogs are much the same. The calmer the dogs at the dog park are, the less likely they will be to chase one another. The less they chase one another, the less likely they will be to nip one another. The less they nip one another, the less likely they will be to get into a fight.

DON'T PUNCH OUT AT THE PARK!

Often, an owner's behavior at the park is as much at fault as is her lack of preparation before she arrives. She gets to the park, lets her dog go, and then spends the rest of the time totally disengaged, standing in one place, gabbing with the other owners. The owner sees this time as a chance to relax from the pressures of having a dog—to "punch out" from the job for a while. But remember, being a pack leader is a 24-7 responsibility. This is not a satisfying pack experience for the dog because the dog is completely on his own, with no guidance from his pack leader. This isn't to say you should be in the middle of the pack, engaging your dog at all times. It does mean, though, that you should be on the alert, not standing in one place, but moving around the park and constantly connecting with your dog through calm-assertive voice, eye contact, and energy. You must know your dog's body language and how to snap him out of it if an interaction seems to be turning into a confrontation. If a dog does misbehave or is challenged or bullied by another dog, don't react with soft energy. Don't nurture dominant, fearful, or aggressive behavior by comforting the dog or petting him. Don't let your dog hide or cower between your legs. Always clean up after your dog, and never, ever leave your dog unsupervised in a dog park! If you have successfully established yourself as your dog's pack leader, your dog will be looking to you for his cues as to how to behave. Don't let him down!

Remember, your dog has four choices when interacting with other dogs—fight, flight, avoid, or submit. If your dog ignores or avoids other dogs at the park, that doesn't mean he's a social misfit! When you're walking in downtown Los Angeles at noon on a workday, you don't say "Hi" to everybody you meet, do you? Of course not. You ignore most of the people you pass. You don't introduce yourself to every stranger you meet in a crowded elevator! For a dog, ignoring is also part of normal social behavior. A healthy, balanced dog knows how to avoid others as a way of preventing conflict and keeping his disposition stable.

There aren't any agreed-upon statistics on dog park fights, injuries, and deaths in the United States, but there have been enough such incidents to provoke many communities to try to ban off-leash parks altogether. Dogs that do best there are usually those socialized to them at a very young age. Clearly, there are some dogs that should simply not be taken to a dog park, period. Dominant-aggressive dogs should never be taken there. A fearful or nervous dog shouldn't be taken there. (However, this is not a solution to helping him overcome that fear.) Fear is a signal for any dominant-type dogs in the park to attack your dog.

Under no circumstances should you ever take a sick dog to the park—not only could he infect other dogs, but dominant dogs will pick up on his illness as weakness. Never take more than three dogs at a time to a dog park, and take more than one only if you are certain of each dog's temperament. Female dogs in heat can cause dog park fights. So can bringing food to the park; the presence of food can trigger fights.

At any public dog park, there is no way you can predict the temperament of every dog that shows up. To socialize your dog around other canines, there are many safer alternatives. You can find dog-walking friends, and walk your dogs together—the best way for dogs to get to know one another as a pack. Then begin by letting these dogs get to know one another in more relaxed play situations, carefully making note of each dog's behavior and response. Stay involved, and correct your dog as necessary, encouraging your human companions to do the same. The dogs in the group will quickly learn the rules. Remember, a wolf pack usually consists of only five to eight dogs at a time. You don't need to be around ten to twenty dogs for your dog to benefit from and enjoy the company of his own kind.

Travel

Any dog owner knows the perils of taking your dog on a trip. When we put our dogs in a car or in carrying cases for airplane, train, or boat travel, some can become dizzy, some will vomit, and some will drool or pant the whole time. Some dogs become overexcited and won't calm down. Other dogs develop a trapped feeling, which produces a defensive type of fear aggression. They'll snarl and bite and won't stop whining or barking. The reason these dogs are miserable when it comes time for them to travel is because they weren't in calm-submissive states of mind before they were put into the car or carrier. We need to condition them to associate travel time with relaxation.

Once again, every time we are going to expose our dogs to something that is unnatural for them—which includes travel in a car or plane—the best thing we can do for them is to prepare them beforehand. Naturally, exercise is the first part of this equation. Before we put them in the car on the kennel or carrier, we have to walk them. Yes, I'm telling you again to take your dog on yet another long, vigorous walk. If it's a very long drive or airplane flight, add a backpack or an extra half hour on the treadmill. Your goal is for your dog to be absolutely tired out by the time you put him in any enclosed space. He'll be in his natural resting mode, so it will make sense for him to stay quiet for a long period of time.

Of course, some dogs naturally love to ride in the car, because their owners let them stick their heads out the window. When your dog has his nose out the car window, it's a more exciting experience for him than it would be for a human going to a 3D, sense-surround, smell-o-rama, virtual-reality movie. That's because of the scents—thousands and thousands of different scents, familiar and unfamiliar, hitting your dog's nose every second. If there are five cars in front of you, your dog is picking up every single scent present in each of those cars. If you're passing by a farm, your dog is picking up the scent of every animal on that farm. Dogs get incredible joy from this experience—entertainment, satisfaction, and psychological stimulation. But I don't suggest you allow this, because it's physically very dangerous for your dog. A pebble or a piece of debris could get in his eyes, and too much air could harm his ears. Also, so much stimulation could get him overexcited. Instead, once you've made sure your dog is in resting mode in the car, crack the window open just a little bit, but not enough for him to get his head through. Though the air he smells this way will not be as intense in concentration, he'll still be able to pick up many fascinating scents, without any risk to his health.

Moving

I have a lot of clients who will come to me for the first time after a big move. They'll say, "My dog was perfect before we got the new house." Now he's showing this or that unwanted behavior. He's become this, he's become that. These clients don't realize how they have contributed to their dog's newfound symptoms. I'd like you to know how those symptoms can be avoided altogether.

In nature, dogs move all the time. There's nothing they love better than exploring a new environment. But the way we humans move is not natural to them. When we're getting ready to move house or apartment, our dogs have no idea that we're going to be migrating to a new territory, but they always sense that something dramatic is about to happen. First, they see everything familiar about their world being taken away. Then they sense all the conflicting energies the humans are bringing to the move—the excitement, the tension, the stress, or the sadness. When people are distressed about leaving their home, this becomes weak, negative energy to a dog. While we're wandering our empty houses, crying about how much we'll miss the old neighborhood and reminiscing about how our children were born there, our dogs only understand that something really bad is happening. Then we throw them in the car or stick them in the kennel and put them on a plane. They don't know they're going to Ohio, they don't know they're going to New York, they don't know they're going to Michigan. When we get to the new, empty house, we let them out and then expect them to adjust even faster than we do! They're already anxious from the move, picking up on our emotions and associating all of it with something very traumatic. That's why, when they arrive at the new house, behaviors that you never saw before will show up. *Dogs are not pieces of furniture!* We can't simply box them up and move them from place to place without expecting them to be affected by it.

If you live in a neighborhood near the place you will be moving, I suggest you take your dog on a walk there two or three times before the move—from your old place and back, if possible. Dogs are very sensitive to new environments, and when the real moving day comes, they'll know that they've been there before. If you live far away, follow the procedures I've outlined for traveling with your dog. Then, when you arrive, guess what you're going to do? Even though you are going through your own grieving process or your own emotional transformation, the moment your dog arrives at your new home, you have to take him for a walk. This walk isn't just to tire him out; it's also to help him adjust to the unfamiliar environment. This is a walk that must last *more than one hour.* Though it's impossible for most people, I'd recommend you make it three hours or more. It'll do you good after all your traveling, and will help you relieve some of your own moving-day stress as well. Perhaps you can switch off dog-walking and unpacking responsibilities with the other members of your household on that first day. Whatever you do, however, consider this walk a milestone event in your dog's life. This is the walk that will bring him back to understanding that you have migrated to a new territory and will make that migration a more natural event.

If you've walked your dog for more than an hour, he should be tired and ready to relax when you bring him into your new house. Feed him and then introduce him to the home, one room

at a time. Don't let him wander around on his own. Many of my
clients made the mistake of doing this simply because they were
too busy unpacking to bother with their dog. They saw that their
dog wanted to explore and they let him roam all over the new
house—even before they had had a chance to explore it themselves. These owners were punching out on discipline.

Remember, it's not his house, it's yours. If he's able to own it
before you, then he becomes the dominant one in that space. I
suggest you introduce your dog to one room—say, the kitchen—
and keep the rest of the house off limits while you're unpacking. If
he's had his introductory walk, he'll be in resting mode and happy
to wait for you. When you're ready, take him from room to room,
inviting him into each one just as you did when you first brought
him into the house. He'll learn that this is the new "den" you share
together, and that you are still the undisputed pack leader there.

Introducing a New Dog to the Pack

Sometimes I see clients who have tried to solve a behavior problem—say, separation anxiety—by bringing another dog into the
home. Despite their best intentions, this can be like dropping a
lighted match into a can of gasoline. If you're dealing with two
dogs, at least one of them has to be balanced. If you're dealing with a multidog household, all of those dogs in the original
pack have to be balanced. There simply cannot be a successful introduction between dogs when more than one of them is
unbalanced. Even if your "pack" consists of only you and one
dog, introducing a new dog into the pack should be a carefully
thought out process that takes the dogs' balance and energy—
not to mention your own—into consideration.

Remember Scarlett, my French bulldog and good-luck charm

at the Center? She had the unfortunate experience of being an unstable dog dropped into the middle of an unstable pack in her owner's home. When Scarlett came along, all the dogs that were already in the household were unstable and living a life free of rules, boundaries, and limitations. One dog was petrified of everything, and another one was fear-aggressive and possessive of everything. Even the humans in the household were unbalanced and undisciplined. Scarlett is a very sensitive dog. The minute she arrived, she picked up on this unstable energy, and her reaction was to fight, to attack the negative energy. She was also the youngest, and the most high-energy and athletic dog in the house. She was just not going to put up with being bossed around by other unstable dogs. Unfortunately for her, her owners had already developed attachments to the dogs that were already living there, so those dogs had seniority. Scarlett was just the newcomer, and because she was the new girl, she got blamed for everything. That's why, when her owners wouldn't change, I had to get Scarlett out of that situation.

Just as you might when choosing a dog for yourself, choose for your existing dog a dog with compatible energy. Don't choose a dog with a higher energy level than your dog! Just as in dating, dogs don't have to like all the same things to get along, but they do need to share the same basic temperament. Most people, when they bring a new dog into a situation, will favor the dog that was already there. They start with favoritism right off the bat because they feel guilty for bringing a "competitor" into their dog's home. They don't want the dog to feel "jealous." We often interpret the very natural period of deciding who's the more dominant and who's the more submissive in a pack of animals as "jealousy." Perhaps dogs do experience something like our emotion of jealousy. But more often, we write the script of that story. The reason behind the "jealousy" is the fact that the new dog has brought a higher level of energy or a competitive energy to the dog that is already comfortable with the environment as it was. Still, many owners will fret about this, thinking, "Now my dog's upset with me. My dog hates me." They then project yet more negative energy. When things between the dogs and the owner continue to go downhill, they take their dog to a pet psychic. The psychic will say that the two dogs were ancient rivals who didn't get along in a past life. Do you think I'm exaggerating? This is a mild version of some of the stories I've heard from my clients!

You need to treat both dogs equally—from the calm-assertive position of pack leader. Dogs who are followers in a pack don't fight one another for the number two and number three positions. They should be concentrating all their energies on following *your* rules, boundaries, and limitations. If you are truly a solid pack leader, the dogs have no choice but to get along. Two submissive minds will be able to live and play together successfully. Two dominant minds will challenge each other, and make your life miserable.

There are certain situations where I would encourage a little more of a dominant-submissive relationship between a new dog and an old one. I recently shot a story for the second season of *Dog Whisperer* that was all about bringing in a companion for a dog that was already in the home. The segment is called "Buford's Blind Date"—Buford being a tough-looking but very calm, stable, but unsocialized boxer. Buford was a prime candidate for getting a companion, but his owner, Bonita, was not a 100 percent committed, 100 percent calm-assertive pack leader. Though a very laid-back lady, she needed a lot of guidance before bringing another boxer into the home, and I knew I couldn't count on her to provide strong leadership for *two* powerful dogs. I went with Bonita to Boxer Rescue in Sun Valley, California, to help her choose Buford's new platonic "bride." Even though Buford, being a mellow guy, could have gotten along well with a number of different dogs, I had to keep Bonita's energy and level of commitment in mind in the selection process. She needed a dog that would ease into the household without making a lot of added work for her. We chose Honey, a petite, friendly, but extremely calm-submissive girl with a coat the color of smooth milk chocolate. Once we got Honey home, I allowed Buford to establish dominance immediately. Though he and Honey both are fixed, I allowed him to mount her in a dominance position. I also instructed Bonita not to give any affection to Honey for two weeks. Bonita is a woman who loves dogs, so this was a terribly difficult assignment for her. But it was important that she gave Buford the space to be dominant over the other dog before Bonita began her relationship with her. In essence, I was giving Buford the job that the human usually has—introducing the new dog to the rules of the house. In his balanced state of mind, Buford would probably do a more consistent job of it in those first two weeks than Bonita would have.

When introducing a new dog to a household, make sure your existing dogs all have had plenty of walks and energy-draining exercise before the big meet-up. Make sure they are calm and submissive. Even if you are feeling nervous about your new dog meeting your "baby," you have to understand that you can't share that fear, tension, nervousness, or insecurity around dogs. By doing so you would be pretty much be ensuring that their first meeting was a bad experience. If you're not feeling comfortable with introducing the dogs inside the house, then do what many people do—introduce them on neutral territory. Then, at the end of the day, invite them both into your home together.

Most important, however, you need to know your dog before you think about expanding your household. Make sure your dog isn't frustrated and doesn't have fear-aggression or dominance-aggression–related issues. If you have access to other dogs, do some research by watching how your dog interacts with them in various situations. Watch them closely at the dog park or on a dog "playdate." This will show you what areas of your dog's behavior you need to work on before you can bring any new friends home for good.

Dogs and the Life Cycle: Aging and Death

When we live with a dog for many years, we inevitably have to watch that dog age. Dogs have a shorter life cycle than we do—an average of 13 years[2] to our 77[3]—so unless we adopt them when we are elderly, there's a likelihood they will go through old age before us. This can be a heartbreaking time for many dog owners and families, but one of the things I believe animals come into our lives to teach us is that aging and death are part of nature, that in living life, we must experience and accept death as merely another phase of nature's life cycle. Dogs celebrate life, and they're okay with death. In fact, they are much better with death than we are. We need to look at them as our teachers in this department. Their natural wisdom can help us find comfort when we are facing our own human frailty and death.

If a dog gets sick—say, is diagnosed with cancer—he does not perceive its illness the same way we do. We'll feel sorry for the dog and flood it with sad, mourning energy every time we look at it, but that energy does nothing but create a negative environment for the dog. If a dog comes back from the vet with a cancer diagnosis, it's not thinking, "Oh my God, I've got only six months to live! I wish I'd gone to China!" Dogs live in the moment, regardless of whether they have cancer or not. Regardless of whether they're blind or not. Regardless of whether they're deaf or not. No matter how dire their situation, dogs keep living in the moment every single day. I recently did a seminar for 350 people in Texas. A dog from a local shelter was sitting near me up front. That dog had been diagnosed with cancer recently but you couldn't imagine a dog that was more downright, utterly happy! Everybody at the seminar was whispering, "That dog has cancer. Oh, poor thing." But the dog didn't care about them feeling sorry for her. She was having a wonderful time, just being a balanced, calm-submissive dog in an interesting new environment. One thing we can learn from dogs is how to appreciate and enjoy life in its smallest detail, every single day.

The decision to put a dog down when it is suffering is one of the hardest ones we humans can face. This highly personal decision, in the end, comes down to your own conscience, spiritual beliefs, and your private connection with your dog. One of my clients described making that decision only at the moment when "all the lights went out" in her pet, despite the fact that he was still living and breathing. The best wisdom I can offer you in such a painful situation is that when your dog does finally pass, he has probably lived a fuller life than you have. Your dog has savored every moment on this earth. He is leaving it with no unfinished business, no regrets.

Human beings are the only animals who actively fear death, who actively dread death, obsess over it, and grieve over it—that is, *before* it happens. Dogs have so much to teach us in this area. A dog lives in the moment, every moment, every day. A dog lives every day to the fullest. Do dogs grieve? Yes. Recent research has proven that many animals grieve their dead, especially family members, mates, or those with whom they've bonded deeply.[4] But for most animals, grief is simply a phase they pass through on the way back to balance. In the wild, if a pack leader dies, the pack will spend some time mourning the loss of their leader, and going through the difficult transition to a new pack structure. Then they'll move on.

As I've said before, psychologically, dogs move on much more quickly than humans—that is, if we let them. If one dog in a two-dog household dies, of course the other dog will mourn the one who passed away. But it's natural for that dog to then move on to his normal level of balance—unless humans prevent him from going there. It's we who hold him back from what his nature is telling him to do—to move forward, to live life to the fullest. You'd be surprised how many cases I have had where one dog in the family died and the surviving dog suddenly had issues he never had before. The family will call me in and say, "He just can't get over Winston's death." I'll look around the room. There will be photos of Winston everywhere. They'll be souvenirs from the funeral, an urn of ashes on the mantel. The curtains will be drawn. The house will be dark and dusty. The dog didn't arrange the house like this. I'll ask when Winston passed away and they'll say, "Six months ago." Six months! Six months is an *eternity* to a dog. For a dog to linger in a state of depression for that long isn't natural. Dogs are more than willing to return to the balance and stability they knew before. In these cases, the human beings were the ones dwelling in a state of grief, unwilling to move on. The dog was merely picking up on the tragic energy and depression emitted by the humans, and was being dragged down by it. These are cases where the humans needed grief counseling in order to stop projecting onto their dog their own unwillingness to move on. They had to first accept and then deal with their own issues.

I also get an inordinate number of cases where a new dog has been brought into a household after the recent death of a dog.

The new dog is supposed to be a "substitute" for the dog who's gone. Many times in these cases, the "substitute" dog was brought in too soon, while the humans (and sometimes the other dogs in the household) were still processing their grief. When you bring an animal into a house full of sadness, you introduce it to an environment that is nothing but soft, weak energy—completely negative energy. There are no strong pack leaders in a home in mourning.

In a recent case of mine, a new Great Dane puppy had taken over the household and was making life miserable for the husband, wife, and the original family dog. The puppy was not a naturally dominant animal, but the moment it walked through the door, it sensed a leadership vacuum. As difficult as it may be, I advise you to wait a little while after your pet dies before you bring in a new one. Wait until you're ready to open the curtains, let the light in, and laugh again. Then, you'll be ready once again to be the pack leader, and to provide a healthy, balanced home for the new dog in your life.

Cesar with Daddy

9

Fulfilling Our Dogs, Fulfilling Ourselves

Though it may be a blow to our oversize human egos, the truth of the matter is, we need dogs more than they need us. If humans were to disappear from the face of the earth tomorrow, dogs would manage to survive. They would follow their genetic blueprints and form packs, in much the same way their wolf relatives still do. They would return to hunting and would establish territories. They would continue to raise their pups very much as they do today. In many ways, they might be happier. Dogs don't need human beings to be balanced. In fact, most of the difficulties and instabilities domestic dogs suffer arise from their being in unnatural situations, living with us behind walls, in this modern, industrialized world.

I've said before that dogs are from Pluto and human beings are from Saturn. It's more accurate to say that dogs are from Earth—and humans are from outer space. In so many ways, we humans are different from every other being that shares this planet with us. We have the power to rationalize, which includes the power to fool ourselves. That's what we do when we humanize animals. We project our own images on to them in order to make ourselves feel better. In doing so, not only do we harm to those animals, but we also distance ourselves even further from the natural world in which they exist.

What we seem to forget is that we still have access to the very same world they inhabit. That's why indigenous peoples in the deserts, in the mountains, in the forests, and in the jungles are able to survive there for generation after generation. They are Homo sapiens, just as we are, yet they are fully in tune with their animal natures. They live comfortably in both worlds. Here, in "civilization," we have detached ourselves from that natural world by defining ourselves exclusively as the superior species, the species that creates, the species that develops. We continue to kill off that better, more natural side of ourselves when we become the species that destroys whole ecosystems for the benefit of money. No other species destroys Mother Nature the way we do. Only humans do that.

Yet no matter how much we ravage the earth, our animal natures yearn to be fulfilled. Why do you think we plant trees along the freeways? Why do we put waterfalls in the lobbies of high rises? Why do we decorate the walls of our homes with paintings of landscapes? Even the tiniest inner-city apartments often have window boxes with plants in them. We'll spend a year's worth of savings just to take a one-week, sanity-saving vacation by the ocean, by the lake, by the mountains. That's because, without some connection with Mother Nature, we feel isolated. Our world feels cold. We feel unbalanced. We die inside.

In America and in some other cultures of the world, dogs and the other animals we bring into our homes serve as one of our most important links to Mother Nature. We may not even know it consciously, but they are our lifelines to a part of ourselves that we are at the brink of losing altogether. When we humanize dogs, we cut ourselves off from the vital lessons they have been put here to teach us: How to experience the world through the truths of our animal instincts. How to live every moment and every day to the fullest.

When we take dogs into our homes, it's our responsibility to fulfill their instinctual needs, so that they can achieve balance. Dogs don't care about doing tricks, they don't care about winning trophies, they don't care if their collars have "bling." They don't care if you live in a big house or even if you have a job. They care about other things . . . like the solidarity of the pack . . . like bonding with their pack leaders during migration . . . like exploring their world . . . like living in the simple joy of a single moment. If you fulfill your dog in these ways—by giving him exercise, discipline, and affection, in that order—your dog will happily and willingly return the favor. You will witness the miracle of two very different species communicating and bonding with each other in ways you never thought possible. You will achieve in your relationship with your dog the kind of deep connection you always dreamed of having.

I sincerely hope that, with this book, I have helped you find a place to begin in your quest for a better, healthier relationship with the dogs in your life.

The golden light of magic hour begins to descend on this deserted Southern California beach as I leap into the middle of a shallow wave and throw a tennis ball with all my might. Yelping with joy,

every dog in the pack bounds after it, competing to be the one that gets to bring it back to me—but never fighting with one another for its possession. Anyone who knows dogs knows what a miracle this is—but I'm a good pack leader and they're good followers. The rules are the rules, and everybody knows it. Carlitos, a three-legged pit bull, gets the prize this time, a testament to his sheer determination. The others bark after him as he hobbles back to me, dropping the soggy ball into my hand and looking at me with utter bliss in his eyes. I rub his head, then run back to the shore and throw the ball again. The dogs leap back into the surf. For a moment, I'm feeling what they're feeling—the cool, salty sea on my skin, the thousands of coastal scents in my nostrils, the soothing rush of the surf in my ears. I'm feeling all the pure joy of this one fleeting moment, and I owe them for that. I owe them everything.

The sun is red on the rim of the Pacific as we trudge up the rocky path back to the van. We're all exhausted but happy. Tonight, all forty plus dogs at the Center will sleep soundly. I'll sleep well, too, knowing that I've helped fulfill their lives—just as they have already succeeded in fulfilling mine.

CESAR'S GLOSSARY OF TERMS

1. Calm-assertive energy

This is the energy you need to project to show your dog you are the calm and assertive pack leader. Note *assertive* does not mean angry or aggressive. Calm-assertive means always compassionate, but quietly in control.

2. Calm-submissive energy

In nature, this is the appropriate energy for a "follower" in a dog pack, and thus the ideal energy for a dog to project when living in a household with humans. Signs of calm-submissive energy include a relaxed posture, ears held back, and a nearly instinctual response to the "pack leader's" commands.

3. Exercise, discipline, and affection . . . in that order!

These are the three ingredients for creating a happy, balanced dog. Most dog owners give only affection, or don't provide these three necessities in the correct order.

a. EXERCISE—walking a dog at least one hour every day, and in the correct way.

b. DISCIPLINE—giving a dog rules, boundaries, and limitations in a nonabusive manner.

c. AFFECTION—a reward we give to our dogs and to ourselves, but only *after* the dog has achieved calm submission in our "pack."

4. Master the walk

The walk is an extremely important ritual for a dog. It needs to take place a minimum of twice a day, for at least thirty to forty-five minutes each time, so that both the dog's mind and its body are given a workout. It's also important that the owner act as the dog's leader during a walk. This means the dog walks next to the owner or behind him/her—not pulling ahead. If a dog is "walking" a human, the dog perceives itself as pack leader at that moment, and the human is not in control.

5. Rules, boundaries, and limitations

a. Dogs need to know that their pack leader is clearly setting the rules, boundaries, and limitations for their life both inside *and* outside the house.

b. Anger, aggression, or abuse toward a dog will *not* establish you as pack leader; an angry, aggressive leader is not in control. Calm-assertive energy and daily, *consistent* leadership behavior will make enforcing the rules easier.

6. Issues

If a dog doesn't trust its owner to be a strong, stable pack leader, it becomes unclear about its correct role within the pack. A dog that is confused about who is in charge is actually concerned about the ability of the pack to *survive,* so it attempts to fill in the missing leadership elements, often erratically. This can cause aggression, anxiety, fear, obsessions, or phobias—what I call "issues."

7. Balance

A balanced dog is in the state Mother Nature wants it to be in—as a calm-submissive pack follower, who is fulfilled physically with exercise; psychologically with rules, boundaries, and limitations; and emotionally with affection from its owner.

8. Dog training

Conditioning a dog to human commands—sit, stay, come, heel—isn't what I do.

9. Dog rehabilitation

This is what I do: help a dog with issues to return to a balanced state of calm submission. Sometimes it may appear that I can "fix" a dog instantly, but as I've said, "a dog is not an appliance that can be sent out for repairs." Permanent dog rehabilitation can occur only with a calm, assertive, stable, and *consistent* owner.

10. Nose, eyes, ears . . . in that order!

I remind dog owners that dogs see the world differently from the way we do. We communicate using our ears first, then our eyes, and lastly, our nose. Dogs begin with the nose, then the eyes, and lastly the ears. Allowing a dog to experience our scent before we engage it in eye contact or speak to it is one way to establish trust early on.

11. Humanizing a dog

Many owners make the well-intentioned mistake of thinking of their dogs as children. I advise people to try to see the world through a dog's eyes. Cute outfits, fancy dog food, and a million-aire's mansion will not make for a happy dog. Regular exercise, a strong stable pack leader, and affection that's *earned* will result in a dog that's calm and balanced.

12. People training

When I am called in on a job, many owners assume it's their dog that's the problem. I try to help people understand that their *own* behavior has a powerful affect on their dog, and I offer them suggestions for "retraining" themselves to be calm-assertive pack leaders.

RECOMMENDATIONS FOR
FURTHER READING

Abrantes, Roger. *Dog Language: An Encyclopedia of Dog Behavior.* Wenatchee, WA: Wakan Tanka Publishers, 1997.

American Kennel Club. *The Complete Dog Book,* 19th edition. New York: Wiley Publications, 1998.

Bekoff, Mark. *Minding Animals: Awareness, Emotion and Heart.* New York: Oxford University Press, 2002.

Dibra, Bash (with Elizabeth Randolph, and Kitty Brown). *Your Dream Dog: A Guide to Choosing the Right Breed for You.* New York: New American Library, 2003.

Fogle, Bruce, DVM. MRCVS. *The Dog's Mind: Understanding Your Dog's Behavior.* New York: Howell Book House, 1990.

Hauser, Marc D. *Wild Minds: What Animals Really Think.* New York: Henry Holt and Company, 2000.

Irvine, Leslie. *If You Tame Me: Understanding Our Connection with Animals.* Philadelphia: Temple University Press, 2004.

McConnell, Patricia B., Ph.D. *The Other End of the Leash: Why We Do What We Do Around Dogs.* New York: Ballantine Books, 2002.

Monks of New Skete. *How to Be Your Dog's Best Friend*. New York: Little, Brown and Company, 2002.

Scott, John Paul, and John L. Fuller. *Genetics and the Social Behavior of the Dog: The Classic Study*. Chicago: University of Chicago Press, 1965.

Whitney, Leon F., DVM. *Dog Psychology: The Basics of Dog Training*. New York: Howell Book House, 1971; 1964.

CESAR RECOMMENDS:

ORGANIZATIONS TO TURN TO

BATTERSEA DOGS HOME
Battersea Dogs & Cats Home
4 Battersea Park Rd
Battersea
London SW8 4AA
t: 020 7622 3626
f: 020 7622 6451

MISSING PETS BUREAU
Missing Pets Bureau
Freepost SEA999
Primrose Lane, Croydon,
Surrey CR9 8WZ
t: 0870 1 999 000 (24hr Main Number)
f: 0870 1 999 011

RSPCA
Enquiries service
RSPCA
Wilberforce Way
Southwater
Horsham
West Sussex
RH13 9RS
t: 0870 55 55 999 (24 hour national cruelty and advice line)

BLUE CROSS HEAD OFFICE
Shilton Road
Burford
Oxon OX18 4PF
t: 01993 822651
f: 01993 823083
Email: info@bluecross.org.uk

DOGS TRUST
17 Wakely Street
London EC1V 7RQ
t: 020 7837 0006

DOGS LOST
PO BOX 227
WORKSOP
NOTTS S81 8WU
t: 01909 733366
Email: admin@doglost.co.uk
www.doglost.co.uk

INTERNATIONAL ANIMAL RESCUE
Lime House
Regency Close
Uckfield
East Sussex TN22 1DS
General Enquiries
t: 01825 767 688
f: 01825 768 012
Email: info@iar.org.uk

Ireland
DOGS AID ANIMAL SANCTUARY
St Margaret's
Co Dublin
t: 00353 1 8347134
Email: dogsaid@eircom.net

Wales
All Creatures Great and Small
Church Farm
Llanfrechfa
Cwmbran
South Wales NP44 8AD
t: 01633 866144 (2-5pm)
Email: info@acgas.org.uk

Scotland
DAWGS (DOG ACTION WORKING GROUP SCOTLAND)
6 Whitemyres Holdings
Lang Stracht
Kingswell
Aberdeen AB15 6NB
t: 01224 208989
f: 01224 313877
Email: dawgsabdn@hotmail.com
www.dawgs.co.uk

Vets

PDSA (People's Dispensary for Sick Animals)
Head Office
Whitechapel Way
Priorslee
Telford
Shropshire TF2 9PQ
t: 01952 290999
f: 01952 291035

Royal College of Veterinary Surgeons
Belgravia House
62-64 Horseferry Road
London SW1P 2AF

t: 0 207222 2001
f: 0 207222 2004
Email: admin@rcvs.org.uk

Trade Organizations

British Institute of Professional Dog Trainers
B.I.P.D.T
Bowstone Gate
Nr. Disley
Cheshire SK12 2AW
t: 01663 762 772
www.bipdt.net

NOTES

Introduction
1. Source: U.S. Humane Society.
2. Mindy Fetterman, "Pampered Pooches Nestle in Lap of Luxury," *USA Today*, 11 Feb. 2005, 1A.
3. Alex Lieber, "Lifetime Costs of Pet Ownership," PetPlace.com, http://petplace.compuserve.com/Articles/artShow.asp?artID=5024.

1: Growing Up with Dogs
1. Robert M. Saponsky, "Social Status and Health in Humans and Other Animals," *Annual Review of Anthropology* 33 (2004): 393–414.

2: If We Could Talk to the Animals
1. Bruce Fogle, *The Dog's Mind: Understanding Your Dog's Behavior*, New York: Macmillan, 1990, 38.
2. Hubert Montagner, *L'Attachement: Les Debuts de la Tendresse (Attachment: The Stages of Affection)*, Paris: Editions Odile Jacob, 1988.
3. Don Oldenburg, "A Sense of Doom: Animal Instinct for Disaster," *The Washington Post*, 8 Jan. 2005, C1.
4. Maryann Mott, "Did Animals Sense Tsunami Was Coming?" *National Geographic News*, 4 Jan. 2005, http://news.nationalgeographic.com/news/2005/01/0104_tsunami_animals.html.

5. Leon F. Whitney, DVM, *Dog Psychology: The Basics of Dog Training,* New York: Macmillan, 1971, 152–53.

6. Carolyn M. Willis, et al., "Olfactory Detection of Human Bladder Cancer by Dogs: Proof of Principal Study," *BMJ* 329 (2004):712.

3: Dog Psychology

1. Marc D. Hauser, *Wild Minds: What Animals Really Think,* New York: Henry Holt and Co., 2000, xiv–xx.

2. H. Varendi, R. H. Porter, and J. Winberg, "Does the Newborn Baby Find the Nipple by Smell?" *The Lancet* 8, no. 344 (8298) (Oct. 1994): 989–90.

3. H. Varendi, R. H. Porter, and J. Winberg, "Attractiveness of Amniotic Fluid Odor: Evidence of Prenatal Olfactory Learning," *Acta Paediatrica* 85, no. 10 (1996): 1223–27.

4. John Paul Scott and John L. Fuller, *Genetics and the Social Behavior of the Dog,* Chicago: University of Chicago Press, 1965, 94–95.

5. Bruce Fogel, *The Dog's Mind: Understanding Your Dog's Behavior,* New York: Macmillan, 1990, 74.

6. Patricia B. McConnell, *The Other End of the Leash: Why We Do What We Do Around Dogs,* New York: Ballantine Books, 2002, 116.

7. Virginia Morell, "The Origin of Dogs: Running with the Wolves," *Science* 276, 5319 (13 June 1997): 1647–48.

8. David L. Mech, *The Wolf: The Ecology and Behavior of an Endangered Species,* New York: Natural History Press, 1970.

9. John Paul Scott and John L. Fuller, *Genetics and the Social Behavior of the Dog,* Chicago: University of Chicago Press, 1965, 400–403.

10. Maryann Mott, "Breed-specific Bans Spark Constitutional Dogfight," *National Geographic News,* 17 June 2004, http://

news.nationalgeographic.com/news/2004/06/0617_
040617_dogbans.html.

4: Power of the Pack

1. "Wolves in Denali Park and Reserve," National Park Service/
   Dept. of the Interior, http://www.nps.gov/akso/ParkWise/
   Students/ReferenceLibrary/DENA/WolvesInDenali.htm.
2. Bruce Fogel, *The Dog's Mind: Understanding Your Dog's
   Behavior,* New York: Macmillan, 1990, 50–51.
3. Elizabeth Pennisi, "How Did Cooperative Behavior Evolve?"
   Science 309, 5731 (1 July 2005): 93.
4. Elizabeth MacDonald and Chana R. Schoenberger, "Special
   Report: The World's Most Powerful Women," *Forbes,* 28 July
   2005.
5. R. Butler and H. F. Harlow, "Persistence of Visual Exploration in Monkeys," *Journal of Comparative and Physiological
   Psychology* 46 (1954): 258.
6. E. E. Shillito, "Exploratory Behavior in the Short-tailed Vole
   Microtus arestis," *Behavior* 21 (1963): 145–54.
7. Source: American Humane Association.

5: Issues

1. Kathy Dye, "Wolves: Violent? Yes. Threat? No," *Juneau Em-
   pire,* 2 Nov. 2000, http://juneauempire.com/smart_search/.

6: Dogs in the Red Zone

1. J. J. Sacks, et al., "Fatal Dog Attacks, 1989–1994," *Pediatrics*
   97, no. 6 (1 June 1996): 891–95.
2. D. Pimental, L. Lach, R. Zuniga, and D. Morrison, "Environmental and Economic Costs Associated with Non-indigenous
   Species in the United States," Cornell University, College of

Agriculture and Life Sciences, Ithaca, N.Y., 1999, http://www.news.cornell.edu/releases/Jan99/species_costs.html.

3. T. A. Karlson, "The Incidence of Facial Injuries from Dog Bites," *JAMA* 251 no. 24 (June 1984): 3265–67.

4. Source: American Society of Plastic Surgeons.

5. Source: American Humane Association.

6. Jaxon Van Derbeken, "Dog Owner Defends Story: Knoller Says Her Memory of Attack 'fades in and out,'" *San Francisco Chronicle*, 13 Mar. 2002, A21.

7. American Kennel Club, *The Complete Dog Book*, 19th edition, revised, New York: Wiley Publishing, 1998, 286–87.

8. Ibid., 271–75.

9. Juan Gonzalez, "News & Views: This Web Site's the Pits," *New York Daily News*, 4 Dec. 2003, http://www.nydailynews.com/news/story/142548p-126284c.html.

10. Maryann Mott, "Breed-Specific Bans Spark Constitutional Dogfight," *National Geographic News*, 17 June 2004, http://news.nationalgeographic.com/news/2004/06/0617_040617_dogbans.html.

11. Kerry Kearsley, "Washington Bill Asks Insurers to Consider Dogs' Deeds, Not Their Breeds," *AP Online*, 18 March 2005.

12. Benjamin N. Gedan, "Even Mild-mannered Dogs Can Be Lethal to Children," *The Providence Journal*, 15 July 2005: B17.

13. Bruce Fogel, *The Dog's Mind: Understanding Your Dog's Behavior*, New York: Macmillan, 1990, 126.

7: Cesar's Fulfillment Formula for a Balanced and Healthy Dog

1. "Wolves in Denali Park and Reserve," National Park Service/Dept. of the Interior, http://www.nps.gov/akso/ParkWise/Students/ReferenceLibrary/DENA/WolvesInDenali.htm.

2. John Paul Scott and John L. Fuller, *Genetics and the Social*

Behavior of the Dog, Chicago: University of Chicago Press, 1965, 46.

8: "Can't We All Just Get Along?"

1. Amanda Covarrubius and Natasha Lee, "Pet Rottweiler Kills Toddler in Glendale," *Los Angeles Times,* 4 Aug 2005: B1.
2. J. J. Brace, "Theories of Aging," *Veterinary Clinics of North America—Small Animal Practice* 11 (1981): 811–14.
3. Source: AARP.
4. Marc D. Hauser, *Wild Minds: What Animals Really Think,* New York: Henry Holt and Company, 2000, 226–67.

ILLUSTRATION CREDITS

Laura Allen: pages 150, 154, 168, 222, 227, 232.

David Boelke: pages 58, 80, 110, 142, 213.

Robin Layton: page 128.

Cheri Lucas: pages ii, 8.

Cesar Millan: pages xv, 12, 20, 33, 50, 51, 55, 75, 76, 90, 91, 145, 170, 183, 193, 200, 209.

MPH Entertainment—Emery/Sumner Productions: pages 135, 163, 166, 187, 196, 204.

www.rintintin.com: page 35.

Alan Weissman: pages 207, 268.

INDEX

Page references in **boldface** refer to illustrations.

innate nature of dogs and, 97–98
introducing oneself to dogs and,
89–93, **90, 91**
living in the moment and, 95–97,
124, 217–18, 245, 264–65
name and personality and, 102–4
"nose, eyes, ears" formula and, 93
pack mentality and, 111–40; *see
also* packs
"problem breed" myth and, 99–102
recognizing animal in your dog
and, 94–97
Dog Psychology (Whitney), 53
Dog Psychology Center, 2, 9–18, **55,**
73, 139, 147, 180–81, 215, 226,
228, **228, 232,** 237
daily routine at, 9–13, 18, 240,
271–72
introducing new dogs at, 12, 78,
252
opening of, 54
profiles of dogs at, 15–18
rehabilitation at, 14–18, 117,
185–87
staff at, 14
Dog's Mind, The (Fogle), 53, 65
dog walkers, professional, 212
Dolittle, Dr. (character), 59–60
dominance, 27, 118, 156, 229
body language of, 115
essential for pack to function,
118–20
pack leadership and, 114, 115,
118–20, 146
"powerbroker paradox" and,
120–26, 201
testosterone and, 113
two dogs in household and,
262–63
dominance aggression, **145,** 145–49,
249, 255, 264
dominance games, 149, 176
dominance ritual, 220–23, **222**

dominant temperament, 103, 221
dangerous animals and, 146,
147–48
human leadership for dogs with,
115, 145–46, 147, 168
doors:
going through ahead of dog,
123–24, 132–33, 205, 238
visitors coming to, 134, 137–38,
156
Dyer, Wayne, 71

Emily (pit bull), 183–89, **187,** 236
emotion, energy and, 66–68, 123,
188
energy, 61–74, 96–97
active-submissive, 27–28, 73–74,
243
alert-dominant, 75
alert-relaxed, 75
body language and, 74
breed and, 101
calm-assertive, *see* calm-assertive
energy
calm-submissive, *see* calm-
submissive energy
choosing a dog and, 101–2, 115,
236–37, 261–62
controlling your projection of,
70–73, 78, 129, 147, 188, 206
of earth, animals in touch with,
67–68
emotion and, 66–68, 123, 188
fear and, 65–66, 71–73, 184,
187–88
high, pack leadership and, 114
human behavior and, 64–66
of puppies, mother's recognition
of, 103
puppies' experience of, 86
redirecting into acceptable
activities, 226–29
status within pack and, 113

ABOUT THE AUTHORS

CESAR MILLAN

Renowned dog behavior expert Cesar Millan is one of the most sought-after professionals in the field of dog rehabilitation. From bullying Chihuahuas to timid Great Danes, Cesar has an uncanny gift for communicating with dogs and seeing the world through their eyes. His celebrity roster of clients includes Will Smith and Jada Pinkett Smith, Vin Diesel, Nicolas Cage, Ridley Scott, Michael Bay, Hilary Duff—and, of course, their dogs. At his Dog Psychology Center in Los Angeles, California, Cesar fields as many as one hundred requests per day from people desperate for his help. By the time people call Cesar, they are confronting a crisis with their beloved pet. He is their emergency responder, and often their last resort.

In addition to his show, *Dog Whisperer with Cesar Millan* on the National Geographic Channel, Cesar has appeared on the *Tonight Show with Jay Leno, Good Morning, America* with Diane Sawyer, *Good Day Live, America's Top Dog, Entertainment Insider,* and three times on *The Oprah Winfrey Show.* He's been profiled in such publications as *People* magazine, *Men's Health* magazine, *The Washington Post,* the *Los Angeles Times,* the *New York Post,* and *US Weekly,* to name but a few. The National Humane Society Genesis Award Committee presented him with a 2005 Special Commendation for his work helping to rehabilitate sheltered animals.

Cesar was born in Culiacan, Mexico, and has more than twenty years of experience with canines. He lives in Los Angeles and spends his spare time with his family—his wife, Ilusion, and two sons, Andre, eleven, and Calvin, six—all of whom help him in his work.

For more information on Cesar Millan, the Dog Psychology Center, and his upcoming seminars, please visit www.cesarmillan inc.com. Cesar's first DVD, *People Training for Dogs,* is also available for purchase on this site.

MELISSA JO PELTIER

Melissa Jo Peltier is co-owner and co-founder of the prolific MPH Entertainment, in Burbank, California. Her film and television writing, and her directing, have been honored with more than fifty international awards and commendations, including Emmy, Humanitas, and Peabody awards and three Writers Guild Award nominations. Her original television movie thriller, *Nightwaves,* starring Sherilyn Fenn, was a hit for Lifetime in 2004. With her two MPH partners, Peltier is also executive producer and co-writer of *Dog Whisperer with Cesar Millan,* on the National Geographic Channel, now in its second season. She divides her time between Los Angeles and New York, where she lives with her family.